C000177975

DAY BY DAY WITH
J.C.RYLE

DAY BY DAY WITH
J.C.RYLE

A NEW DAILY DEVOTIONAL
OF RYLE'S WRITINGS

EDITED BY | ERIC RUSSELL

CHRISTIAN HERITAGE

J. C. Ryle

John Charles Ryle (1816–1900) was the first Bishop of Liverpool, a post he held for twenty years. His impact on the Church of his time was immense, but since his death his writings have been widely read and hugely appreciated. His life and writings stand as an example to us all of how to combine firm faith with warm Christ-like compassion.

Eric Russell

Eric Russell was ordained as a Church of England minister. He is also a college lecturer training teachers in religious studies. He has written a well-received biography of J. C. Ryle *'That Man of Granite with a Heart of a Child'* (ISBN 1-85792-631-5).

ISBN 1-85792-959-4

© Copyright Christian Focus Publications 2004

Published in 2004
in the
Christian Heritage Imprint
by
Christian Focus Publications, Ltd.
Geanies House, Fearn, Tain,
Ross-shire, IV20 1TW, Scotland.

Cover Design by Alister MacInnes

Printed and bound by
Bell & Bain, Thornliebank, Glasgow.

All rights reserved. No part of this publication may be reproduced, stored in a retrieval system, or transmitted, in any form, by any means, electronic, mechanical, photocopying, recording or otherwise without the prior permission of the publisher or a licence permitting restricted copying. In the U.K. such licences are issued by the Copyright Licensing Agency, 90 Tottenham Court Road, London W1P 9HE.

PREFACE

It is longer than I care to remember when I first came across a book by J. C. Ryle. I believe it was *Knots Untied*, one of his books on Christian doctrine, and I found it so thoroughly biblical and evangelical, and his writing so clear and easy to follow, that it gave me a desire to read more of his many volumes on doctrine, *Holiness, Principles for Churchmen*, *Practical Religion*, his sermon in *The Upper Room*, and, of course, his *Expository Thoughts on the Gospels*. I appreciate his uncompromising stand in all his writings on the supremacy of Scripture, his clear statements on the fundamentals of evangelical faith and all in plain English.

I have had a lifelong interest in his life and ministry, during which I collected much information about this remarkable man and evangelical leader, who became the first Bishop of Liverpool. Eventually I realized I had gathered sufficient material, and I hope a sufficient understanding of his strengths and weaknesses, to write a biography of this exceptional Christian leader.

Shortly after my biography on Ryle, *That Man of Granite with the Heart of a Child*, was published by Christian Focus, I was asked if I would compile a series of Daily Readings for the Year based on Ryle's *Expository Thoughts on the Gospels*.

Ryle was a daily reader of the Bible, and in his mid-Suffolk parish he began writing comments, with the help of the Spirit, on his study of verses in St Matthew's Gospel. He wrote in 'a plain and pointed style', in language which the folks in his country parish would understand. The first volume was published in 1856, and in the Preface he explained the work was intended for private devotional reading and for use at family prayers. The work was warmly received, and as time allowed he compiled further short expositions on the rest of the Gospels, and completed his seventh and final volume on St John's Gospel in 1873. In his careful preparation of the readings he found the commentaries of others helpful, particularly the works of Reformation and Puritan writers, but he insisted that Scripture itself must always have the supremacy, in interpreting the Word of God.

It is a 'labour of love' to read carefully through Ryle's 'Thoughts' on the ministry and teaching of Jesus in the Gospels, and I pray the reader will enjoy pondering over the selected excerpts, find encouragement and accept the challenge to be a more faithful follower of the Lord Jesus.

Eric Russell
2004

JANUARY

January 1

And knew her not till she had brought forth her firstborn son:
and he called his name JESUS.
Matthew 1:25

The two names given to our Lord.
One is 'Jesus': the other 'Emmanuel'. One describes His office: the other His nature. Both are deeply interesting.

The name Jesus means 'Saviour': it is the same name as Joshua, in the Old Testament. It is given to our Lord because 'he shall save his people from their sins'. This is His special office. He saves them from the guilt of sin, by washing them in His own atoning blood; He saves them from the dominion of sin, by putting in their hearts the sanctifying Spirit; He saves them from the presence of sin, when He takes them out of this world to rest with Him: He will save them from all the consequences of sin, when He shall give them a glorious body at the last day. Blessed and holy are Christ's people! From sorrow, cross and conflict they are not saved; but they are 'saved from sin' for evermore. They are cleansed from guilt by Christ's blood: they are made meet for heaven by Christ's Spirit. This is salvation! He who cleaves to sin is not yet saved.

Jesus is a very encouraging name to heavy-laden sinners. He who is King of kings and Lord of lords might lawfully have taken some more high-sounding title. But He did not do so. The rulers of this world have often called themselves Great, Conqueror, Bold, Magnificent and the like. The Son of God was content to call Himself 'Saviour'. The souls which desire salvation may draw nigh to the Father with boldness, and have access with confidence through Christ. It is His office and His delight to show mercy. 'God sent not his son into the world to condemn the world; but that the world through him might be saved' (John 3:17).

Jesus is the name which is peculiarly sweet and precious to believers. It has often done them good, when the favour of kings and princes would have been heard of with unconcern; it has given them what money cannot buy – even inward peace; it has eased their consciences, and given rest to their heavy hearts.

January 2

*And the Word was made flesh, and dwelt among us, (and we beheld his
glory, the glory as of the only begotten of the Father,)
full of grace and truth.*
John 1:14

The reality of our Lord Jesus Christ's incarnation, or
being made man.

St John tells us that 'the Word was made flesh, and dwelt
among us'.

The plain meaning of these words is, that our divine Saviour really
took human nature upon Him, in order to save sinners. He really became
a man like ourselves in all things, sin only excepted. Like ourselves, He
was born of a woman, though born in a miraculous manner. Like
ourselves, He grew from infancy to boyhood, and from boyhood to
man's estate, both in wisdom and in stature (Luke 2:52). Like ourselves,
He hungered, thirsted, ate, drunk, slept, was wearied, felt pain, wept,
rejoiced, marvelled, was moved to anger and to compassion. Having
become flesh, and taken a body, He prayed, read the Scriptures, suffered
being tempted and submitted His human will to the will of God the
Father. And finally, in the same body, He really suffered and shed His
blood, really died, was really buried, really rose again, and really
ascended up into heaven. And yet all this time He was God as well as
man!

This union of two natures in Christ's one Person is doubtless one of
the greatest mysteries of the Christian religion. It needs to be carefully
stated. It is just one of those great truths which are not meant to be
curiously pried into, but to be reverently believed. Nowhere, perhaps,
shall we find a more wise and judicious statement than in the second
article of the Church of England. 'The Son, which is the Word of the
Father, begotten from everlasting of the Father, the very and eternal
God, and of one substance with the Father, took man's nature in the
womb of the blessed Virgin of her substance: so that two whole and
perfect natures, that is to say, the Godhead and the manhood, were
joined together in one Person, never to be divided, whereof is one
Christ, very God and very man.' This is a most valuable declaration.
This is 'sound speech, which cannot be condemned'.

January 3

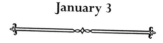

And lo a voice from heaven, saying,
This is my beloved Son, in whom I am well pleased.
Matthew 3:17

The peculiarly solemn circumstances by which the baptism of our Lord Jesus Christ was attended.

Such a baptism never will be again, so long as the world stands. We are told of the presence of all three Persons of the blessed Trinity. God the Son, manifest in the flesh, is baptized; God the Spirit descends like a dove, and lights upon Him; God the Father speaks from heaven with a voice. In a word, we have the manifested presence of Father, Son and Holy Ghost. We may regard this as a public announcement that the work of Christ was the result of the eternal counsels of all the three Persons of the blessed Trinity. It was the whole Trinity, which at the beginning of the creation said, 'Let us make man'; it was the whole Trinity again, which at the beginning of the Gospel seemed to say, 'Let us save man.'

We are told of 'a voice from heaven' at our Lord's baptism: the 'heavens were opened', and words were heard. This was a most significant miracle. We read of no voice from heaven before this, except at the giving of the law on Sinai. Both occasions were of peculiar importance; it therefore seemed good to our Father in heaven to mark both with peculiar honour. At the introduction both of the law and gospel He Himself spoke. 'God spake all these words' (Exod. 20:1).

How striking and deeply instructive are the Father's words: 'This is my beloved Son, in whom I am well pleased'. He declares, in these words, that Jesus is the divine Saviour sealed and appointed from all eternity to carry out the work of redemption: He proclaims that He accepts Him as the Mediator between God and man; He publishes to the world that He is satisfied with Him as the propitiation, the Substitute, the ransom-payer for the lost family of Adam and the Head of a redeemed people. In Him He sees His holy law magnified and made honourable: through Him He can be just and yet the justifier of the ungodly (Isa. 42:21; Rom. 3:26).

January 4

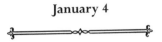

*Go ye therefore, and teach all nations, baptizing them in the name of
the Father, and of the Son, and of the Holy Ghost...*
Matthew 28:19

The public profession which Jesus requires of those who
believe His gospel.

He tells His apostles to 'baptize' those whom they received as
disciples. It is very difficult to conceive, when we read this last command
of our Lord's, how men can avoid the conclusion that baptism is
necessary, when it may be had. It seems impossible to explain the word
that we have here of any but an outward ordinance, to be administered
to all who join His Church. That outward baptism is not absolutely
necessary to salvation, the case of the penitent thief plainly shows: he
went to paradise unbaptized. That outward baptism alone often confers
no benefit, the case of Simon Magus plainly shows: although baptized
he remained 'in the gall of bitterness, and in the bond of iniquity' (Acts
8:23). But that baptism is a matter of entire indifference, and need not
be used at all, is an assertion which seems at variance with our Lord's
words in this place.

The plain practical lesson of the words is the necessity of a public
confession of faith in Christ. It is not enough to be a secret disciple: we
must not be ashamed to let men see whose we are, and whom we serve.
We must not behave as if we did not like to be thought Christians; but
take up our cross, and confess our Master before the world. His words
are very solemn: 'Whosoever therefore shall be ashamed of me ... of
him also shall the Son of man be ashamed, when he cometh in the glory
of his Father with the holy angels' (Mark 8:38).

Let us observe the obedience which Jesus requires of all who profess
themselves His disciples. He bids the apostles teach them to observe all
things, whatsoever He has commanded them.

This is a searching expression. It shows the uselessness of a mere
name and form of Christianity; it shows that they only are to be counted
true Christians who live in practical obedience to His word, and strive
to do the things that He has commanded.

January 5

And there came a voice from heaven, saying,
Thou art my beloved Son, in whom I am well pleased.
Mark 1:11

The voice from heaven which was heard at our Lord's baptism.

We read, 'there came a voice from heaven, saying, Thou art my beloved Son, in whom I am well pleased'.

That voice was the voice of God the Father. It declared the wondrous and ineffable love which has existed between the Father and the Son from all eternity. 'The Father loveth the Son, and hath given all things into his hand' (John 3:35). It proclaimed the Father's full and complete approbation of Christ's mission to seek and save the lost. It announced the Father's acceptance of the Son as the Mediator, Substitute and Surety of the new covenant.

There is a rich mine of comfort in these words, for all Christ's believing members. In themselves, and in their own doings, they see nothing to please God. They are daily sensible of weakness, shortcoming and imperfection in all their ways. But let them recollect that the Father regards them as members of His beloved Son Jesus Christ. He sees no spot in them (Cant. 4:7).

He beholds them as 'in Christ', clothed in His righteousness, and invested with His merit. They are 'accepted in the Beloved', and when the holy eye of God looks at them, He is 'well pleased'.

That voice was the voice of God the Father. It declared the wondrous and ineffable love which has existed between the Father and the Son from all eternity. 'The Father loveth the Son, and hath given all things into his hand' (John 3:35). It proclaimed the Father's full and complete approbation of Christ's mission to seek and save the lost. It announced the Father's acceptance of the Son as Mediator, Substitute and Surety of the new covenant.

January 6

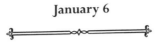

Now when all the people were baptized, it came to pass, that Jesus also being baptized, and praying, the heaven was opened...
Luke 3:21

Т he high honour the Lord Jesus has put on baptism. We find that among others who came to John the Baptist, the Saviour of the world came, and was 'baptized'.

An ordinance which the Son of God was pleased to use, and afterwards to appoint for the use of His whole Church, ought always to be held in peculiar reverence by His people. Baptism cannot be a thing of slight importance, if Christ Himself was baptized. The use of baptism would never have been enjoined on the Church of Christ if it had been a mere outward form, incapable of conveying any blessing.

It is hardly necessary to say that errors of every sort and description abound on the subject of baptism. Some make an idol of it, and exalt it far above the place assigned to it in the Bible. Some degrade it and dishonour it, and seem almost to forget that it was ordained by Christ Himself. Some limit the use of it so narrowly that they will baptize none unless they are grown up, and can give full proof of their conversion. Some invest the baptismal water with such magic power, that they would like missionaries to go into heathen lands and baptize all persons, old and young indiscriminately, and believe that however ignorant the heathen may be, baptism must do them good. On no subject, perhaps in religion, have Christians more need to pray for a right judgment and a sound mind.

Let it suffice us to hold firmly the general principle, that baptism was graciously intended by our Lord to be a help to His Church, and 'a means of grace', and that when rightly and worthily used, we may confidently look upon it for a blessing. But let us never forget that the grace of God is not tied to any sacrament, and that we may be baptized with water without being baptized with the Holy Ghost.

January 7

*Now when all the people were baptized, it came to pass, that Jesus also
being baptized, and praying, the heaven was opened...*
Luke 3:21

The close connection that ought to exist between the
administration of baptism and prayer.

We are specially told by St Luke that when our Lord was baptized
He was also 'praying'.

We need not doubt that there is a great lesson in this fact, and one
that the Church of Christ has too much overlooked. We are meant to
learn that the baptism which God blesses must be a baptism accompanied
by prayer. The sprinkling of water is not sufficient. The use of the name
of the blessed Trinity is not enough. The form of the sacrament alone
conveys no grace. There must be something else beside all this. There
must be 'the prayer of faith'. A baptism without prayer, it may be
confidently asserted, is a baptism on which we have no right to expect
God's blessing.

Why is it that the sacrament of baptism appears to bear so little
fruit? How is it that thousands are every year baptized, and never give
the slightest proof of having received benefit from it? The answer to
these questions is short and simple. In the vast majority of baptisms
there is no prayer except the prayer of the officiating minister. Parents
bring their children to the font, without the slightest sense of what
they are doing. Sponsors stand up and answer for the child, in evident
ignorance of the nature of the ordinance they are attending, and as a
mere matter of form. What possible reason have we for expecting such
baptisms to be blessed by God? None: none at all! Such baptisms may
well be barren of results. They are not baptisms according to the mind
of Christ. Let us pray that the eyes of Christians on this important subject
may be opened. It is one on which there is great need of change.

January 8

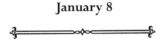

But while men slept, his enemy came and sowed tares among the
wheat, and went his way.
Matthew 13:25

Good and evil will always be found together in the professing Church, until the end of the world.

The visible Church is set before us as a mixed body: it is a vast 'field' in which 'wheat and tares' grow side by side. We must expect to find believers and unbelievers, converted and unconverted, 'the children of the kingdom and the children of the wicked one', all mingled together in every congregation of baptized people.

The purest preaching of the gospel will not prevent this. In every age of the Church, the same state of things has existed: it was the experience of the early Fathers; it was the experience of the Reformers; it is the experience of the best ministers at the present hour. There has never been a visible Church or a religious assembly of which the members have been all 'wheat'. The devil, that great enemy of souls, has always taken care to sow 'tares'.

The most strict and prudent discipline will not prevent this: Episcopalians, Presbyterians and Independents, all alike find it to be so. Do what we will to purify a Church, we shall never succeed in obtaining a perfectly pure communion: tares will be found among the wheat; hypocrites and deceivers will creep in; and, worst of all, if we are extreme in our efforts to obtain purity, we do more harm than good: we run the risk of encouraging many a Judas Iscariot, and breaking many a bruised reed. In our zeal to 'gather up the tares', we are in danger of 'rooting up the wheat with them': such zeal is not according to knowledge, and has often done much harm. Those who care not what happens to the wheat, provided they can root up the tares, show little of the mind of Christ: and after all, there is deep truth in the charitable saying of Augustine, 'Those who are tares today, may be wheat tomorrow.'

January 9

Moreover if thy brother shall trespass against thee,
go and tell him his fault between thee and him alone:
if he shall hear thee, thou hast gained thy brother.
Matthew 18:15

W hat a clear argument we have in these verses for the exercise of discipline in a Christian congregation. Our Lord commands disagreements between Christians, which cannot be otherwise settled, to be referred to the decision of the Church, or Christian assembly to which they belong. '[T]ell it', He says, to 'the church'. It is evident, from this, that He intends every congregation of professing Christians to take cognizance of the moral conduct of its members, either by the action of the whole body collectively, or of heads and elders to whom its authority may be delegated. It is evident also that He intends every congregation to have the power of excluding disobedient and refractory members from participation in its ordinances. '[I]f he neglect', He says, 'to hear the church, let him be unto thee as an heathen man and a publican'. He says not a word about temporal punishment, and civil disabilities: spiritual penalties are the only penalty He permits the Church to inflict; and when rightly inflicted they are not to be lightly regarded. 'Whatsoever ye shall bind on earth shall be bound in heaven.' Such appears to be the substance of our Lord's teaching about ecclesiastical discipline.

It is vain to deny that the whole subject is surrounded with difficulties. On no point has the influence of the world weighed so heavily on the action of Churches: on no point have Churches made so many mistakes, sometimes on the side of sleepy remissness, sometimes on the side of blind severity. No doubt the power of excommunication has been fearfully abused and perverted, and as Quesnel says, 'we ought to be more afraid of our sins than of all the excommunications in the world'. Still it is impossible to deny, with such a passage as this before us, that Church discipline is according to the mind of Christ, and, when wisely exercised, is calculated to promote a Church's health and well-being.

January 10

*For where two or three are gathered together in my name,
there am I in the midst of them.*
Matthew 18:20

What gracious encouragement Christ holds out to those who meet together in His name.
He says, 'where two or three are gathered together in my name, there am I in the midst of them'.

That saying is a striking proof of our Lord's divinity. God alone can be in more places than one at the same time.

There is a comfort in these words for all who love to meet together for religious purposes. At every assembly for public worship, at every gathering for prayer and praise, at every missionary meeting, at every Bible reading, the King of kings is present, Christ Himself attends. We may be often disheartened by the small number who are present on such occasions, compared with the number of those who meet for worldly ends; we may sometimes find it hard to bear the taunts and ridicule of an ill-natured world, which cries like the enemy of old, 'What do these feeble Jews?' (Neh. 4:2). But we have no reason for despondency: we may boldly fall back on these words of Jesus. At all such meetings we have the company of Christ Himself.

There is solemn rebuke in these words for all who neglect the public worship of God, and never attend meetings for any religious purpose. They turn their backs on the society of the Lord of lords; they miss the opportunity of meeting Christ Himself. It avails nothing to say that the proceedings of religious meetings are marked by weakness and infirmity, or that as much good is got by staying at home as going to church: the words of our Lord should silence such arguments at once. Surely men are not wise when they speak contemptuously of any gathering where Christ is present.

May we all ponder these things! If we have met together with God's people for spiritual purposes in times past, let us persevere, and not be ashamed. If we have hitherto despised such meetings, let us consider our ways and learn wisdom.

January 11

And cast ye the unprofitable servant into outer darkness:
there shall be weeping and gnashing of teeth.
Matthew 25:30

Unfruitful members of Christ's Church will be condemned and cast away in the day of judgment. The parable tells us that the servant who buried his master's money, was reminded that he 'knew' his master's character and requirements, and was therefore without excuse; it tells us that he was condemned as 'wicked', 'slothful', and 'unprofitable', and cast into 'outer darkness': and our Lord adds the solemn words, 'there shall be weeping and gnashing of teeth'.

There will be no excuse for an unconverted Christian at the last day. The reasons with which he now pretends to satisfy himself will prove useless and vain: the Judge of all the earth will be found to have done right; the ruin of the lost soul will be found to be his own fault. Those words of our Lord, 'thou knewest', are words that ought to ring loudly in many a man's ears, and prick him to the heart. Thousands are living at this day 'without Christ' and without conversion, and yet pretending that they cannot help it! And all this time they 'know', in their own conscience, that they are guilty. They are burying their talent: they are not doing what they can. Happy are they who find this out betimes! It will all come out at the last day.

Let us leave this parable with a solemn determination, by God's grace, never to be content with a profession of Christianity without practice. Let us not only *talk* about religion, but act; let us not only *feel* the importance of religion, but do something too. We are not told that the unprofitable servant was a murderer, or a thief, or even a waster of his Lord's money: but he *did nothing*, and this was his ruin! Let us beware of a do-nothing Christianity: such Christianity does not come from the Spirit of God. 'To do no harm,' says Baxter, 'is the praise of a stone, not a man.'

January 12

And he said, Whereunto shall we liken the kingdom of God?
or with what comparison shall we compare it?
Mark 4:30

C hrist's visible Church was to be small and weak in its
beginnings.

A grain of mustard seed was a proverbial expression among
the Jews for something very small and insignificant. Our Lord calls it
less than all the seeds that be in the earth. Twice in the Gospels we find
our Lord using the figure as a word of comparison, when speaking of a
weak faith (Matt. 17:20; Luke 17:6).

The idea was doubtless familiar to a Jewish mind, however strange
it may sound to us. Here, as in other places, the Son of God shows us
the wisdom of using language familiar to the minds of those who we
address.

It would be difficult to find an emblem which more faithfully
represents the history of the visible Church of Christ than this grain of
mustard seed.

Weakness and apparent insignificance were undoubtedly the
characteristics of its beginning. How did its Head and King come into
the world? He came as a feeble infant, born in a manger at Bethlehem,
without riches, or armies, or attendants, or power. Who were the men
that the Head of the Church gathered round Himself, and appointed
His apostles? They were poor and unlearned persons, fishermen,
publicans, and men of like occupations, to all appearance the most
unlikely people to shake the world. What was the last public act of the
earthly ministry of the great Head of the Church? He was crucified,
like a malefactor, between two thieves, after having been forsaken by
nearly all His disciples, betrayed by one, and denied by another. What
was the doctrine which the first builders of the Church went forth
from the upper chamber in Jerusalem to preach to mankind? It was a
doctrine which to the Jews was a stumbling-block, and to the Greeks
foolishness. It was a proclamation that the great Head of their new
religion had been put to death on a cross, and that notwithstanding
this, they offered life through His death to the world!

January 13

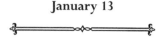

And ought not this woman, being a daughter of Abraham,
whom Satan hath bound, lo, these eighteen years,
be loosed from this bond on the sabbath day?
Luke 13:16

A **striking example of diligence in the use of means of grace.** We are told of a 'woman which had a spirit of infirmity eighteen years, and was bowed together, and could in no wise lift up herself'.

We know not who this woman was. Our Lord's saying that she was 'a daughter of Abraham', would lead us to infer that she was a true believer; but her name and history are hidden from us. This only we know, that when Jesus was 'teaching in one of the synagogues on the sabbath', this woman was there. Sickness was no excuse with her for tarrying from God's house. In spite of suffering and infirmity, she found her way to the place where the day and the Word of God were honoured, and where the people of God met together. And truly she was blessed in her deed! She found a rich reward for all her pains. She came sorrowing, and went home rejoicing.

The conduct of this suffering Jewess may well put to shame many a strong and healthy professing Christian. How many in the full enjoyment of bodily vigour, allow the most frivolous excuses to keep them away from the house of God! How many are constantly spending the whole Sunday in idleness, pleasure-seeking, or business, and scoffing and sneering at those who 'keep the Sabbath holy'! How many think it a great matter if they attend the public worship of God once on Sunday, and regard a second attendance as a needless excess of zeal, akin to fanaticism! How many find religious services a weariness while they attend them, and feel relieved when they are over! How few know anything of David's spirit, when he said, 'I was glad when they said unto me, Let us go in to the house of the LORD.' 'How amiable are thy tabernacles, O LORD of hosts!' (Ps. 122:1; Ps. 84:1).

January 14

I tell you, in that night there shall be two men in one bed;
the one shall be taken, and the other shall be left.
Luke 17:34

What an awful separation there will be in the professing Church when Christ comes again. Our Lord describes this separation by a very striking picture. He says, 'in that night there shall be two men in one bed; the one shall be taken, and the other shall be left. Two women shall be grinding together; the one shall be taken, and the other left.'

The meaning of these expressions is clear and plain. The day of Christ's second advent shall be the day when good and evil, converted and unconverted, shall at length be divided into two distinct bodies. The visible Church shall no longer be a mixed body; the wheat and the tares shall no longer grow side by side; the good fish and the bad shall at length be sorted into two bodies. The angels shall come forth and gather together the godly, that they may be rewarded, and leave the wicked behind to be punished. 'Converted or unconverted?' will be the only object of inquiry. It will matter nothing that people have worked together, and slept together, and lived together for many years: they will be dealt with at last according to their religion. Those members of the family who have loved Christ will be taken up to heaven; and those who have loved the world will be cast down to hell. Converted and unconverted shall be separated for evermore when Jesus comes again.

Let us lay to heart these things. He that loves his relatives and friends is specially bound to consider them. If those whom he loves are true servants of Christ, let him know that he must cast in his lot with them, if he would not one day be parted with them for ever. If those whom he loves are yet dead in trespasses and sins, let him know that he must work and pray for their conversion, lest he should be separated from them by and by to all eternity. Life is the only time for such work. Life is fast ebbing away from us all. Partings, and separations, and the breaking up of families are at all times painful things; but all the separations that we see now are nothing compared to those which will be seen when Christ comes again.

January 15

But Thomas, one of the twelve, called Didymus,
was not with them when Jesus came.
John 20:24

How much Christians may lose by not regularly attending the assemblies of God's people. Thomas was absent the first time that Jesus appeared to the disciples after His resurrection, and consequently Thomas missed a blessing. Of course we have no certain proof that the absence of the apostle could not admit of explanation. Yet, at such a crisis in the lives of the eleven, it seems highly improbable that he had any good reason for not being with his brethren, and it is far more likely that in some way he was to blame. One thing, at any rate, is clear and plain. By being absent he was kept in suspense and unbelief a whole week, while all around him were rejoicing in the thought of a risen Lord. It is difficult to suppose that this would have been the case if there had not been a fault somewhere. It is hard to avoid the suspicion that Thomas was absent when he might have been present.

We shall all do well to remember the charge of the Apostle St Paul: forsake not 'the assembling of ourselves together, as the manner of some is' (Heb. 10:25).

Never to be absent from God's house on Sundays, without good reason – never to miss the Lord's Supper when administered in our own congregation – never to let our place be empty when means of grace are going on – this is one way to be a growing and prosperous Christian. The very sermon that we needlessly miss, may contain a precious word in season for our souls. The very assembly for prayer and praise from which we stay away, may be the very gathering that would have cheered, and stablished, and quickened our hearts. We little know how dependent our spiritual health is on little, regular, habitual helps, and how much we suffer if we miss our medicine. It may satisfy those who are blind to their own state, and destitute of grace, but it should never satisfy a real servant of Christ.

January 16

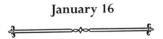

For whosoever shall do the will of my Father which is in heaven,
the same is my brother, and sister, and mother.
Matthew 12:50

The tender affection with which the Lord Jesus regards His true disciples.

We should mark how He speaks of every one who does the will of His Father in heaven. He says, 'the same is my brother, and sister, and mother'. What gracious words these are! Who can conceive the depth of our dear Lord's love towards His relatives according to the flesh? It was a pure, unselfish love. It must have been a mighty love, a love that passes man's understanding. Yet here we see that all His believing people are counted as His relatives: He loves them, feels for them, cares for them, as members of His family, bone of His bone, and flesh of His flesh.

There is a solemn warning here to all who mock and persecute true Christians on account of their religion. They consider not what they are doing; they are persecuting the near relatives of the King of kings. They will find at the last day that they have mocked those whom the Judge of all regards as His 'brother, and sister, and mother'.

There is rich encouragement here for all believers. They are far more precious in their Lord's eyes than they are in their own. Their faith may be feeble, their repentance weak, their strength small: they may be poor and needy in this world; but there is a glorious 'whosoever' in the last verse of this chapter which ought to cheer them. 'Whosoever' believes is a near relative of Christ; the Elder Brother will provide for him in time and eternity, and never let him be cast away. There is not one 'little sister' in the family of the redeemed, whom Jesus does not remember (Cant. 8:8). Joseph provided richly for all his relatives, and the Lord Jesus will provide for His.

January 17

*And as soon as he had spoken,
immediately the leprosy departed from him, and he was cleansed.*
Mark 1:42

The wondrous and almighty power of the Lord Jesus Christ.

We are told that the unhappy leper came to our Lord, 'beseeching him, and kneeling down to him, and saying unto him, If thou wilt, thou canst make me clean'. We are told that 'Jesus, moved with compassion, put forth his hand, and touched him, and saith unto him, I will; be thou clean'. At once the cure was effected. That very instant the deadly plague departed from the poor sufferer, and he was healed. It is but a word, and a touch, and there stands before our Lord, not a leper, but a sound and healthy man.

Who can conceive the greatness of the change in the feelings of this leper, when he found himself healed? The morning sun rose upon him, a miserable being, more dead than alive, his whole frame a mass of sores and corruption, his very existence a burden. The evening sun saw him full of hope and joy, free from pain, and fit for the society of his fellow men. Surely the change must have been like life from the dead. Let us bless God that the Saviour with whom we have to do is almighty. It is a cheering and comfortable thought that with Christ nothing is impossible. No heart disease is so deep-seated but He is able to cure it. No plague of soul is so virulent but our Great Physician can heal it. Let us never despair of anyone's salvation, so long as he lives. The worst of spiritual lepers may yet be cleansed. No cases of spiritual leprosy could be worse than those of Manasseh, Saul and Zacchaeus, yet they were all cured: Jesus Christ made them whole. The chief of sinners may yet be brought nigh to God by the blood and Spirit of Christ. Men are not lost, because they are too bad to be saved, but because they will not come to Christ that He may save them.

January 18

And Jesus, when he came out, saw much people, and was moved with compassion toward them, because they were as sheep not having a shepherd: and he began to teach them many things.
Mark 6:34

The feelings of our Lord Jesus Christ towards the people who came together to Him.

We read that He 'was moved with compassion toward them, because they were as sheep not having a shepherd'. They were destitute of teachers. They had no guides but the blind scribes and Pharisees. They had no spiritual food but man-made traditions. Thousands of immortal souls stood before our Lord, ignorant, helpless and on the high road to ruin. It touched the gracious heart of our Lord Jesus Christ. He was 'moved with compassion toward them … he began to teach them many things'.

Let us never forget that our Lord is the same yesterday, today and for ever. He never changes. High in heaven, at God's right hand, He still looks with compassion on the children of men. He still pities the ignorant, and them that are out of the way. He is still willing to 'teach them many things'. Special as His love is towards His own sheep who hear His voice, He still has a mighty general love towards all mankind, a love of real pity, a love of compassion. We must not overlook this. It is a poor theology which teaches that Christ cares for none except believers. There is warrant in Scripture for telling the chief of sinners that Jesus pities them and cares for their souls, that Jesus is willing to save them, and invites them to believe and be saved.

Let us ask ourselves, as we leave the passage, whether we know anything of the mind of Christ? Are we like Him, tenderly concerned about the souls of the unconverted? Do we, like Him, feel deep compassion for all who are yet as sheep without a shepherd? Do we care about the impenitent and ungodly near our own doors? Do we care about the heathen, the Jew, the Mahometan and the Roman Catholic in foreign lands? Do we use every means, and give our money willingly, to spread the gospel in the world?

January 19

*Are not five sparrows sold for two farthings,
and not one of them is forgotten before God?*
Luke 12:6

Christ's encouragement to persecuted believers.
He reminds them of God's providential care over the least of
His creatures: 'not one sparrow is forgotten before God.' He
goes on to assure them that the same Fatherly care is engaged on behalf
of each one of themselves: 'the very hairs of your head are all numbered'.
Nothing whatever, whether great or small, can happen to a believer,
without God's ordering and permission.

The providential government of God over everything in this world
is a truth of which the Greek and Roman philosophers had no
conception. It is a truth which is specially revealed to us in the Word of
God. Just as the telescope and microscope show us that there is order
and design in all the works of God's hand, from the greatest planet
down to the least insect, so does the Bible teach us that there is wisdom,
order and design in all the events of our daily life. There is no such thing
as 'chance', 'luck', or 'accident' in the Christian's journey through this
world. All is arranged and appointed by God: and all things are 'working
together' for the believer's good (Rom. 8:28).

Let us seek to have an abiding sense of God's hand in all that befalls
us, if we profess to be believers in Jesus Christ. Let us strive to realize
that a Father's hand is measuring out our daily portion, and that our
steps are ordered by Him. A daily practical faith of this kind is one
grand secret of happiness, and a mighty antidote against murmuring
and discontent. We should try to feel in the day of trial and
disappointment, that all is right and all is well done. We should try to
feel on the bed of sickness, that there must be a 'needs-be'. We should
say to ourselves, 'God could keep away from me these things if He
thought fit. But He does not do so, and therefore they must be for my
advantage. I will lie still, and bear them patiently. I have "an everlasting
covenant, ordered in all things, and sure" (2 Sam. 23:5). What pleases
God shall please me.'

January 20

And Jesus stood, and commanded him to be brought unto him:
and when he was come near, he asked him ...
Luke 18:40

An encouraging instance of Christ's kindness and compassion.

Passages like these in the Gospels are intended for the special comfort of all who feel their sins and come to Christ for peace. Such persons may be sensible of much infirmity in all their approaches to the Son of God. Their faith may be very feeble, their sins many and great, their prayers very poor and stammering, their motives far short of perfection; but, after all, do they really come to Christ with their sins? Are they really willing to forsake all other confidence, and commit their souls to Christ's hands? If this be so, they may hope and not be afraid. That same Jesus still lives who heard the blind man's cry, and granted his request. He will never go back from His own words: 'him that cometh to me I will in no wise cast out' (John 6:37).

We see lastly in this passage a striking example of the conduct which becomes one who has received mercy from Christ. We are told that when the blind man was restored to sight, he followed Jesus, 'glorifying God'. He felt deeply grateful: he resolved to show his gratitude by becoming one of our Lord's followers and disciples. Pharisees might cavil at our Lord; Sadducees might sneer at His teaching: it mattered nothing to this new disciple; he had the witness in himself that Christ was a Master worth following. He could say, 'I was blind, now I see' (John 9:25).

January 21

*And immediately he received his sight, and followed him, glorifying
God: and all the people, when they saw it, gave praise unto God.*
Luke 18:43

A striking example of the conduct which becomes one who has received mercy from Christ.

We are told that when the blind man was restored to sight, he followed Jesus, 'glorifying God'. He felt deeply grateful: he resolved to show his gratitude by becoming one of our Lord's followers and disciples. Pharisees might cavil at our Lord; Sadducees might sneer at His teaching: it mattered nothing to this new disciple; he had the witness in himself that Christ was a Master worth following. He could say, 'I was blind, now I see' (John 9:25).

Grateful love is the true spring of real obedience to Christ. Men will never take up the cross and confess Jesus before the world, and live to Him, until they feel that they are indebted to Him for pardon, peace and hope. The ungodly are what they are, because they have no sense of sin, and no consciousness of being under any special obligation to Christ. The godly are what they are, because they love Him who first loved them, and washed them from sin in His own blood. Christ has healed them, and therefore they follow Christ.

Let us leave the passage with solemn self-inquiry. If we would know whether we have any part or lot in Christ, let us look at our lives. Whom do we follow? What are the great ends and objects for which we live? The man who has a real hope in Jesus may always be known by the general bias of his life.

January 22

And when Jesus came to the place, he looked up, and saw him,
and said unto him, Zacchaeus, make haste, and come down;
for today I must abide at thy house.
Luke 19:5

Christ's free compassion towards sinners, and Christ's power to change hearts.

A more striking instance than that before us it is impossible to conceive. Unasked, our Lord stops and speaks to Zacchaeus; unasked, He offers Himself to be a guest in the house of a sinner; unasked, He sends into the heart of a publican the renewing grace of the Spirit, and put him that very day among the children of God (Jer. 3:19).

It is impossible, with such a passage as this before us, to exalt too highly the grace of our Lord Jesus Christ. We cannot maintain too strongly that there is in Him an infinite readiness to receive, and an infinite ability to save sinners; above all, we cannot hold too firmly that salvation is not of works, but of grace. If ever there was a soul sought and saved, without having done anything to deserve it, that soul was the soul of Zacchaeus. Let us grasp these doctrines firmly, and never let them go. Their price is above rubies. Grace, free grace, is the only thought which gives men rest in a dying hour. Let us proclaim these doctrines confidently to everyone to whom we speak about spiritual things; let us bid them come to Jesus Christ, just as they are, and not wait in the vain hope that they can make themselves fit and worthy to come. Not least, let us tell them that Jesus Christ waits for them, and would come and dwell in their poor sinful hearts, if they would only receive Him. 'Behold,' He says, 'I stand at the door, and knock: if any man hear my voice, and open the door, I will come in to him, and will sup with him, and he with me' (Rev. 3:20).

We are told that Zacchaeus stood, and said unto the Lord, 'the half of my goods I give to the poor; and if I have taken any thing from any man by false accusation, I restore him fourfold'. There was reality in that speech: there was unmistakable proof that Zacchaeus was a new creature. Freely pardoned, and raised from death to life, Zacchaeus felt that he could not begin too soon to show whose he was and whom he served.

January 23

And the Lord turned, and looked upon Peter. And Peter remembered the
word of the Lord, how he had said unto him,
Before the cock crow, thou shalt deny me thrice.
Luke 22:61

The infinite mercy of our Lord Jesus Christ.
This is a lesson which is brought out most forcibly by a fact
which is only recorded in St Luke's Gospel. We are told that
when Peter denied Christ the third time, and the cock crew, 'the Lord
turned, and looked upon Peter'. Those words are deeply touching!
Surrounded by bloodthirsty and insulting enemies, in the full prospect
of horrible outrages, an unjust trial and a painful death, the Lord Jesus
yet found time to think kindly of His poor erring disciple: even then
He would have Peter know He did not forget him. Sorrowfully no doubt,
but not angrily, He 'turned, and looked upon Peter'. There was deep
meaning in that look. It was a sermon which Peter never forgot.

The love of Christ towards His people is a deep well which has no
bottom. Let us never measure it by comparison with any kind of love of
man or woman: it exceeds all other love, as far as the sun exceeds the
rushlight. There is about it a mine of compassion, and patience, and
readiness to forgive sin, of whose riches we have but a faint conception.
Let us not be afraid to trust that love, when we first feel our sins: let us
never be afraid to go on trusting it after we have once believed. No man
need despair, however far he may have fallen, if he will only repent and
turn to Christ. If the heart of Jesus was so gracious when He was prisoner
in the judgment hall, we surely need not think it is less gracious when
He sits in glory at the right hand of God.

We are told that when Peter remembered the warning he had
received, and saw how far he had fallen, he 'went out, and wept bitterly'.
Sorrow like this, let us always remember, is an inseparable companion
of true repentance. Here lies the grand distinction between 'repentance
unto salvation' and unvailing remorse.

January 24

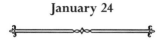

Jesus saith unto her, I that speak unto thee am he.
John 4:26

Christ's gracious willingness to reveal Himself to the chief of sinners.

He concludes His conversation with the Samaritan woman by telling her openly and unreservedly that He is the Saviour of the world. 'I that speak unto thee', He says, 'am he.' Nowhere in all the Gospels do we find our Lord making such a full avowal of His nature and office as He does in this place. And this avowal, be it remembered, was made not to learned scribes, or moral Pharisees, but to one who up to that day had been an ignorant, thoughtless and immoral person!

Dealings with sinners, such as these, form one of the grand peculiarities of the gospel. Whatever a man's past life may have been, there is hope and a remedy for him in Christ. If he is only willing to hear Christ's voice and follow Him, Christ is willing to receive him at once as a friend, and to bestow on him the fullest measure of mercy and grace. The Samaritan woman, the penitent thief, the Philippian scribe, the publican Zacchaeus, are all patterns of Christ's readiness to show mercy, and to confer full and immediate pardons. It is His glory that, like a great physician, He will undertake to cure those who are apparently incurable, and that none are too bad for Him to love and heal. Let these things sink down into our hearts. Whatever else we doubt, let us never doubt that Christ's love to sinners passeth knowledge, and that Christ is as willing to receive as He is almighty to save.

What are we ourselves? This is the question, after all, which demands our attention. We may have been up to this day careless, thoughtless, sinful as the woman whose story we have been reading. But yet there is hope. He who talked with the Samaritan woman at the well is yet living at God's right hand, and never changes. Let us only ask, and He will 'give us living water'.

January 25

*When Jesus therefore saw her weeping, and the Jews also weeping
which came with her, he groaned in the spirit, and was troubled.*
John 11:33

What a depth of tender sympathy there is in Christ's heart towards His people.

We read that when our Lord saw Mary weeping, and the Jews also weeping with her, 'he groaned in the spirit, and was troubled'. We read even more than this. He gave outward expression to His feelings: He 'wept'. He knew perfectly well that the sorrow of the family of Bethany would soon be turned into joy, and that Lazarus in a few minutes would be restored to his sisters. But though He knew all this, He 'wept'.

This weeping of Christ is deeply instructive. It shows us that it is not sinful to sorrow. Weeping and mourning are sadly trying to flesh and blood, and make us feel the weakness of our mortal nature. But they are not in themselves wrong. Even the Son of God wept. It shows us that deep feeling is not a thing of which we need be ashamed. To be cold and stoical and unmoved in the sight of sorrow is no sign of grace. There is nothing unworthy of a child of God in tears. Even the Son of God could weep. It shows us, above all, that the Saviour in whom believers trust is a most tender and feeling Saviour. He is One who can be touched with sympathy for our infirmities. When we turn to Him in the hour of trouble, and pour out our hearts before Him, He knows what we go through, and can pity. And He is One who never changes. Though He now sits at God's right hand in heaven, His heart is still the same that it was upon earth. We have an Advocate with the Father, who, when He was upon earth, could weep.

Let us remember these things in daily life, and never be ashamed of walking in our Master's footsteps. Let us strive to be men and women of a tender heart and a sympathizing spirit. Let us never be ashamed to weep with them that weep, and rejoice with them that rejoice. Well would it be for the Church and the world if there were more Christians of this stamp and character! The Church would be far more beautiful, and the world would be far more happy.

January 26

And a certain scribe came, and said unto him,
Master, I will follow thee withersoever thou goest.
Matthew 8:19

Our Lord's wisdom in dealing with those who professed a willingness to be His disciples.
The passage throws so much light on a subject frequently misunderstood in these days, that it deserves more than ordinary attention.

A certain scribe offers to follow our Lord whithersoever He goes. It was a remarkable offer, when we consider the class to which the man belonged, and the time at which it was made. But the offer receives a remarkable answer. It is not directly accepted, nor yet flatly rejected. Our Lord only makes the solemn reply, 'The foxes have holes, and the birds of the air have nests; but the Son of man hath not where to lay his head'.

Another follower of our Lord next comes forward, and asks to be allowed to bury his father, before going any further in the path of a disciple. The request seems, at first sight, a natural and lawful one. But it draws from our Lord's lips a reply no less solemn than that already referred to: 'Follow me; and let the dead bury their dead'.

There is something deeply impressive in both these sayings. They ought to be well weighed by all professing Christians. They teach us plainly, that people who show a desire to come forward and profess themselves true disciples of Christ, should be warned plainly to 'count the cost', before they begin. Are they prepared to endure hardship? Are they ready to carry the cross? If not, they are not yet fit to begin. They teach us plainly that there are times when a Christian must literally give up all for Christ's sake, and when even such duties as attending to a parent's funeral must be left to be performed by others. Such duties some will always be ready to attend to; and at no time can they be put in comparison with the greater duty of preaching the gospel, and doing Christ's work in the world.

January 27

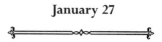

Again, the kingdom of heaven is like unto treasure hid in a field;
the which when a man hath found, he hideth, and for joy thereof
goeth and selleth all that he hath, and buyeth that field.
Matthew 13:44

Men really convinced of the importance of salvation will give up everything to win Christ and eternal life.
What was the conduct of the two men our Lord describes? The one was persuaded that there was a 'treasure hid in a field' which would amply repay him, if he bought the field, however great the price that he might give. The other was persuaded that the 'pearl' he had found was so immensely valuable, that it would answer to him to purchase it at any cost. Both were convinced that they had found a thing of great value: both were satisfied that it was worth a great present sacrifice to make this thing their own. Others might wonder at them; others might think them foolish for paying such a sum of money for the 'field' and 'pearl': but they knew what they were about. They were sure that they were making a good bargain.

We see, in this simple picture, the conduct of a true Christian explained. He is what he is, and does what he does in his religion, because he is thoroughly persuaded that it is worthwhile. He comes out from the world; he puts off the old man; he forsakes the vain companion of his past life. Like Matthew, he gives up everything, and, like Paul, he 'counts all things loss' for Christ's sake. And why? Because he is convinced that Christ will make amends to him for all he gives up. He sees in Christ an endless 'treasure'; he sees in Christ a precious 'pearl'; to win Christ he will make any sacrifice. This is true faith: this is the stamp of a genuine work of the Holy Ghost.

We see in these two parables the real clue to the conduct of many unconverted people. They are what they are in religion, because they are not fully persuaded that it is worthwhile to be different. They flinch from decision; they shrink from taking up the cross; they halt between two opinions; they will not commit themselves: they will not come forward boldly on the Lord's side. And why? Because they are not convinced that it will answer: they have not faith.

January 28

—◦◦◦—

And every one that hath forsaken houses, or brethren, or sisters,
or father, or mother, or wife, or children, or lands, for my name's sake,
shall receive an hundredfold, and shall inherit everlasting life.
Matthew 19:29

The immense encouragement the gospel offers to those who give up everything for Christ's sake.

We are told that Peter asked our Lord what he and the other apostles, who had forsaken their little all for His sake, should receive in return. He obtained a most gracious reply. A full recompense shall be made to all who make sacrifices for Christ's sake: they 'shall receive an hundredfold, and shall inherit everlasting life'.

There is something very cheering in this promise. Few in the present day, excepting converts among the heathen, are ever required to forsake homes, relatives and lands, on account of their religion; yet there are few true Christians who have not much to go through, in one way or another, if they are really faithful to their Lord. The offence of the cross is not yet ceased: laughter, ridicule, mockery and family persecution, are often the portion of an English believer. The favour of the world is often forfeited, places and situations are often perilled, by a conscientious adherence to the demands of the gospel of Christ. All who are exposed to trials of this kind may take comfort in the promise of these verses. Jesus foresaw their need, and intended these words to be their consolation.

We may rest assured that no man shall ever be a real loser by following Christ. The believer may seem to suffer loss for a time, when he first begins the life of a decided Christian; he may be much cast down by the afflictions that are brought upon him on account of his religion: but let him rest assured that he will never find himself a loser in the long run. Christ can raise up friends for us who shall more than compensate for those we lose; Christ can open hearts and homes to us far more warm and hospitable than those that are closed against us; above all, Christ can give us peace of conscience, inward joy, bright hopes and happy feelings, which shall far outweigh every pleasant earthly thing that we have cast away for His sake.

January 29

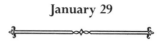

And whosoever will be chief among you, let him be your servant ...
Matthew 20:27

A **life of self-denying kindness to others is the true secret of greatness in the kingdom of Christ.**
What saith the Scripture? '[W]hosoever will be great among you, let him be your minister ... whosoever will be chief among you, let him be your servant'.

The standard of the world, and the standard of the Lord Jesus, are widely different. They are more than different: they are flatly contradictory one to the other. Among the children of this world he is thought the greatest man who has most land, most money, most servants, most rank and most earthly power: among the children of God he is reckoned the greatest who does most to promote the spiritual and temporal happiness of his fellow creatures. True greatness consists, not in receiving, but in giving, not in selfish absorption of good things, but in imparting good to others, not in being served, but in serving, not in sitting still, and being ministered to, but in going about and ministering to others. The angels of God see far more beauty in the work of the missionary than in the work of the Australian digger for gold. They take far more interest in the labours of men like Howard and Judson than in the victories of generals, the political speeches of statesmen or the council-chambers of kings. Let us remember these things. Let us beware of seeking false greatness: let us aim at that greatness which alone is true. There is a mine of profound wisdom in that saying of our Lord's, 'It is more blessed to give than to receive' (Acts 20:35).

What saith the Scripture? We ought to serve one another, 'Even as the Son of man came not to be ministered unto, but to minister'.

The Lord God has mercifully provided His people with everything necessary to their sanctification. He has given those who follow after holiness the clearest of precepts, the best of motives and the most encouraging of promises: but this is not all. He has furthermore supplied them with the most perfect pattern and example – even the life of His own Son.

January 30

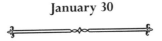

Now when he had left speaking, he said unto Simon, Launch out into the deep, and let down your nets for a draught.
Luke 5:4

What encouragement our Lord gives to unquestioning obedience.

We are told, that after preaching He bade Simon 'Launch out into the deep, and let down his nets for a draught'. He receives an answer which exhibits in a striking manner the mind of a good servant. 'Master,' says Simon, 'we have toiled all the night, and have taken nothing: nevertheless at thy word I will let down the net'. And what was the reward of this ready compliance with the Lord's commands? At once, we are told 'they inclosed a great multitude of fishes: and their net brake'.

We need not doubt that a practical lesson for all Christians is contained under these simple circumstances. We are meant to learn the lesson of ready, unhesitating obedience to every plain command of Christ. The path of duty may sometimes be hard and disagreeable. The wisdom of the course we propose to follow may not be apparent to the world. But none of these things must move us. We are not to confer with flesh and blood. We are to go straight forward when Jesus says, 'Go'; and do a thing boldly, unflinchingly and decidedly, when Jesus says, 'Do it.' We are to walk by faith and not by sight, and believe that what we see not now to be right and reasonable, we shall see hereafter. So acting, we shall never find in the long run that we are losers. So acting, we shall find, sooner or later, that we reap a great reward.

In measuring these words of Peter, we must of course remember the time at which they were spoken. He was at best, but a babe in grace, weak in faith, weak in experience and weak in knowledge. At a later period in his life he would, doubtless, have said, 'Abide with me', and not, 'Depart'. But still, after every deduction of this kind, the words of Peter exactly express the first feelings of man when he is brought into anything like close contact with God. The sight of divine greatness and holiness makes him feel strongly his own littleness and sinfulness.

Cost

January 31

If any man come to me, and hate not his father, and mother,
and wife, and children, and brethren, and sisters, yea,
and his own life also, he cannot be my disciple.
Luke 14:26

True Christians must be ready, if need be, to give up
everything for Christ's sake.

This is a lesson which is taught in very remarkable language.
Our Lord says, 'If any man come to Me, and hate not his father, and
mother, and wife, and children, and brethren, and sisters, yea, and his
own life also, he cannot be my disciple.'

This expression must doubtless be interpreted with some
qualification. We must never explain any text of Scripture in such a
manner as to make it contradict another. Our Lord did not mean us to
understand that it is the duty of Christians to hate their relatives. This
would have been to contradict the fifth commandment. He only meant
that those who follow Him must love Him with a deeper love even than
their nearest and dearest connections, or their own lives. He did not
mean that it is an essential part of Christianity to quarrel with our
relatives and friends. But He did mean that if the claims of our relatives
and the claims of Christ come into collision, the claims of relatives
must give way. We must choose rather to displease those we love most
upon earth, than to displease Him who died for us on the cross.

The demand which our Lord makes upon us here is peculiarly
stringent and heart-searching. Yet it is a wise and a necessary one.
Experience shows, both in the church at home, and in the mission-field
abroad, that the greatest foes to a man's soul are sometimes those of his
own house. It sometimes happens that the greatest hindrance in the
way of an awakened conscience is the opposition of relatives and friends.
Ungodly fathers cannot bear to see their sons, 'taking up new views' of
religion; worldly mothers are vexed to see their daughters unwilling to
enter into the gaieties of the world. A collision of opinion takes place
frequently, as soon as grace enters into a family, and then comes the
time when the true Christian must remember the spirit of our Lord's
words in this passage. He must be willing to offend his family, rather
than offend Christ.

FEBRUARY

February 1

*So likewise, whosoever he be of you that forsaketh not all that he hath,
he cannot be my disciple.*
Luke 14:33

Those who are thinking of following Christ should be warned to 'count the cost'.

This is a lesson which was intended for the multitudes who followed our Lord without thought and consideration, and was enforced by examples drawn from building and from war. It is a lesson which will be found useful in every age of the Church.

It costs something to be a true Christian. Let that never be forgotten. To be a mere nominal Christian, and go to church, is cheap and easy work; but to hear Christ's voice, and follow Christ, and believe in Christ, and confess Christ, requires much self-denial. It will cost us our sins, and our self-righteousness, and our ease, and our worldliness. All – all must be given up. We must fight an enemy, who comes against us with twenty thousand followers. We must build a tower in troublous times. Our Lord Jesus Christ would have us thoroughly understand this. He bids us 'count the cost'.

Now, why did our Lord use this language? Did He wish to discourage men from becoming His disciples? Did He mean to make the gate of life appear more narrow than it is? It is not difficult to find an answer to these questions. Our Lord spoke as He did to prevent men following Him lightly and inconsiderately, from mere animal feeling or temporary excitement, who in time of temptation would fall away. He knew that nothing does so much harm to the cause of true religion as backsliding, and that nothing causes so much backsliding as enlisting disciples without letting them know what they take in hand. He had no desire to swell the number of His followers by admitting soldiers who would fail in the hour of need. For this reason He raises a warning voice. He bids all who think of taking service with Him count the cost before they begin.

February 2

Then said Jesus to those Jews which believed on him,
If ye continue in my word, then are ye my disciples indeed ...
John 8:31

The importance of steady perseverance in Christ's service.

There were many, it seems, at this particular period, who professed to believe on our Lord, and expressed a desire to become His disciples. There is nothing to show that they had true faith. They appear to have acted under the influence of temporary excitement, and without considering what they were doing. And to them our Lord addresses this instructive warning – 'If ye continue in my word, then are ye my disciples indeed'.

This sentence contains a mine of wisdom. To make a beginning in religious life is comparatively easy. Not a few mixed motives assist us. The love of novelty, the praise of well-meaning but indiscreet professors, the secret of self-satisfaction of feeling 'how good I am', the universal excitement attending a new position – all these things combine to aid a young beginner. Aided by them he begins to run the race that leads to heaven, lays aside many bad habits, takes up many good ones, has many comfortable frames and feelings, and gets on swimmingly for a time. But when the newness of his position is past and gone, when the freshness of his feelings is rubbed off and lost, when the world and the devil begin to pull hard at him, when the weakness of his own heart begins to appear – then it is that he finds out the real difficulties of vital Christianity. Then it is that he discovers the deep wisdom of our Lord's saying now before us. It is not beginning, but 'continuing' a religious profession, that is the test of true grace.

We should remember these things in forming our estimate of other people's religion. No doubt we ought to be thankful when we see any one ceasing to do evil and learning to do well. We must not despise 'the day of small things' (Zech. 4:10). But we must not forget that to begin is one thing, and to go on is quite another. Patient continuance in well-doing is the only sure evidence of grace. Not he that runs fast and furiously at first, but he that keeps up his speed, is he that 'runs so as to obtain'.

February 3

Even as the Son of man came not to be ministered unto,
but to minister, and to give his life a ransom for many.
Matthew 20:28

Christ's death was an atonement for sin.
What saith the Scripture? '[T]he Son of man came ... to give his life a ransom for many'.

This is the mightiest truth in the Bible. Let us take care that we grasp it firmly, and never let it go. Our Lord Jesus Christ did not die merely as a martyr, or as a splendid example of self-sacrifice and self-denial: those who can see no more than that in His death, fall infinitely short of the truth; they lose sight of the very foundation-stone of Christianity, and miss the whole comfort of the gospel. Christ died as a sacrifice for man's sin; He died to make reconciliation for man's iniquity; He died to purge our sins by the offering of Himself; He died to redeem us from the curse which we all deserved, and to make satisfaction to the justice of God, which must otherwise have condemned us. Never let us forget this!

We are all by nature debtors. We owe to our holy Maker ten thousand talents, and are not able to pay. We cannot atone for our own transgressions, for we are weak and frail, and only adding to our debts every day. But, blessed be God, what we could not do, Christ came into the world to do for us; what we could not pay, He undertook to pay for us: to pay it, He died for us upon the cross. He 'offered Himself ... to God' (Heb. 9:14).

He 'suffered for sins, the just for the unjust, that he might bring us to God' (1 Pet. 3:18). Once more, never let us forget this! Let us leave these verses without asking ourselves, where is our humility? what is our idea of true greatness? what is our example? what is our hope? Life, eternal life, depends on the answer we give to these questions. Happy is that man who is truly humble, strives to do good in his day, walks in the steps of Jesus and rests all his hopes on the ransom paid for him by Christ's blood. Such a man is a true Christian!

February 4

For even the Son of man came not to be ministered unto,
but to minister, and to give his life a ransom for many.
Mark 10:45

The language which our Lord uses in speaking of His own death.

He says, 'the Son of man came ... to give his life a ransom for many'.

This is one of those expressions which ought to be carefully treasured up in the minds of all true Christians. It is one of the texts which prove incontrovertibly the atoning character of Christ's death. That death was no common death, like the death of a martyr, or of other holy men. It was the public payment by an almighty Representative of the debts of sinful man to a holy God. It was the ransom which a divine Surety undertook to provide, in order to procure liberty for sinners tied and bound by the chain of their sins. By that death Jesus made a full and complete satisfaction for man's countless transgressions. He bore our sins in His own body on the tree. The Lord laid on Him the iniquity of us all. When He died, He died for us. When He suffered, He suffered in our stead. When He hung on the cross, He hung there as our Substitute. When His blood flowed, it was the price of our souls.

Let all who trust in Christ take comfort in the thought that they build on a sure foundation. It is true that we are sinners, but Christ has borne our sins. It is true that we are poor, helpless debtors, but Christ has paid our debts. It is true that we deserve to be shut up for ever in the prison of hell. But, thanks be to God, Christ hath paid a full and complete ransom for us. The door is wide open. The prisoners may go free. May we all know this privilege by heartfelt experience, and walk in the blessed liberty of the children of God.

February 5

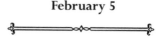

And it came to pass, when the time was come that he should be
received up, he stedfastly set his face to go to Jerusalem.
Luke 9:51

The steady determination with which our Lord Jesus Christ regarded His own crucifixion and death.

We read that 'when the time was come that he should be received up, he stedfastly set his face to go to Jerusalem'. He knew full well what was before Him. The betrayal, the unjust trial, the mockery, the scourging, the crown of thorns, the spitting, the nails, the spear, the agony on the cross – all, all were doubtless spread before His mind's eye, like a picture. But He never flinched for a moment from the work that He had undertaken. His heart was set on paying the price of our redemption, and going even to the prison of the grave, as our Surety. He was full of tender love towards sinners. It was the desire of His whole soul to procure for them salvation. And so, 'for the joy that was set before him endured the cross, despising the shame' (Heb. 12:2).

For ever let us bless God that we have such a ready and willing Saviour. For ever let us remember that as He was ready to suffer, so He is always ready to save. The man that comes to Christ by faith should never doubt Christ's willingness to receive him. The mere fact that the Son of God willingly came into the world to die, and willingly suffered, should silence such doubts entirely. All the unwillingness is on the part of man, not of Christ. It consists in the ignorance, and pride, and unbelief, and half-heartedness of the sinner himself.

But there is nothing wanting in Christ. Let us strive and pray that the same mind may be in us which was in our blessed Master. Like Him, let us be willing to go anywhere, do anything, suffer anything, when the path for duty is clear, and the voice of God calls. Let us set our faces steadfastly to our work, when our work is plainly marked out, and drink our bitter cups patiently, when they come from a Father's hand.

February 6

For he shall be delivered unto the Gentiles, and shall be mocked,
and spitefully entreated, and spitted on ...
Luke 18:32

The clear and plain prediction which our Lord makes about His own death.

We see Him telling the disciples that He would be 'delivered unto the Gentiles, mocked ... spitefully entreated ... spitted on ... scourged ... and put to death.'

The importance of our Lord's death appears in the frequency with which He foretold it, and referred to it during His life. He knew well that it was the principal end for which He came into the world. He was to give His life a ransom for many; He was to make His soul an offering for sin, and to bear our transgressions in His own body on the tree; He was to give His body and blood for the life of the world. Let us seek to be of the same mind with Christ in our estimate of His death: let our principal thoughts about Jesus be inseparably bound up with His crucifixion. The corner stone of all truth concerning Christ is this, that 'while we were yet sinners, Christ died for us' (Rom. 5:8).

The love of our Lord Jesus Christ towards sinners is strikingly shown in His steady purpose of heart to die for them. All through His life He knew that He was about to be crucified. There was nothing in His cross and passion which He did not foresee distinctly, even to the minutest particular: long before it came upon Him He tasted all the well-known bitterness of anticipated suffering. Yet He never swerved from His path for a moment. He was straitened in spirit till He had finished the work He came to do (Luke 12:50). Such love passeth knowledge; it is unspeakable, unsearchable: we may rest on that love without fear. If Christ so loved us before we thought of Him, He will surely not cease to love us after we have believed.

The calmness of our Lord Jesus Christ in the prospect of certain death ought to be a pattern to all His people. Like Him, let us drink the bitter cup which our Father gives us, without a murmur, and say, 'Not my will but Thine be done.'

February 7

And when Jesus had cried with a loud voice, he said, Father, into thy hands I
commend my spirit: and having said thus, he gave up the ghost.
Luke 23:46

The remarkable words which our Lord spoke when He
died.

We read that when He had cried with a loud voice, He said,
'Father, into thy hands I commend my Spirit: and having said thus, he
gave up the ghost'.

There is a depth of meaning, no doubt, in these words, which we
have no line to fathom. There was something mysterious about our Lord's
death, which made it unlike the death of any mere man. He who spoke
the words before us, we must carefully remember, was God as well as
man: His divine and human nature were inseparably united. His divine
nature of course could not die. He says Himself, 'I lay down my life,
that I might take it again. No man taketh it from me, but I lay it down of
myself. I have power to lay it down, and I have power to take it again'
(John 10:17, 18). Christ died, not as we die when our hour is come,
not because He was compelled and could not help dying, but voluntarily,
and of His own free will.

There is a sense, however, in which our Lord's words supply a lesson
to all true Christians: they show us the manner in which death should
be met by all God's children; they afford an example which every
believer should strive to follow. Like our Master, we should not be
afraid to confront the king of terrors: we should regard him as a
vanquished enemy, whose sting has been taken away by Christ's death;
we should think of him as a foe who can hurt the body for a little season,
but after that has no more that he can do; we should await his approaches
with calmness and patience, and believe that when flesh fails our soul
will be in good keeping. This was the mind of dying Stephen: 'Lord
Jesus,' he said, 'receive my spirit.' This was the mind of Paul the aged,
when the time of his departure was at hand. He says 'I know whom I
have believed, and am persuaded that he is able to keep that which I
have committed unto him against that day' (Acts 7:59; 2 Tim. 1:12).
Happy indeed are those who have a last end like this!

February 8

And he took it down, and wrapped it in linen, and laid it in a
sepulchre that was hewn in stone, wherein never man before was laid.
Luke 23:53

The reality of Christ's death.
This is a fact which is placed beyond dispute, by the circumstances related about His burial. Those who took His body from the cross, and wrapped it in linen, could not have been deceived: their own senses must have been witnesses to the fact that He whom they handled was a corpse, their own hands and eyes must have told them that He whom they laid in Joseph's sepulchre was not alive but dead.

The importance of the fact before us is far greater than a careless reader supposes. If Christ did not really die, there would be an end of all the comfort of the gospel: nothing short of His death could have paid man's debt to God. His incarnation, and sermons, and parables, and miracles, and sinless obedience to the law would have availed nothing, if He had not died. The penalty threatened to the first Adam was death eternal in hell; if the Second Adam had not really and actually died in our stead, as well as taught us truth, the original penalty would have continued in full force against Adam and all his children. It was the life blood of Christ which was to save our souls.

For ever let us bless God that our great Redeemer's death is a fact beyond all dispute. The centurion who stood by the cross, the friends who took out the nails, and laid the body in the grave, the women who stood by and beheld, the priest who sealed up the grave, the soldiers who guarded the sepulchre – all, all are witnesses that Jesus actually was dead. The great sacrifice was really offered; the life of the Lamb was actually taken away: the penalty due to sin has actually been discharged by our divine Substitute. Sinners believing in Jesus may hope and not be afraid. In themselves they are guilty: but Christ hath died for the ungodly, and their debt is now completely paid.

February 9

And said unto them, Thus it is written, and thus it behoved Christ to
suffer, and to rise from the dead the third day ...
Luke 24:46

The remarkable manner in which the Lord Jesus speaks of His own death on the cross.

He does not speak of it as a misfortune, or as a thing to be lamented, but as a necessity. He says, 'It behoved Christ to suffer, and to rise from the dead the third day'.

The death of Christ was necessary to our salvation. His flesh and blood offered in sacrifice on the cross were 'the life of the world' (John 6:51). Without the death of Christ, so far as we can see, God's law could never have been satisfied, sin could never have been pardoned, man could never have been justified before God and God could never have shown mercy to man. The cross of Christ was the solution of a mighty difficulty: it untied a vast knot; it enabled God to be 'just, and the justifier' of the ungodly (Rom. 3:26). It enabled man to draw near to God with boldness, and to feel that though a sinner he might have hope. Christ by suffering as a Substitute in our stead, the just for the unjust, has made a way by which we can draw near to God. We may freely acknowledge that in ourselves we are guilty and deserve death; but we may boldly plead, that One has died for us, and that for His sake, believing on Him, we claim life and acquittal.

Let us ever glory in the cross of Christ; let us regard it as the source of all our hopes, and the foundation of all our peace. Ignorance and unbelief may see nothing in the sufferings of Calvary but the cruel martyrdom of an innocent person: faith will look far deeper; faith will see in the death of Jesus the payment of man's enormous debt to God, and the complete salvation of all who believe.

February 10

As the Father knoweth me, even so know I the Father:
and I lay down my life for the sheep.
John 10:15

When Christ died, He died of His own voluntary free will.

He uses a remarkable expression to teach this: 'I lay down my life, that I might take it again. No man taketh it from me, but I lay it down of myself. I have power to lay it down, and I have power to take it again.'

The point before us is of no mean importance. We must never suppose for a moment that our Lord had no power to prevent His sufferings, and that He was delivered up to His enemies and crucified because He could not help it. Nothing could be further from the truth than such an idea. The treachery of Judas, the armed band of priests' servants, the enmity of scribes and Pharisees, the injustice of Pontius Pilate, the rude hands of Roman soldiers, the scourge, the nails, and the spear, all these could not have harmed a hair of our Lord's head, unless He had allowed them. Well might He say those remarkable words, 'Thinkest thou that I cannot now pray to my Father, and he shall presently give me more than twelve legions of angels? But how then shall the scriptures be fulfilled' (Matt. 26:53).

The plain truth is, that our Lord submitted to death of His own free will, because He knew that His death was the only way of making atonement for man's sins. He poured out His soul unto death with all the desire of His heart, because He had determined to pay our debt to God, and redeem us from hell. For the joy set before Him He willingly endured the cross, and laid down His life, in order that we, through His death, might have eternal life. His death was not the death of a martyr, who sinks at last overwhelmed by enemies, but the death of a triumphant conqueror, who knows that even in dying He wins for Himself and His people a kingdom and a crown of glory.

February 11

Now is my soul troubled; and what shall I say? Father, save me from this hour: but for this cause came I unto this hour.
John 12:27

A great doctrine indirectly proved.

That doctrine is the imputation of man's sin to Christ. We see the Saviour of the world, the eternal Son of God troubled and disturbed in mind: 'Now is my soul troubled'. We see Him who could heal diseases with a touch, cast out devils with a word, and command the waves and winds to obey Him, in great agony and conflict of spirit. Now how can this be explained?

To say, as some do, that the only cause of our Lord's trouble was the prospect of His own painful death on the cross, is a very unsatisfactory explanation. At this rate it might justly be said that many a martyr has shown more calmness and courage than the Son of God. Such a conclusion is, to say the least, most revolting. Yet this is the conclusion to which men are driven if they adopt the modern notion, that Christ's death was only a great example of self-sacrifice.

Nothing can ever explain our Lord's trouble of soul, both here and in Gethsemane, except the old doctrine, that He felt the burden of man's sin pressing Him down. It was the mighty weight of a world's guilt imputed to Him and meeting on His head, which made Him groan and agonize, and cry, 'Now is my soul troubled'. For ever let us cling to that doctrine, not only as untying the knot of the passage before us, but as the only ground of solid comfort for the heart of a Christian. That our sins have been really laid on our divine Substitute, and borne by Him, and that His righteousness is really imputed to us and accounted ours, this is the real warrant for Christian peace. And if any man asks how we know that our sins were laid on Christ, we bid him read such passages as that which is before us, and explain them on any other principle if he can. Christ has borne our sins, carried our sins, groaned under the burden of our sins, been 'troubled' in soul by the weight of our sins and really taken away our sins. This, we may rest assured, is sound doctrine: this is scriptural theology.

February 12

When Jesus therefore had received the vinegar, he said, It is finished:
and he bowed his head, and gave up the ghost.
John 19:30

The peculiarly solemn saying which came from our Lord's lips just before He died.

St John relates that when He 'had received the vinegar, he said, It is finished: and he bowed his head and gave up the ghost.' It is surely not too much to say, that of all the seven famous sayings of Christ on the cross, none is more remarkable than this, which John alone has recorded.

The precise meaning of this wondrous expression, 'It is finished', is a point which the Holy Ghost has not thought good to reveal to us. There is a depth about it, we must all instinctively feel, which man has probably no line to fathom. Yet there is perhaps no irreverence in conjecturing the thoughts that were in our Lord's mind when the word was spoken. The finishing of all the known and unknown sufferings which He came to endure, as our Substitute, the finishing of the ceremonial law, which He came to wind up and fulfil, as the true Sacrifice for sin, the finishing of the many prophecies, which He came to accomplish, the finishing of the great work of man's redemption, which was now close at hand, all this, we need not doubt, our Lord had in view when He said, 'It is finished'. There may have been more behind, for aught we know. But in handling the language of such a Being as our Saviour, on such an occasion, and at so mysterious a crisis of His history, it is well to be cautious. 'The place whereon we stand is holy ground.' One comfortable thought, at all events, stands out most clearly on the face of this famous expression. We rest our souls on a 'finished work', if we rest them on the work of Jesus Christ the Lord. We need not fear that either sin, or Satan, or law shall condemn us at the last day. We may lean back on the thought, that we have a Saviour who has done all, paid all, accomplished all, performed all that is necessary for our salvation.

e DEATH

February 13

While he yet spake, there cometh one from the ruler of the synagogue's house, saying to him, Thy daughter is dead; trouble not the Master.
Luke 8:49

How universal is the dominion which death holds over the sons of men.

We see him coming to a rich man's house, and tearing from him the desire of his eyes with a stroke. '[T]here cometh one from the ruler of the synagogue's house, saying to him, Thy daughter is dead....' Such tidings as these are the bitterest cups which we have to drink in this world. Nothing cuts so deeply into man's heart as to part with beloved ones, and lay them in the grave. Few griefs are so crushing and heavy as the grief of a parent over an only child.

Death is indeed a cruel enemy! He makes no distinction in his attacks. He comes to the rich man's hall as well as to the poor man's cottage. He does not spare the young, the strong and the beautiful, any more than the old, infirm and the grey-haired. Not all the gold of Australia, nor all the skill of doctors, can keep the hand of death from our bodies in the day of his power. When the appointed hour comes, and God permits him to smite, our worldly schemes must be broken off, and our darlings must be taken away and buried out of our sight.

These thoughts are melancholy, and few like to hear of them. The subject of death is one that men blink, and refuse to look at. 'All men think all men mortal but themselves.' But why should we treat this great reality in this way? Why should we not rather look the subject of death in the face, in order that when our turn comes we may be prepared to die? Death will come to our houses, whether we like it or not. Death will take each of us away, despite our dislike to hearing about it. Surely it is the part of a wise man to get ready for this great change. Why should we not be ready? There is One who can deliver us from the fear of death (Heb. 2:15). Christ has overcome death, and 'brought life and immortality to light through the gospel' (2 Tim. 1:10). He that believeth on Him hath everlasting life, and though he were dead yet shall he live (John 6:47; 11:25). Let us believe in the Lord Jesus, and then death will lose his sting.

f 52

February 14

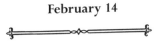

And he put them all out, and took her by the hand,
and called, saying, Maid, arise.
Luke 8:54

The almighty power which our Lord Jesus Christ possesses even over death.

We are told that He came to the house of Jairus and turned the mourning into joy. He took by the hand the breathless body of the ruler's daughter, 'and called saying, Damsel, arise'. At once, by that all-powerful voice, life was restored. 'Her spirit came again, and she arose straightway.'

Let us take comfort in the thought that there is a limit to death's power. The king of terrors is very strong. How many generations he has mowed down and swept into the dust! How many of the wise, and strong, and fair, he has swallowed down and snatched away in their prime! How many victories he has won, and how often he has written, 'Vanity of vanities', on the pride of man! Patriarchs and kings and prophets and apostles, have all in turn been obliged to yield to him. They have all died. But, thanks be unto God, there is One stronger than death. There is One who has said, 'O death, I will be thy plagues; O grave, I will be thy destruction' (Hos. 13:14). That One is the Friend of sinners, Christ Jesus the Lord. He proved His power frequently when He came to earth the first time, in the house of Jairus, by the tomb of Bethany, in the gate of Nain. He will prove it to all the world when He comes again. 'The last enemy that shall be destroyed is death' (1 Cor. 15:26). '[T]he earth shall cast out the dead' (Isa. 26:19).

Let us leave the passage with the consoling thought that the things which happened in Jairus' house are a type of good things to come. The hour cometh and will soon be here, when the voice of Christ shall call all His people from their graves, and gather them together to part no more. Believing husbands shall once more see believing wives. Believing parents shall once more see believing children. Christ shall unite the whole family in the great home in heaven, and all tears shall be wiped from all eyes.

February 15

And Jesus answering said unto them, Suppose ye that these Galilaeans were sinners above all the Galilaeans, because they suffered such things?
Luke 13:2

How much more ready people are to talk of the deaths of others than their own. The death of the Galilaeans, mentioned here, was probably a common subject of conversation in Jerusalem and all Judaea: we can well believe that all the circumstances and particulars belonging to it were continually discussed by thousands who never thought of their own latter end. It is just the same in the present day. A murder, a sudden death, a shipwreck or a railway accident, will completely occupy the minds of a neighbourhood, and be in the mouth of every one you meet; and yet these very persons dislike talking of their own deaths, and their own prospects in the world beyond the grave. Such is human nature in every age. In religion, men are ready to talk of anybody's business rather than their own.

The state of our own souls should always be our first concern. It is eminently true that real Christianity will always begin at home. The converted man will always think first of his own heart, his own life, his own deserts and his own sins. Does he hear of a sudden death? He will say to himself, 'Should I have been found ready, if this had happened to me?' Does he hear of some awful crime, or deed of wickedness? He will say to himself, 'Are my sins forgiven? and have I really repented of my own transgressions?' Does he hear of worldly men running into every excess of sin? He will say to himself, 'Who has made me to differ? What has kept me from walking in the same road, except the free grace of God?' May we ever seek to be men of this frame of mind! Let us take a kind interest in all around us. Let us feel tender pity and compassion for all who suffer violence, or are removed by sudden death. But let us never forget to look at home, and to learn wisdom for ourselves from all that happens to others.

February 16

These things said he: and after that he saith unto them, Our friend
Lazarus sleepeth; but I go, that I may awake him out of sleep.
John 11:11

How tenderly Christ speaks of the death of believers.
He announces the fact of Lazarus being dead in language of
singular beauty and gentleness: 'Our friend Lazarus sleepeth'.
Every true Christian has a Friend in heaven, of almighty power and
boundless love. He is thought of, cared for and provided for, defended
by God's eternal Son. He has an unfailing Protector, who never slumbers
or sleeps, and watches continually over his interests. The world may
despise him, but he has no cause to be ashamed. Father and mother
even may cast him out, but Christ having once taken him up will never
let him go. He is the 'friend of Christ' even after he is dead! The
friendships of this world are often fair-weather friendships, and fail us
like summer-dried fountains, when our need is the sorest; but the
friendship of the Son of God is stronger than death, and goes beyond
the grave. The Friend of sinners is a Friend that sticketh closer than a
brother.

The death of true Christians is 'sleep', and not annihilation. It is a
solemn and miraculous change, no doubt, but not a change to be
regarded with alarm. They have nothing to fear for their souls in the
change, for their sins are washed away in Christ's blood. The sharpest
sting of death is the sense of unpardoned sin. Christians have nothing to
fear for their bodies in the change: they will rise again by and by, refreshed
and renewed, after the image of the Lord. The grave itself is a conquered
enemy. It must render back its tenants safe and sound, the very moment
that Christ calls for them at the last day.

Let us remember these things when those whom we love fall asleep
in Christ, or when we ourselves receive our notice to quit this world.
Let us call to mind in such an hour, that our great Friend takes thought
for our bodies as well as for our souls, and that He will not allow one
hair of our heads to perish. Let us never forget that the grave is the
place where the Lord Himself lay, and that as He rose again triumphant
from that cold bed, so also shall all His people.

February 17

And as Jesus passed forth from thence, he saw a man, named Matthew,
sitting at the receipt of custom: and he saith unto him,
Follow me. And he arose, and followed him.
Matthew 9:9

The wonderful call of the Apostle Matthew to be Christ's disciple.

We find the man, who afterwards was the first to write a Gospel, sitting at the receipt of custom: we see him absorbed in his worldly calling, and possibly thinking of nothing but money and gain; but suddenly the Lord Jesus calls on him to follow Him, and become His disciple. At once Matthew obeys: He 'made haste, and delayed not' to keep Christ's commandments (Ps. 119:60). He arises and follows Him.

We should learn, from Matthew's case, that with Christ nothing is impossible. He can take a tax gatherer, and make him an apostle: He can change any heart, and make all things new. Let us never despair of any one's salvation. Let us pray on, and speak on, and work on, in order to do good to souls, even to the souls of the worst. 'The voice of the Lord is powerful' (Ps. 29:4). When He says by the power of the Spirit, 'follow Me', He can make the hardest and most sinful obey.

We should observe Matthew's decision. He waited for nothing: he did not tarry for 'a convenient season' (Acts 24:25); and he reaped in consequence a great reward. He wrote a book which is known all over the earth; he became a blessing to others as well as blessed in his own soul; he left a name behind him which is better known than the names of princes and kings. The richest man of the world is soon forgotten when he dies, but as long as the world stands millions will know the name of Matthew the publican.

February 18

And he said unto her, What wilt thou? She saith unto him,
Grant that these my two sons may sit, the one on thy right hand,
and the other on the left, in thy kingdom.
Matthew 20:21

The mixture of ignorance and faith that may be found even in true-hearted Christians.

We see the mother of James and John coming to our Lord with her two sons, and preferring on their behalf a strange petition. She asks that they may sit, one on His right hand, and the other on His left, in His kingdom. She seems to have forgotten all He had just been saying about His suffering: her eager mind can think of nothing but His glory. His plain warnings about the crucifixion appear to have been thrown away on her sons: their thoughts were full of nothing but His throne, and the day of His power. There was much of faith in their request, but there was much more of infirmity. There was something to be commended, in that they could see in Jesus of Nazareth a coming king; but there was also much to blame, in that they did not remember that He was to be crucified before He could reign. Truly 'the flesh lusteth against the spirit' in all God's children, and Luther well remarks, 'the flesh ever seeks to be glorified before it is crucified'.

There are many Christians who are very like this woman and her sons. They see in part, and know in part, the things of God, they have faith enough to follow Christ; they have knowledge enough to hate sin, and come out from the world: and yet there are many truths of Christianity of which they are deplorably ignorant. They talk ignorantly, they act ignorantly and commit many sad mistakes. Their acquaintance with the Bible is very scanty: their insight into their own hearts very small. But we must learn from these verses to deal gently with such people, because the Lord has received them. We must not set them down as graceless and godless, because of their ignorance: we must remember that true faith may lay at the bottom of their hearts, though there is much rubbish at the top. We must reflect that the sons of Zebedee, whose knowledge was at one time so imperfect, became at a later period pillars of the Church of Christ.

February 19

*Watch and pray, that ye enter not into temptation: the spirit indeed is
willing, but the flesh is weak.*
Matthew 26:41

A great weakness, even in true disciples of Christ, and
that they have need to watch and pray against it.
We see Peter, James and John, those three chosen apostles,
sleeping when they ought to have been watching and praying; and we
find our Lord addressing them in these solemn words, 'Watch and pray,
that ye enter not into temptation: the spirit indeed is willing, but the
flesh is weak.'

There is a double nature in all believers. Converted, renewed,
sanctified as they are, they still carry about with them a mass of
indwelling corruption, a body of sin. St Paul speaks of this, when he
says, 'I find then a law, that, when I would do good, evil is present with
me. For I delight in the law of God after the inward man: But I see
another law in my members, warring against the law of my mind' (Rom.
7:21-23). The experience of all true Christians in every age confirms
this. They find within two contrary principles, and a continual strife
between the two; to these two principles our Lord alludes when He
addresses His half-awakened disciples: He calls the one 'flesh', and the
other 'spirit'. He says 'the spirit is willing, but the flesh is weak'.

But does our Lord excuse this weakness of His disciples? Be it far
from us to think so: those who draw this conclusion mistake His meaning.
He uses that very weakness as an argument for watchfulness and prayer;
He teaches us that the very fact that we are encompassed with infirmity,
should stir us up continually to 'watch and pray'.

February 20

Teaching them to observe all things whatsoever I have commanded you: and, lo, I am with you always, even unto the end of the world. Amen.
Matthew 28:20

The obedience which Jesus requires of all who profess themselves His disciples.

He bids the apostles teach them to observe all things, whatsoever He has commanded them.

This is a searching expression. It shows the uselessness of a mere name and form of Christianity; it shows that they only are to be counted true Christians who live in a practical obedience to His word, and strive to do the things that He has commanded. The water of baptism, and the bread and wine of the Lord's Supper alone will save no man's soul. It profits nothing that we go to a place of worship and hear Christ's ministers, and approve of the gospel, if our religion goes no further than this. What are our lives? What is our daily conduct at home and abroad? Is the Sermon on the Mount our rule and standard? Do we strive to copy Christ's example? Do we seek to do the things that He commanded? These are questions that must be answered in the affirmative, if we would prove ourselves born again, and children of God. Obedience is the only proof of reality. 'faith without works is dead', being alone (Jas. 2:17, 20, 26). 'Ye are my friends,' says Jesus, 'if ye do whatsoever I command you' (John 15:14).

He says to His disciples, 'I am with you always, even unto the end of the world.'

It is impossible to conceive words more comforting, strengthening, cheering and sanctifying than these. Though left alone, like orphan children in a cold, unkind world, the disciples were not to think they were deserted: their Master would be ever 'with them'. Though commissioned to do a work as hard as that of Moses when sent to Pharaoh, they were not to be discouraged: their Master would certainly be 'with them'. No words could be more suited to the position of those to whom they were first spoken; no words could be imagined more consolatory to believers in every age of the world.

February 21

Now as he walked by the sea of Galilee, he saw Simon and Andrew his brother casting a net into the sea: for they were fishers.
Mark 1:16

The occupation of those who were first called to be Christ's disciples.

We read that our Lord called Simon and Andrew, when they were 'casting a net into the sea', and James and John while they were 'mending their nets'.

It is clear from these words, that the first followers of our Lord were not the great of this world. They were men who had neither riches, nor rank, nor power. But the kingdom of Christ is not dependent on such things as these. His cause advances in the world, 'Not by might, nor by power, but by my Spirit, saith the LORD of hosts' (Zech. 4:6). The words of St Paul will always be found true: 'not many wise men after the flesh, not many mighty, not many noble, are called: But God hath chosen the foolish things of the world to confound the wise; and God hath chosen the weak things of the world to confound the things which are mighty' (1 Cor. 1:26, 27). The Church which began with a few fishermen, and yet overspread half the world, must have been founded by God.

We must beware of giving way to the common notion, that there is anything disgraceful in being poor, and in working with our own hands. The Bible contains many instances of special privileges conferred on working men. Moses was keeping sheep, when God appeared to him in the burning bush. Gideon was thrashing wheat, when the angel brought him a message from heaven. Elisha was ploughing, when Elijah called him to be a prophet in his stead. The apostles were fishing, when Jesus called them to follow Him. It is disgraceful to be covetous, or proud, or a cheat, or a gambler, or a drunkard, or a glutton, or unclean. But it is no disgrace to be poor. The labourer who serves Christ faithfully is far more honourable in God's eyes, than the nobleman who serves sin.

February 22

*And he called unto him the twelve, and began to send them forth by
two and two; and gave them power over unclean spirits.*
Mark 6:7

Christ sent forth His apostles 'two and two'.
St Mark is the only evangelist who mentions this fact. It is one
that deserves special notice.

There can be no doubt that this fact is meant to teach us the
advantages of Christian company to all who work for Christ. The wise
man had good reason for saying, 'Two are better than one' (Eccles.
4:9). Two men together will do more work than two men singly. They
will help one another in judgment, and commit fewer mistakes. They
will aid one another in difficulties, and less often fail of success. They
will stir one another up when tempted to idleness, and less often relapse
into indolence and indifference. They will comfort one another in times
of trial, and be less often cast down. '[W]oe to him that is alone when
he falleth; for he hath not another to help him up' (Eccles. 4:10).

It is probable that this principle is not sufficiently remembered in
the Church of Christ in these latter days. The harvest is undoubtedly
great all over the world, both at home and abroad. The labourers are
unquestionably few, and the supply of faithful men far less than the
demand. The arguments for sending out men 'one by one', under existing
circumstances, are undeniably strong and weighty. But still the conduct
of our Lord in this place is a striking fact. The fact that there is hardly a
single case in the Acts where we find Paul or any other apostle working
entirely alone is another remarkable circumstance. It is difficult to avoid
the conclusion, that if the rule of going forth 'two and two' had been
more strictly observed, the missionary field would have yielded larger
results than it has.

One thing at all events is clear, and that is the duty of all workers for
Christ to work together and help one another whenever they can. As
'Iron sharpeneth iron; so a man sharpeneth the countenance of his
friend.'

February 23

*And the apostles gathered themselves together unto Jesus, and told him
all things, both what they had done, and what they had taught'.*

Mark 6:30

The conduct of the apostles when they returned from
their first mission as preachers.

We read that they 'gathered themselves together unto Jesus, and
told him all things, both what they had done, and what they had taught'.

These words are deeply instructive. They are a bright example to all
ministers of the gospel, and to all labourers in the great work of doing
good to souls. All such should daily do as the apostles did on this occasion.
They should tell all their proceedings to the great Head of the Church.
They should spread all their work before Christ, and ask of Him counsel,
guidance, strength and help.

Prayer is the main secret of success in spiritual business. It moves
Him who can move heaven and earth. It brings down the promised aid
of the Holy Ghost, without whom the finest sermons, the clearest
teaching and the most diligent working, are all alike in vain. It is not
always those who have the most eminent gifts who are most successful
labourers for God. It is generally those who keep up closest communion
with Christ and are most instant in prayer. It is those who cry with the
prophet Ezekiel, 'Come from the four winds, O breath, and breathe
upon these slain, that they may live' (Ezek. 37:9). It is those who follow
most exactly the apostolic model, and 'give ourselves continually to
prayer, and to the ministry of the word' (Acts 6:4). Happy is that Church
which has a praying as well as a preaching ministry! The question we
should ask about a new minister is not merely, 'Can he preach well?'
but, 'Does he pray much for his people and his work?'

February 24

*And he said unto them, Come ye yourselves apart into a desert place,
and rest a while: for there were many coming and going,
and they had no leisure so much as to eat.*
Mark 6:31

The words of our Lord to the apostles, when they returned from their first public ministry.

'[H]e said unto them, Come ye yourselves apart into a desert place, and rest a while'.

These words are full of tender consideration. Our Lord knows well that His servants are flesh as well as spirit, and have bodies as well as souls. He knows that at best they have a treasure in earthen vessels, and are themselves compassed with many infirmities. He shows them that He does not expect from them more than their bodily strength can do. He asks for what we can do, and not for what we cannot do. 'Come ye yourselves apart', He says, 'and rest awhile'.

These words are full of deep wisdom. Our Lord knows well that His servants must attend to their own souls as well as the souls of others. He knows that a constant attention to public work is apt to make us forget our own private soul-business, and that while we are keeping the vineyards of others we are in danger of neglecting our own (Cant. 1:6). He reminds us that it is good for ministers to withdraw occasionally from public work, and look within. 'Come ye yourselves apart', He says, 'into a desert place'.

There are few unhappily in the Church of Christ, who need these admonitions. There are but few in danger of overworking themselves, and injuring their own bodies and souls by excessive attention to others. The vast majority of professing Christians are indolent and slothful, and do nothing for the world around them. There are few comparatively who need the bridle nearly so much as the spur. Yet these few ought to lay to heart the lessons of this passage. They should economize their health as a talent, and not squander it away like gamblers. They should be content with spending their daily income of strength, and should not draw recklessly on their principle. They should remember that to do a little, and do it well, is often the way to do most in the long run.

February 25

And they reasoned among themselves, saying, It is because we have no bread.
Mark 8:16

The dull understanding of the disciples.
When our Lord gave the warning of this passage, they thought that the 'leaven' of which He spoke must be the leaven of bread. It never struck them that He was speaking of doctrine. They drew from Him the sharp reproof, 'perceive ye not yet, neither understand? have ye your heart yet hardened? ... How is it that ye do not understand?' Believers, converted, renewed, as the disciples were, they were still dull of apprehension in spiritual things. Their eyes were still dim, and their perception slow in the matters of the kingdom of God.

We shall find it useful to ourselves to remember what is here recorded of the disciples. It may help to correct the high thoughts which we are apt to entertain of our own wisdom, and to keep us humble and lowly minded. We must not fancy that we know everything as soon as we are converted. Our knowledge, like all our graces, is always imperfect, and never so far from perfection as at our first beginning in the service of Christ. There is more ignorance in our hearts than we are at all aware of. '[I]f any man think that he knoweth any thing, he knoweth nothing yet as he ought to know' (1 Cor. 8:2).

Above all, we shall find it useful to remember what is here recorded, in dealing with young Christians. We must not expect perfection in a new convert. We must not set him down as graceless, and godless, and a false professor, because at first he sees but half the truth, and commits many mistakes. His heart may be right in the sight of God, and yet, like the disciples, he may be very slow of understanding in the things of the Spirit. We must bear with him patiently, and not cast him aside. We must give him time to grow in grace and knowledge, and his latter end may find him ripe in wisdom, like Peter and John. It is a blessed thought that Jesus, our Master in heaven, despises none of His people. Marvellous and blameworthy as their slowness to learn undoubtedly is, His patience never gives way. He goes on teaching them, 'line upon line, precept upon precept'. Let us do likewise.

February 26

And he said unto them, Go ye into all the world,
and preach the gospel to every creature.
Mark 16:15

The parting commission which our Lord gives to His apostles.

He is addressing them for the last time. He marks out their work till He comes again, in words of wide and deep significance, 'Go ye into all the world, and preach the gospel to every creature'.

The Lord Jesus would have us know that all the world needs the Gospel. In every quarter of the globe man is the same, sinful, corrupt and alienated from God. Civilized or uncivilized, in China, or in Africa, he is by nature everywhere the same, without knowledge, without holiness, without faith and without love. Wherever we see a child of Adam, whatever be his colour, we see one whose heart is wicked, and who needs the blood of Christ, the renewing of the Holy Ghost and reconciliation with God.

The Lord Jesus would have us know that the salvation of the gospel is to be offered freely to all mankind. The glad tidings that 'God so loved the world that He gave His only begotten Son', and that 'Christ has died for the ungodly', is to be proclaimed freely 'to every creature'. We are not justified in making any exception in the proclamation. We have no warrant for limiting the offer to the elect. We come short of the fullness of Christ's words, and take away from the breadth of His sayings, if we shrink from telling any one, 'God is full of love to you, Christ is willing to save you. "[W]hosoever will, let him take him of the water of life freely"' (Rev. 22:17).

Let us see in these words of Christ, the strongest argument in favour of missionary work, both at home and abroad. Remembering these words, let us be unwearied in trying to do good to the souls of all mankind. If we cannot go to the heathen in China and Hindostan let us seek to enlighten the darkness which we shall easily find within reach of our own door. Let us labour on, unmoved by the sneers and taunts of those who disapprove missionary operations and hold them up to scorn.

February 27

And so was also James, and John, the sons of Zebedee, which were partners with Simon. And Jesus said unto Simon, Fear not; from henceforth thou shalt catch men.

Luke 5:10

The mighty promise which Jesus holds out to Peter: 'Fear not;' He says, 'from henceforth thou shalt catch men'.

That promise, we may well believe, was not intended for Peter only, but for all the apostles, and not for all the apostles only, but for all faithful ministers of the gospel who walk in the apostles' steps. It was spoken for their encouragement and consolation. It was intended to support them under that sense of weakness and unprofitableness by which they are sometimes almost overwhelmed. They certainly have a treasure in earthen vessels (2 Cor. 4:7). They are men of like passions with others. They find their own hearts weak and frail, like the hearts of any of their hearers. They are often tempted to give up in despair, and to leave off preaching. But here stands a promise, on which the great Head of the Church would have them daily lean: 'Fear not ... thou shalt catch men'.

Let us pray daily for all ministers that they may be true successors of Peter and his brethren, that they may preach the same full and free gospel which they preached, and live the same holy lives which they lived. These are the only ministers who will ever prove successful fishermen. To some of them God may give more honour, and to others less. But all true and faithful preachers of the gospel have a right to believe that their labour shall not prove in vain. They may often preach the Word with many tears, and see no result of their labour. But God's word shall not return void (Isa. 55:11). The last day shall show that no work for God was ever thrown away. Every faithful fisherman shall find his Master's words made good: 'thou shalt catch men'.

February 28

But one thing is needful: and Mary hath chosen that good part,
which shall not be taken away from her.
Luke 10:42

What a solemn rebuke our Lord Jesus Christ gave to His servant Martha.

Like a wise physician He saw the disease which was preying upon her, and at once applied the remedy. Like a tender parent, He exposed the fault into which His erring child had fallen, and did not spare the chastening which was required. 'Martha, Martha,' He said, 'thou art careful and troubled about many things: But one thing is needful'. Faithful are the wounds of a friend! That little sentence was precious balm indeed! It contained a volume of practical divinity in a few words.

'[O]ne thing is needful …' How true that saying! The longer we live in the world, the more true it will appear. The nearer we come to the grave, the more thoroughly we shall assent to it. Health, and money, and lands, and rank, and honours, and property, are all well in their way. But they cannot be called needful. Without them thousands are happy in this world, and reach glory in the world to come. The 'many things' which men and women are continually struggling for, are not really necessaries. The grace of God which bringeth salvation is the one thing needful.

Let this little sentence be continually before the eyes of our minds. Let it check us when we are ready to murmur at earthly trials. Let it strengthen us when we are tempted to deny our Master on account of persecution. Let it caution us when we begin to think too much of the things of this world. Let it quicken us when we are disposed to look back, like Lot's wife. In all such seasons, let the words of our Lord ring in our ears like a trumpet, and bring us to a right mind. '[O]ne thing is needful …' If Christ is ours, we have all and abound.

February 29

———◆═══◇◇═══◆———

But one thing is needful: and Mary hath chosen that good part,
which shall not be taken away from her.
Luke 10:42

W hat high commendation our Lord Jesus Christ
pronounced on Mary's choice.

We read that He said, 'Mary hath chosen that good part,
which shall not be taken away from her'. There was a deep meaning in
these words. They were spoken not for Mary's sake only, but for the
sake of all Christ's believing people in every part of the world. They
were meant to encourage all true Christians to be single-eyed and whole-
hearted, to follow the Lord fully, and to walk closely with God, to
make soul-business immeasurable their first business, and to think
comparatively little of the things of this world.

The true Christian's portion is the grace of God. This is the 'good
part' which he has chosen, and it is the only portion which really deserves
the name of 'good'. It is the only good thing which is substantial,
satisfying, real and lasting. It is good in sickness and good in health,
good in youth and good in age, good in adversity and good in prosperity,
good in life and good in death, good in time and good in eternity. No
circumstance and no position can be imagined in which it is not good
for man to have the grace of God.

The true Christian's possession shall never be taken from him. He
alone, of all mankind, shall never be stripped of his inheritance. Kings
must one day leave their palaces. Rich men must one day leave their
money and lands. They only hold them till they die. But the poorest
saint on earth has a treasure of which he will never be deprived. The
grace of God, and the favour of Christ, are riches which no man can
take from him. They will go with him to the grave when he dies. They
will rise with him in the resurrection morning, and be his to all eternity.

MARCH

March 1

*And they understood none of these things: and this saying was hid
from them, neither knew they the things which were spoken.*
Luke 18:34

The slowness of the disciples to understand Christ's death.
We find that when our Lord described His coming sufferings, the disciples 'understood none of these things: and this saying was hid from them, neither knew they the things which were spoken'.

We read such passages as these, perhaps, with a mixture of pity and surprise. We wonder at the darkness and blindness of these Jews. We marvel that in the face of plain teaching, and in the light of plain types of the Mosaic law, the sufferings of Messiah should have been lost sight of in His glory, and His cross hidden behind His crown.

But we are not forgetting that the vicarious death of Christ has always been a stumbling-block and an offence to proud human nature? Do we not know that even now, after Christ has risen from the dead and ascended into glory, the doctrine of the cross is still foolishness to many, and that Christ's substitution for us on the cross is a truth which is often denied, rejected and refused? Before we wonder at these first weak disciples for not understanding our Lord's words about His death we should do well to look around us: it may humble us to remember that thousands of so-called Christians neither understand nor value Christ's death at the present day.

Let us look well to our own hearts. We live in a day when false doctrines about Christ's death abound on every side. Let us see that Christ crucified is really the foundation of our own hopes, and that Christ's atoning death for sin is indeed the whole life of our souls. Let us beware of adding to Christ's sacrifice on the cross, as the Roman Catholic does. Its value was infinite: it admits of no addition. Let us beware of taking away from Christ's sacrifice, as the Socinian does. To suppose that the Son of God only died to leave us an example of self-denial, is to contradict a hundred plain texts of Scripture. Let us walk in the old paths.

March 2

But before all these, they shall lay their hands on you, and persecute
you, delivering you up to the synagogues, and into prisons,
being brought before kings and rulers for my name's sake.
Luke 21:12

Christ's prediction concerning His own disciples.
He does not prophesy smooth things, and promise them an
uninterrupted course of temporal comfort. He says that they
shall be 'persecuted', put in 'prison', 'brought before kings and rulers',
'betrayed', 'put to death', and 'hated of all men for my name's sake'.

The words of this prophecy were doubtless intended to apply to
every age of the Church of Christ. They began to be fulfilled in the days
of the apostles. The book of Acts supplies us with many an instance of
their fulfilment. They have been repeatedly fulfilled during the last
eighteen hundred years: wherever there have been disciples of Christ,
there has always been more or less persecution. They will yet receive a
more full accomplishment before the end comes: the last tribulation
will probably be marked by special violence and bitterness: it will be a
'great tribulation' (Rev. 7:14).

Let it be a settled principle in our minds that the true Christian
must always enter the kingdom of God 'through much tribulation' (Acts
14:22). His best things are yet to come. This world is not our home. If
we are faithful and decided servants of Christ, the world will certainly
hate us, as it hated our Master. In one way or another grace will always
be persecuted: no consistency of conduct, however faultless, no kindness
and amiability of character, however striking, will exempt a believer
from the world's dislike, so long as he lives. It is foolish to be surprised
at this; it is a mere waste of time to murmur at it: it is a part of the
cross, and we must bear it patiently.

'Marvel not, my brethren,' says St John, 'if the world hate you.' 'If
ye were of the world,' says our Lord, 'the world would love his own:
but because ye are not of the world, but I have chosen you out of the
world, therefore the world hateth you' (1 John 3:13; John 15:18, 19).

March 3

And he said unto them, When I sent you without purse, and scrip,
and shoes, lacked ye any thing? And they said, Nothing.
Luke 22:35

The servant of Christ ought to use all reasonable means in doing his Master's work.

We read that our Lord said to His disciples, 'he that hath a purse, let him take it, and likewise his scrip: and he that hath no sword, let him sell his garment, and buy one'.

It is safest to take these remarkable words in a proverbial sense. They apply to the whole period of time between our Lord's first and second advents. Until our Lord comes again believers are to make a diligent use of all the faculties which God has implanted in them: they are not to expect miracles to be worked, in order to save them trouble; they are not to expect bread to fall into their mouths, if they will not work for it; they are not to expect difficulties to be surmounted, and enemies to be overcome, if they will not wrestle, and struggle, and take pains. They are to remember that it is 'the hand of the diligent maketh rich' (Prov. 10:4).

We shall do well to lay to heart our Lord's words in this place, and to act habitually on the principle which they contain. Let us labour, and toil, and give, and speak, and act, and write for Christ, as if all depended on our exertions. And yet let us never forget that success depends entirely on God's blessing! To expect success by our own 'purse' and 'sword' is pride and self-righteousness; but to expect success without the 'purse' and 'sword' is presumption and fanaticism. Let us do as Jacob did when he met his brother Esau. He used all innocent means to conciliate and appease him; but when he had done all, he spent all night in prayer (Gen. 32:1-24).

March 4

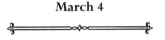

And they remembered his words …
Luke 24:8

How dull the memory of the disciples was about some of our Lord's sayings.

We are told that the angels who appeared to the women, reminded them of their Master's words in Galilee, foretelling His own crucifixion and resurrection; and then we read, 'they remembered his words'. They had heard them, but made no use of them: now, after many days, they call them to mind.

This dullness of memory is a common spiritual disease among believers. It prevails as widely now as it did in the days of the first disciples: it is one among many proofs of our fallen and corrupt condition. Even after men have been renewed by the Holy Ghost, their readiness to forget the promises and precepts of the gospel is continually bringing them into trouble. They hear many things which they ought to store up in their hearts, but seem to forget as fast as they hear; and then, perhaps after many days, affliction brings them up before their recollection, and at once it flashes across their minds that they heard them long ago! They find that they had heard, but heard in vain.

The true cure for a dull memory in religion, is to get deeper love toward Christ, and affections more thoroughly set on things above. We do not readily forget the things we love, and the objects which we keep continually under our eyes: the names of our parents and children are always remembered; the face of the husband or wife we love is graven on the tablets of our hearts. The more our affections are engaged in Christ's service, the more easy shall we find it to remember Christ's words. The words of the apostle ought to be carefully pondered. '[W]e ought to give the more earnest heed to the things which we have heard, lest at any time we should let them slip' (Heb. 2:1). Do we not see, after eighteen centuries of additional proofs that Christ has risen from the dead, a general want of faith, which is truly deplorable? Do we not see myriads of professing Christians who seem not to believe that Jesus died and rose again, and is coming to judge the world? These are painful questions. Strong faith is indeed a rare thing.

March 5

And they worshipped him, and returned to Jerusalem with great joy...
Luke 24:52

The feelings of our Lord's disciples when He finally left them and was carried up into heaven.

We read that they 'returned to Jerusalem with great joy: And were continually in the temple, praising and blessing God'.

How shall we account for these joyful feelings? How shall we explain the singular fact, that this little company of weak disciples, left for the first time like orphans in the midst of an angry world, was not cast down, but was full of joy? The answer to this question is short and simple. The disciples rejoiced, because now for the first time they saw all things clearly about their Master: the veil was removed from their eyes; the darkness had at length passed away. The meaning of Christ's humiliation and low estate; the meaning of His mysterious agony, and cross, and passion; the meaning of His being Messiah and yet a sufferer, the meaning of His being crucified, and yet being Son of God – all, all was at length unravelled and made plain. They saw it all: they understood it all. Their doubts were removed; their stumbling-blocks were taken away: now at last they possessed clear knowledge, and possessing clear knowledge felt unmingled joy.

Let it be a settled principle with us, that the little degree of joy which many believers feel arises often from want of knowledge. Weak faith and inconsistent practice are doubtless two great reasons why many of God's children enjoy so little peace; but it may well be suspected that dim and indistinct views of the gospel are the true cause of many a believer's discomfort. When the Lord Jesus is not clearly known and understood, it must needs follow that there is little 'joy in the Lord'.

Too many believers only scratch the surface of Scripture, and know nothing of digging down into its hid treasures: let the Word dwell in us more richly; let us read our Bibles more diligently: so doing we shall taste more of joy and peace in believing, and shall know what it is to be 'continually ... praising and blessing God'.

March 6

Then said Jesus to those Jews which believed on him,
If ye continue in my word, then are ye my disciples indeed ...
John 8:31

The importance of steady perseverance in Christ's service.

There were many, it seems, at this particular period, who professed to believe on our Lord, and expressed a desire to become His disciples. There is nothing to show that they had true faith. They appear to have acted under the influence of temporary excitement, without considering what they were doing. And to them our Lord addresses this instructive warning, 'If ye continue in my word, then are ye my disciples indeed'.

This sentence contains a mine of wisdom. To make a beginning in religious life is comparatively easy. Not a few mixed motives assist us. The love of novelty, the praise of well-meaning but indiscreet professors, the secret self-satisfaction of feeling 'how good I am', the universal excitement attending a new position – all these things combine to aid the young beginner. Aided by them he begins to run the race that leads to heaven, lays aside many bad habits, takes up many good ones, has many comfortable frames and feelings, and gets on swimmingly for a time. But when the newness of his position is past and gone, when the freshness of his feelings is rubbed off and lost, when the world and the devil begin to pull hard at him, when the weakness of his own heart begins to appear, then it is that he finds out the real difficulties of vital Christianity. Then it is that he discovers the deep wisdom of our Lord's saying now before us. It is not beginning, but 'continuing' a religious profession, that is the test of true grace.

We should remember these things in forming our estimate of other people's religion. No doubt we ought to be thankful when we see any one ceasing to do evil and learning to do well. We must not despise 'the day of small things' (Zech. 4:10).

March 7

*To him the porter openeth; and the sheep hear his voice: and he calleth
his own sheep by name, and leadeth them out.*
John 10:3

A peculiar picture of true Christians.

Our Lord describes them as sheep who 'hear the voice of a true Shepherd, and know His voice'; and as 'sheep who will not follow a stranger, but will flee from him, for they know not the voice of strangers'.

The thing taught in these words is a very curious one, and may seem 'foolishness' to the world. There is a spiritual instinct in most true believers, which generally enables them to distinguish between true and false teaching. When they hear unsound religious instruction, there is something within them which says, 'This is wrong.' When they hear the real truth as it is in Jesus, there is something in their hearts which responds, 'This is right.' The careless man of the world may see no difference whatever between minister and minister, sermon and sermon. The poorest sheep of Christ, as a general rule, will 'distinguish things that differ', though he may sometimes be unable to explain why.

Let us beware of despising this spiritual instinct. Whatever a sneering world may please to say, it is one of the peculiar marks of the indwelling of the Holy Ghost. As such, it is specially mentioned by St John, when he says, '[Y]e have an unction from the Holy One, and ye know all things' (1 John 2:20). Let us rather pray for it daily, in order that we may be kept from the influence of false shepherds. To lose all power of distinguishing between bitter and sweet, is one of the worst symptoms of bodily disease. To be unable to see any difference between law and gospel, truth and error, Protestantism and Popery, the doctrine of Christ and the doctrine of man, is a sure proof that we are yet dead in heart, and need conversion.

How can I be justified? How can a sinner like me be reconciled to my Maker? The Lord Jesus Christ has provided an answer to these mighty questions. By His sacrifice for us on the cross, He has opened a way through the great barrier, and provided pardon and peace for sinners.

March 8

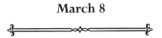

Then said Martha unto Jesus, Lord, if thou hadst been here,
my brother had not died.
John 11:21

What a strange mixture of grace and weakness is to be found even in the hearts of true believers. We see this strikingly illustrated in the language used by Martha and Mary. Both these holy women had faith enough to say, 'Lord, if thou hadst been here, my brother had not died'. Yet neither of them seems to have remembered that the death of Lazarus did not depend on Christ's absence, and that our Lord, had He thought fit, could have prevented his death with a word, without coming to Bethany. Martha had knowledge enough to say, 'I know, that even now, whatsoever thou wilt ask of God, God will give it thee. I know that my brother shall rise again at the last day; I believe that thou art the Christ, the Son of God': but even she could get no further. Her dim eyes and trembling hands could not grasp the grand truth that He who stood before her had the keys of life and death, and that in her Master dwelt 'all the fullness of the Godhead bodily' (Col. 2:9). She saw indeed, but through a glass darkly. She knew, but only in part. She believed, but her faith was mingled with much unbelief. Yet both Martha and Mary were genuine children of God, and true Christians.

These things are graciously written for our learning. It is good to remember what true Christians really are. Many and great are the mistakes into which people fall, by forming a false estimate of the Christian's character. Many are the bitter things which people write against themselves, by expecting to find in their hearts what cannot be found on this side of heaven. Let us settle it in our minds that saints on earth are not perfect angels, but only converted sinners. They are sinners renewed, changed, sanctified, no doubt; but they are yet sinners, and will be till they die.

Happy is that child of God who understands these things, and has learned to judge rightly both of himself and others. Rarely indeed shall we find the saint who does not often need that prayer, 'Lord I believe: help Thou mine unbelief.'

March 9

If any man serve me, let him follow me; and where I am, there shall
also my servant be: if any man serve me, him will my Father honour.
John 12:26

If we profess to serve Christ, we must follow Him.

'If any man serve me,' is the saying, 'let him follow me'.

That expression, 'following', is one of wide signification, and brings before our minds many familiar ideas. As the soldier follows his general, as the servant follows his master, as the scholar follows his teacher, as the sheep follows its shepherd, just so ought the professing Christian to follow Christ. Faith and obedience are the leading marks of real followers, and will always be seen in true believing Christians. Their knowledge may be very small, and their infirmities very great; their grace very weak, and their hope very dim: but they believe what Christ says, and strive to do what Christ commands. And of such Christ declares, 'They serve Me: they are mine.'

Christianity like this, receives little praise from man. It is too thorough, too decided, too strong, too real. To serve Christ in name and form is easy work, and satisfies most people, but to follow Him in faith and life demands more trouble that the generality of men will take about their souls. Laughter, ridicule, opposition, persecution, are often the only reward which Christ's followers get from the world. Their religion is one, 'whose praise is not of men, but of God' (Rom. 2:29).

Yet to him that followeth, let us never forget, the Lord Jesus holds out abundant encouragement: 'where I am,' He declares, 'there shall my servant be: if any man serve me, him will my Father honour'. Let us lay to heart these comfortable promises, and go forward in the narrow way without fear. The world may cast out our name as evil, and turn us out of its society; but when we dwell with Christ in glory, we shall have a home from which we can never be ejected. The world may pour contempt on our religion, and laugh us and our Christianity to scorn; but when the Father honours us at the last day, before the assembly of angels and men, we shall find that His praise makes amends for all.

March 10

*Jesus answered him, Wilt thou lay down thy life for my sake? Verily, verily, I say
unto thee, The cock shall not crow, till thou hast denied me thrice.*

John 13:38

How much self-ignorance there may be in the heart of
a true believer.

We see Simon Peter declaring that he was ready to lay down
his life for his Master. We see his Master telling him that in that very
night he would deny Him thrice. And we all know how the matter
ended. The Master was right, and Peter was wrong.

Let it be a settled principle in our religion, that there is an amount
of weakness in all our hearts, of which we have no adequate conception,
and that we never know how far we might fall if we were tempted. We
fancy sometimes, like Peter, that there are some things we could not
possibly do. We look pitifully upon others who fall into certain sins,
and please ourselves in the thought that at any rate we should not have
done so! We know nothing at all. The seeds of every sin are latent in our
hearts, even when renewed, and they only need occasion, or carelessness,
or the withdrawal of God's grace for a season, to put forth an abundant
crop. Like Peter, we may think we can do wonders for Christ, and, like
Peter, we may learn by bitter experience that we have no power and
might at all.

The servant of Christ will do wisely to remember these things. '[L]et
him that thinketh he standeth take heed lest he fall' (1 Cor. 10:12). A
humble sense of our own innate weakness, a constant dependence on
the Strong One for strength, a daily prayer to be held up, because we
cannot hold up ourselves, these are the true secrets of safety. The great
apostle of the Gentiles said, '[W]hen I am weak, then am I strong' (2
Cor. 12:10).

March 11

Herein is my Father glorified, that ye bear much fruit;
so shall ye be my disciples.
John 15:8

Fruitfulness in Christian practice will not only bring glory to God, but will supply the best evidence to our own hearts that we are real disciples of Christ. Assurance of our own interest in Christ, and of our consequent eternal safety, is one of the highest privileges in religion. To be always doubting and fearing is miserable work. Nothing is worse than suspense in any matter of importance, and above all in the matters of our souls. He that would know one of the best receipts for obtaining assurance, should diligently study Christ's words now before us. Let him strive to bear 'much fruit' in his life, his habits, his temper, his words and his works. So doing he shall feel the 'witness of the Spirit' in his heart, and give abundant proof that he is a living branch of the true Vine. He shall find inward evidence in his own soul that he is a child of God, and shall supply the world with outward evidence that cannot be disputed. He shall leave no room for doubt that he is a disciple.

Would we know why so many professing Christians have little comfort in their religion, and go fearing and doubting along the road to heaven? The question receives a solution in the saying of our Lord we are now considering. Men are content with a little Christianity, and a little fruit of the Spirit, and do not labour to be 'holy in all manner of conversation' (1 Pet. 1:15). They must not wonder if they enjoy little peace, feel little hope and leave behind them little evidence. The fault lies with themselves. God has linked together holiness and happiness; and what God has joined together we must not think to put asunder.

By the grace of God we may make Christ's laws our rule of life, and show daily that we desire to please Him. So doing, our gracious Master will give us a constant sense of His favour, and make us feel His face smiling on us, like the sun shining on a fine day. 'The secret of the LORD is with them that fear him; and He will shew them his covenant' (Ps. 25:14).

March 12

If the world hate you, ye know that it hated me before it hated you.
John 15:18

What true Christians must expect to meet in this world – hatred and persecution.

If the disciples looked for kindness and gratitude from man, they would be painfully disappointed. They must lay their account to be ill-treated like their Master. 'The world hateth you. Be not moved or surprised. If they have persecuted Me, they will also persecute you; if they have kept my saying, they will keep your's also.'

Facts, painful facts in every age, supply abundant proof that our Lord's warning was not without cause. Persecution was the lot of the apostles and their companions wherever they went. Not more than one or two of them, probably, died quietly in his bed. Persecution has been the lot of true believers throughout the eighteen centuries of Church history. The doings of Roman emperors and Roman popes, the Spanish Inquisition, the martyrdoms of Queen Mary's reign, all tell the same story. Persecution is the lot of all really godly people at this very day. Ridicule, mockery, slander, misrepresentation, still show the feeling of unconverted people against the true Christian. As it was in St Paul's day, so it is now. In public and in private, at school and at college, at home and abroad, 'all that will live godly in Christ Jesus shall suffer persecution' (2 Tim. 3:12). Mere churchmanship and outward profession are a cheap religion, of course, and cost a man nothing. But real vital Christianity will always bring with it a cross.

To know and understand these things is of the utmost importance to our comfort. Nothing is so mischievous as the habit of indulging false expectations. Let us realize that human nature never changes, that 'the carnal mind is enmity against God', and against God's image in His people (Rom. 8:7). Let us settle it in our minds that no holiness of life or consistency of conduct will ever prevent wicked people hating the servants of Christ, just as they hated their blameless Master. Let us remember these things, and then we shall not be disappointed.

March 13

And ye also shall bear witness,
because ye have been with me from the beginning.
John 15:27

The special office of the apostles.

They were to be His witnesses in the world. '[Y]e also shall bear witness'.

The expression is singularly instructive and full of meaning. It taught the eleven what they must expect their portion to be, so long as they lived. They would have to bear testimony to facts which many would not believe, and to truths which the natural heart would dislike. They would often have to stand alone, a few against many, a little flock against a great multitude. None of these things must move them. They must count it no strange thing to be persecuted, hated, opposed and discredited. They must not mind it. To witness was their grand duty, whether men believed them or not. So witnessing, their record would be on high, in God's book of remembrance; and so witnessing, sooner of latter, the Judge of all would give them a crown of glory that fadeth not away (1 Pet. 5:4).

Let us never forget, as we leave this passage, that the position of the apostles is that which, in a certain sense, every true Christian must fill, as long as the world stands. We must all be witnesses for Christ. We must not be ashamed to stand up for Christ's cause, to speak out for Christ and to persist in maintaining the truth of Christ's gospel. Wherever we live, in town or in country, in public or in private, abroad or at home, we must boldly confess our Master on every opportunity. So doing, we shall walk in the steps of the apostles, though at a long interval. So doing, we shall please our Master, and may hope at last that we shall receive the apostle's reward.

March 14

And there came also Nicodemus, which at the first came to Jesus by
night, and brought a mixture of myrrh and aloes,
about an hundred pound weight.
John 19:39

There are some servants of Christ whose latter end is better than their beginning.

The case of Nicodemus teaches that lesson very plainly. The only man who dared to help Joseph in his holy work of burying our Lord was one who at first 'came to Jesus by night', and was nothing better than an ignorant inquirer after truth. At a later period in our Lord's ministry we find this same Nicodemus coming forward with somewhat more boldness, and raising in the Council of the Pharisees the question, 'Doth our law judge any man, before it hear him, and know what he doeth?' (John 7:51). Finally, we see him in the passage before us, ministering to our Lord's dead body, and not ashamed to take an active part in giving to the despised Nazarene an honourable burial. How great the contrast between the man who timidly crept into the Lord's lodging to ask a question, and the man who brought a hundred pounds in weight of myrrh and aloes to anoint His dead body! Yet it was the same Nicodemus. How great may be a man's growth in grace, and faith, and knowledge, and courage, in the short space of three years.

We shall do well to store up these things in our minds, and to remember the case of Nicodemus, in forming our estimate of other people's religion. We must not condemn others as graceless and godless, because they do not see the whole truth at once, and only reach decided Christianity by slow degrees. The Holy Ghost always leads believers to the same foundation truths, and into the same highway to heaven. In these there is invariable uniformity. But the Holy Ghost does not always lead believers through the same experience, or at the same rate of speed. In this there is much diversity in His operations. He that says conversion is a needless thing, and that an unconverted man may be saved, is undoubtedly under a strange delusion. But he that says that no-one is converted except he becomes a full-blown and established Christian in a single day, is no less under a delusion. Let us not judge others rashly and hastily.

March 15

*Jesus saith unto her, Touch me not; for I am not yet ascended to my
Father: but go to my brethren, and say unto them, I ascend unto my
Father, and your Father; and to my God, and your God.*

John 20:17

How kindly and graciously our Lord speaks of His disciples.

He bids Mary Magdalene carry a message to them, as His brethren. He bids her tell them that His Father was their Father, and His God their God. It was but three days before that they had all forsaken Him shamefully, and fled. Yet this merciful Master speaks as if all was forgiven and forgotten. His first thought is to bring back the wanderers, to bind up the wounds of their consciences, to reanimate their courage, to restore them to their former place. This was indeed a love that passeth knowledge. To trust deserters, and to show confidence in backsliders, was a compassion which man can hardly understand. So true is that word of David: 'Like as a father pitieth his children, so the LORD pitieth them that fear him. For he knoweth our frame; he remembereth that we are dust' (Ps. 103:13, 14).

Let us leave the passage with the comfortable reflection that Jesus Christ never changes. He is the same yesterday, today and for ever. As He dealt with His erring disciples in the morning of His resurrection, so will He deal with all who believe and love Him, until He comes again. When we wander out of the way He will bring us back. When we fall He will raise us again. But He will never break His royal word: 'him that cometh to Me I will in no wise cast out' (John 6:37). The saints in glory will have one anthem in which every voice and heart will join, 'He hath not dealt with us after our sins; nor rewarded us according to our iniquities' (Ps. 103:10).

March 16

There were together Simon Peter, and Thomas called Didymus,
and Nathanael of Cana in Galilee,
and the sons of Zebedee, and two other of his disciples.
John 21:2

The different characters of different disciples of Christ.
Once more, on this deeply interesting occasion, we see Peter
and John side by side in the same boat, and once more, as at the
sepulchre, we see these two good men behaving in different ways. When
Jesus stood on the shore, in the dim twilight of the morning, John was
the first to perceive who it was and to say, 'It is the Lord'; but Peter was
the first to spring into the water, and to struggle to get close to his
Master. In a word, John was the first to see; but Peter was the first to
act. John's gentle loving spirit was quickest to discern; but Peter's fiery,
impulsive nature, was quickest to stir and move. And yet both were
believers, both were true-hearted disciples, both loved the Lord in life,
and were faithful to Him unto death. But their natural temperaments
were not the same.

Let us never forget the practical lesson before us. As long as we live,
let us diligently use it in forming our estimate of believers. Let us not
condemn others as graceless and unconverted, because they do not see
the path of duty from our standpoint, or feel things exactly as we feel
them. '[T]here are diversities of gifts, but the same Spirit' (1 Cor. 12:4).
The gifts of God's children are not to bestowed precisely in the same
measure and degree. Some have more of one gift, and some have more
of another. Some have gifts which shine more in public, and others have
gifts which shine more in private. Some are more bright in a passive
life, and some are more bright in an active one. Yet each and all the
members of God's family, in their own way and in their own season,
bring glory to God. Martha was careful and troubled about much
serving, when Mary sat at the feet of Jesus and heard His word. Yet
there came a day, at Bethany, when Mary was crushed and prostrated
by overmuch sorrow, and Martha's faith shone more brightly than her
sister's (Luke 10:39, 40; John 11:20-28). Nevertheless both were loved
by our Lord. The one thing needful is to have the grace of the Holy
Spirit, and to love Christ.

March 17

And all they in the synagogue, when they heard these things,
were filled with wrath ...
Luke 4:28

How bitterly human nature dislikes the doctrine of the sovereignty of God.

We see this in the conduct of the men of Nazareth, when our Lord reminded them that God was under no obligation to work miracles among them. Were there not many widows in Israel in the days of Elijah? No doubt there were. Yet to none of them was the prophet sent. All were passed over in favour of a Gentile widow at Sarepta. Were there not many lepers in Israel in the days of Elisha? No doubt there were. Yet to none of them was the privilege of healing granted. Naaman the Syrian was the only one who was cleansed. Such doctrine as this was intolerable to the men of Nazareth. It wounded their pride and self-conceit. It taught them that God was no man's debtor, and that if they themselves were passed over in the distribution of His mercies, they had no right to find fault. They could not bear it. They were 'filled with wrath'. They thrust our Lord out of their city, and had it not been for an exercise of miraculous power on His part, they would doubtless have put Him to a violent death.

Of all the doctrines of the Bible, none is so offensive to human nature as the doctrine of God's sovereignty. To be told that God is great, and just, and holy, and pure, man can bear. But to be told that 'He hath mercy on whom He will have mercy' – that He 'giveth no account of His matters' – that it is 'not of him that willeth, nor of him that runneth, but of God that showeth mercy' – these are truths that the natural man cannot stand; they often call forth all his enmity against God, and fill him with wrath. Nothing, in short, will make him submit to them but the humbling teaching of the Holy Ghost.

Let us settle it in our minds that, whether we like it or not, the sovereignty of God is a doctrine clearly revealed in the Bible, and a fact clearly to be seen in the world.

March 18

And shall not God avenge his own elect, which cry day and night unto
him, though he bear long with them?
Luke 18:7

G od has an elect people upon earth, who are under
His special care.
  Election is one of the deepest truths of Scripture. It is clearly
and beautifully stated in the seventeenth Article of the Church of
England. It is 'the everlasting purpose of God, whereby, before the
foundations of the world were laid, He hath decreed by His counsel,
secret to us, to deliver from curse and damnation those whom He hath
chosen in Christ out of mankind, and to bring them by Christ to
everlasting salvation'. This testimony is true. This is 'Sound speech that
cannot be condemned' (Titus 2:8).

Election is a truth which should call forth praise and thanksgiving
from all true Christians. Except God had chosen and called them, they
would never have chosen and called on Him. Except He had chosen
them of His own good pleasure, without respect to any goodness of
theirs, there would never have been anything in them to make them
worthy of His choice. The worldly and the carnal-minded may rail at
the doctrine of election; the false professor may abuse it, and turn 'the
grace of God into lasciviousness' (Jude 4); but the believer who knows
his own heart will ever bless God for election. He will confess that
without election there would be no salvation.

But what are the marks of election? By what token shall a man know
whether he is one of God's elect? These marks are clearly laid down in
Scripture. Election is inseparably connected with faith in Christ, and
conformity to His image (Rom. 8:29, 30). It was when St Paul saw the
working 'faith', and patient 'hope', and labouring 'love' of the
Thessalonians, that he knew their 'election of God' (1 Thess. 1:3, 4).

Above all, we have a plain mark described by our Lord in the passage
before us: God's elect are a people who 'cry unto Him night and day'.
They are essentially a praying people. No doubt there are many persons
whose prayers are formal and hypocritical. But one thing is very clear:
a prayerless man must never be called one of God's elect. Let that never
be forgotten.

March 19

Ye have not chosen me, but I have chosen you, and ordained you, that ye
should go and bring forth fruit, and that your fruit should remain: that
whatsoever ye shall ask of the Father in my name, He may give it you.
John 15:16

How our Lord speaks of the doctrine of election. He says, 'Ye have not chosen me, but I have chosen you … that ye should go and bring forth fruit'. The choosing here mentioned is evidently two fold. It includes not only the election to the apostolic office, which was peculiar to the eleven, but the election to eternal life, which is the privilege of all believers. To this last choosing, as it specially concerns ourselves, we may profitably direct our attention.

Election to eternal life is a truth of Scripture which we must receive humbly, and believe implicitly. Why the Lord Jesus calls some and does not call others, quickens whom He will, and leaves others alone in their sins, these are deep things which we cannot explain. Let it suffice us to know that it is a fact. God must begin the work of grace in a man's heart, or else a man will never be saved. Christ must first choose us and call us by His Spirit, or else we shall never choose Christ. Beyond doubt, if not saved, we shall have none to blame but ourselves. But if saved, we shall certainly trace up the beginning of our salvation to the choosing grace of Christ. Our song to all eternity will be that which fell from the lips of Jonah: 'Salvation is of the LORD' (Jonah 2:9).

Election is always to sanctification. Those whom Christ chooses out of mankind, He chooses not only that they may be saved, but that they may bear fruit, and fruit that can be seen. All other election beside this is a mere vain delusion, and a miserable invention of man. It was the faith and hope and love of the Thessalonians, which made St Paul say, I know 'your election of God' (1 Thess. 1:4). Where there is no visible fruit of sanctification, we may be sure there is no election.

Armed with such principles as these, we have no cause to be afraid of the doctrine of election. Like any other truth of the gospel, it is liable to be abused and perverted. But to a pious mind, as the seventeenth Article of the Church of England truly says, it is a doctrine 'full of sweet, pleasant, and unspeakable comfort'.

March 20

*And when they were come into the house, they saw the young child
with Mary his mother, and fell down, and worshipped him: and when
they had opened their treasures, they presented unto him gifts:
gold, and frankincense and myrrh.*
Matthew 2:11

A **striking example of faith.**
These wise men believed in Christ when they had never seen
Him; but that was not all. They believed in Him when the scribes
and Pharisees were unbelieving; but that again was not all. They believed
in Him when they saw Him a little infant on Mary's knees, and
worshipped Him as King: this was the crowning point of their faith.
They saw no miracles to convince them; they heard no teaching to
persuade them; they beheld no signs of divinity and greatness to overawe
them; they saw nothing but a newborn infant, helpless and weak, and
needing a mother's care, like any one of ourselves. And yet when they
saw that infant, they believed that they saw the divine Saviour of the
world! They 'fell down, and worshipped Him'.

We read of no greater faith than this in the whole volume of the
Bible. It is a faith that deserves to be placed side by side with that of
the penitent thief. The thief saw one dying the death of a malefactor,
and yet prayed to Him, and 'called him Lord'; the wise men saw a
newborn babe on the lap of a poor woman, and yet worshipped Him,
and confessed that He was Christ. Blessed indeed are they that can
believe in this fashion!

This is the kind of faith that God delights to honour. We see the
proof of that at this very day. Wherever the Bible is read the conduct
of these wise men is known, and told as a memorial of them. Let us
walk in the steps of their faith; let us not be ashamed to believe in
Jesus and confess Him, though all around us remain careless and
unbelieving. Have we not a thousandfold more evidence than the wise
men had, to make us believe that Jesus is the Christ? Beyond doubt we
have. Yet where is our faith?

March 21

The centurion answered and said, Lord, I am not worthy that thou shouldest come under my roof: but speak the word only, and my servant shall be healed.
Matthew 8:8

What a precious thing is the grace of faith. We know little about the centurion described in these verses; his name, his nation, his past history, are all hidden from us: but one thing we know, and that is, that he believed. 'Lord,' he says, 'I am not worthy that thou shouldest come under my roof: but speak the word only, and my servant shall be healed'. He believed, let us remember, when scribes and Pharisees were unbelievers; he believed, though a Gentile born, when Israel was blinded: and our Lord pronounced upon him the commendation, which has been read all over the world from that time to this, 'I have not found so great faith, no, not in Israel'.

Let us lay firm hold on this lesson. It deserves to be remembered. To believe in Christ's power and willingness to help, and to make a practical use of our belief, is a rare and precious gift: let us ever be thankful if we have it. To be willing to come to Jesus as helpless, lost sinners, and commit our souls into His hands is a mighty privilege: let us ever bless God if this willingness is ours, for it is His gift. Such faith is better than all other gifts and knowledge in the world. Many poor, converted heathen, who knows nothing but that he is sick of sin, and trusts in Jesus, shall sit down in heaven, while many learned English scholars are rejected for evermore. Blessed indeed are they that believe!

What do we each know of this faith? This is the great question. Our learning may be small: but do we believe? – Our opportunities of giving and working for Christ's cause may be few: but do we believe? – We may neither be able to preach, nor write, nor argue for the gospel: but do we believe? – May we never rest till we can answer this inquiry! Faith in Christ appears a small and simple thing to the children of this world. They see it as nothing great or grand. But faith in Christ is most precious in God's sight, and, like most precious things, is rare. By it true Christians live; by it they stand; by it they overcome the world. Without this faith no-one can be saved.

March 22

*Therefore I say unto you, What things soever ye desire, when ye pray,
believe that ye receive them, and ye shall have them.*
Mark 11:24

The immense importance of faith.
This is a lesson which our Lord teaches first by a proverbial saying. Faith shall enable a man to accomplish works and overcome difficulties as great and formidable as the removing of a mountain, and casting it into the sea. Afterwards the lesson is impressed upon us still further, by a general exhortation to exercise faith when we pray. 'What things soever ye desire, when ye pray, believe that ye receive them, and ye shall have them'. This promise must of course be taken with a reasonable qualification. It assumes that a believer will ask things which are not sinful, and which are in accordance with the will of God. When he asks such things, he may confidently believe that his prayer will be answered. To use the words of St James, 'let him ask in faith, nothing wavering' (Jas. 1:6).

The faith here commended must be distinguished from that faith which is essential to justification. In principle undoubtedly all true faith is one and the same. It is always trust or belief. But in the object and operations of faith there are diversities which it is useful to understand. Justifying faith is that act of the soul by which man lays hold on Christ and has peace with God. Its special object is the atonement for sin which Jesus made on the cross. The faith spoken of in the passage now before us is a grace of more general signification, the fruit and companion of justifying faith, but still not to be confounded with it. It is rather a general confidence in God's power, wisdom and goodwill towards believers. And its special objects are the promises, the word and the character of God in Christ.

Confidence in God's power and will to help every believer in Christ, and in the truth of every word that God has spoken, is the grand secret of success and prosperity in our religion. In fact, it is the very root of saving Christianity.

March 23

He that believeth and is baptized shall be saved; but he that believeth
not shall be damned.
Mark 16:16

T he terms which our Lord tells us should be offered to all who hear the gospel.

'He that believeth and is baptized shall be saved; but he that believeth not shall be damned.'

Every word in that sentence is of deep importance. Every expression in it deserves to be carefully weighed.

We are taught here the importance of baptism. It is an ordinance generally necessary to salvation, where it can be had. Not 'He that believeth' simply, but 'He that believeth and is baptized shall be saved'. Thousands no doubt receive not the slightest benefit from their baptism. Thousands are washed in sacramental water, who are never washed in the blood of Christ. But it does not follow therefore that baptism is to be despised and neglected. It is an ordinance appointed by Christ Himself, and when used reverently, intelligently and prayerfully, is doubtless accompanied by a special blessing. The baptismal water itself conveys no grace. We must look far beyond the mere outward element, to Him who commanded it to be used. But the public confession of Christ, which is implied in the use of that water, is a sacramental act, which our Master Himself has commanded; and when the ordinance is rightly used, we may confidently believe that He seals it by His blessing. We are taught here, furthermore, the absolute necessity of faith in Christ to salvation. This is the one thing needful. '[H]e that believeth not' is the man that shall be lost for evermore. He may have been baptized, and made a member of the visible Church. He may be a regular communicant at the Lord's Table. He may even believe intellectually all the leading articles of the creed. But all shall profit him nothing if he lacks saving faith in Christ. Have we this faith? This is the great question that concerns us all. Except we feel our sins, and feeling them flee to Christ by faith, and lay hold on Him, we shall find at length we had better never have been born.

March 24

And looking round about upon them all, he said unto the man, Stretch forth thy hand. And he did so: and his hand was restored whole as the other.

Luke 6:10

The nature of the first act of faith, when a soul is converted to God.

The lesson is conveyed to us in a striking manner, by the history of the cure which is here described. We read that our Lord said to the man whose hand was withered, 'Stretch forth thy hand'. The command, at first sight, seems unreasonable, because the man's obedience was apparently impossible. But the poor sufferer was not stopped by any doubts or reasonings of this kind. At once we read that he made the attempt to stretch forth his hand, and, in making it, was cured. He had faith enough to believe that He who bade him stretch forth his hand was not mocking him, and ought to be obeyed. And it was precisely in this act of implicit obedience, that he received a blessing. '[H]is hand was restored whole as the other.'

Let us see in this simple history the best answer to those doubts, and hesitations, and questionings, by which anxious inquirers often perplex themselves, in the matter of coming to Christ. 'How can they believe?' they ask us, 'How can they come to Christ? How can they lay hold on the hope set before them?' The best answer to all such inquiries, is to bid men do as he did who had the withered hand. Let them not stand still reasoning, but act. Let them not torment themselves with metaphysical speculations, but cast themselves, just as they are, on Jesus Christ. So doing, they will find their course made clear. How, or in what manner, we may not be able to explain. But we may boldly make the assertion, that in the act of striving to draw near to God, they shall find God drawing near to them, but that if they deliberately sit still, they must never expect to be saved.

March 25

Wherefore neither thought I myself worthy to come unto thee: but say in a word, and my servant shall be healed.
Luke 7:7

The centurion's faith.
We have a beautiful example of it in the request that he made to our Lord: 'say in a word, and my servant shall be healed'. He thinks it needless for our Lord to come to the place where his servant lay dying. He regards our Lord as one possessing authority over diseases, as complete as his own authority over his soldiers, or a Roman emperor's authority over himself. He believes that a word of command from Jesus is sufficient to send sickness away. He asks to see no sign or wonder. He declares his confidence that Jesus is an almighty Master and King, and that diseases, like obedient servants, will at once depart at His orders.

Faith like this was indeed rare when the Lord Jesus was upon earth. 'Show us a sign from heaven,' was the demand of the sneering Pharisees. To see something wonderful was the great desire of the multitudes who crowded after our Lord. No wonder that we read the remarkable words, Jesus 'marvelled at him', and said unto the people, 'I have not found so great faith, no, not in Israel'. None ought to have been so believing as the children of those who were led through the wilderness, and brought into the promised land. But the last was first and the first last. The faith of a Roman soldier proved stronger than that of the Jews.

Let us not forget to walk in the steps of this blessed spirit of faith which the centurion here exhibited. Our eyes do not yet behold the book of life. We see not our Saviour pleading for us at God's right hand. But have we the word of Christ's promises? Then let us rest on it and fear nothing. Let us not doubt that every word that Christ has spoken shall be made good. The word of Christ is a sure foundation. He that leans upon it shall never be confounded. Believers shall all be found pardoned, justified and glorified at the last day. 'Jesus says so', and therefore it shall be done.

March 26

*And he answered and said unto them, My mother and my brethren are
these which hear the word of God, and do it.*
Luke 8:21

The great privileges of those who hear the Word of God,
and do it.

Our Lord Jesus Christ declares that He regards them as His
mother and His brethren.

The man who hears the Word of God, and does it, is the true
Christian. He hears the call of God to repent and be converted, and he
obeys it. He ceases to do evil, and learns to do well. He puts off the old
man, and puts on the new. He hears the call of God to believe on Jesus
Christ for justification, and he obeys it. He forsakes his own
righteousness, and confesses his need of a Saviour. He receives Christ
crucified as his only hope, and counts all things loss for the knowledge
of Him. He hears the call of God to be holy, and he obeys it. He strives
to mortify the deeds of his body, and to walk after the Spirit. He labours
to lay aside every weight, and the sin that so easily besets him. This is
true vital Christianity. All men and women who are of this character
are true Christians.

Now the troubles of all who 'hear the word of God, and do it' are
neither few nor small. The world, the flesh, and the devil continually
vex them. They often groan, being burdened (2 Cor. 5:4). They often
find the cross heavy, and the way to heaven rough and narrow. They
often feel disposed to cry with St Paul, 'O wretched man that I am!
who shall deliver me from the body of this death?' (Rom. 7:24).

Let all such take comfort in the words of our Lord Jesus Christ
which we are now considering. Let them remember that the Son of
God Himself regards them as His own near relations! Let them not
heed the laughter, and mockery, and persecution of this world. The
woman of whom Christ says, she is My mother, and the man of whom
Christ says, he is My brother, have no cause to be ashamed.

March 27

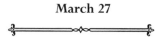

And he said unto them, Where is your faith? And they being afraid
wondered, saying one to another, What manner of man is this! for he
commandeth even the winds and water, and they obey him.

Luke 8:25

How needful it is for Christians to keep their faith ready for use.**

We read that our Lord said to His disciples, when the storm had ceased, and their fears had subsided, 'Where is your faith?' Well might He ask that question! Where was the profit of believing, if they could not believe in the time of need? Where was the real value of faith, unless they kept it in active exercise? Where was the benefit of trusting, if they were to trust their Master in sunshine only, but not in storms? The lesson now before us is one of deep practical importance. To have true saving faith is one thing. To have that faith always ready for use is quite another. Many receive Christ as their Saviour, and deliberately commit their souls to Him for time and eternity, who yet often find their faith sadly failing when something unexpected happens, and they are suddenly tried. These things ought not so to be. We ought to pray that we may have a stock of faith ready for use at a moment's notice, and may never be found unprepared. The highest style of Christian is the man who lives like Moses, 'seeing him who is invisible' (Heb. 2:27).

That man will never be greatly shaken by any storm. He will see Jesus near Him in the darkest hour, and blue sky behind the blackest cloud.

March 28

And Jesus said, Who touched me? When all denied, Peter and they that
were with him said, Master, the multitude throng thee and press thee,
and sayest thou, Who touched me?
Luke 8:45

A striking picture of the first beginnings of saving faith, and its effect.

We are told that she 'Came behind' our Lord, and 'touched the border of His garment: and immediately her issue of blood stanched'. The act appeared a most simple one, and utterly inadequate to produce any great result. But the effect of that act was most marvellous! In an instant the poor sufferer was healed. The relief that many physicians had failed to give in 'twelve years', was obtained in one moment. It was but one touch, and she was well!

It is hard to conceive a more lively image of the experience of many souls than the history of the woman's cure. Hundreds could testify that, like her they long sought spiritual help from physicians, of no value, and wearied their souls by using remedies which brought no cure. At last, like her, they heard of One who healed labouring consciences and forgave sinners, 'without money and without price', if men would only come to Him by faith. The terms seemed too easy to be credible. The tidings sounded too good to be true. But, like the woman before us, they resolved to try. They came to Christ by faith, with all their sins, and to their amazement at once found relief. And now they feel more comfort and hope than they ever felt before. The burden seems rolled off their backs. The weight seems taken off their minds. Light seems breaking in on their hearts. They begin to 'rejoice in the hope of the glory of God' (Rom. 5:2). And all, they would tell us, is owing to one simple thing: they came to Jesus just as they were. They touched Him by faith, and were healed.

For ever let it be graven on our hearts that faith in Christ is the grand secret of peace with God. Without it we shall never find inward rest, whatever we may do in religion.

March 29

He said unto them, But whom say ye that I am?
Peter answering said, The Christ of God.
Luke 9:20

The singular knowledge and faith displayed by the Apostle Peter.

We read, that when our Lord said to His disciples, 'whom say ye that I am? Peter answering said, The Christ of God'.

This was a noble confession, and one of which, in these days, we can hardly realize the full value. To estimate it aright we should place ourselves in the position of our Lord's disciples. We should call to mind that the great, and wise, and learned of their own nation, saw no beauty in their Master, and would not receive Him as the Messiah. We should recollect that they saw no royal dignity about our Lord – no crown – no army – no earthly dominion. They saw nothing but a poor Man, who often had no place in which to lay His head. And yet it was at this time, and under these circumstances, that Peter boldly declares his belief that Jesus is the Christ of God. Truly, this was a great faith! It was mingled, no doubt, with much of ignorance and imperfection. But such as it was, it was a faith that stood alone. He that had it was a remarkable man, and far in advance of the age in which he lived.

We should pray frequently that God would raise up more Christians of the stamp of the Apostle Peter. Erring, and unstable, and ignorant of his own heart as he sometimes proved, that blessed apostle was in some respects one in ten thousand. He had faith and zeal, and love to Christ's cause, when almost all Israel was unbelieving and cold. We want more men of this sort. We want men who are not afraid to stand alone, and to cleave to Christ when the many are against Him. Such men, like Peter, may err sadly at times, but in the long run of life will do more good than any. Knowledge, no doubt, is an excellent thing; but knowledge without zeal and warmth will never do much for the world.

March 30

And the apostles said unto the Lord, Increase our faith.
Luke 17:5

The important request which the Apostles made. They said unto the Lord, 'Increase our faith'.

We know not the secret feelings from which this request sprung. Perhaps the hearts of the apostles failed within them, as they heard one weighty lesson after another fall from our Lord's lips. Perhaps the thought rose up in their minds, 'Who is sufficient for these things? Who can receive such high doctrines? Who can follow such a lofty standard of practice?' These, however, are only conjectures. One thing, at any rate, is clear and plain. The request which they made was most deeply important: 'Increase our faith'.

Faith is the root of saving religion. '[H]e that cometh unto God must believe that he is, and that he is a rewarder of them that diligently seek him' (Heb. 11:6). It is the hand by which the soul lays hold on Jesus Christ, and is united to Him and saved: it is the secret of all Christian comfort, and spiritual prosperity. According to a man's faith will be his peace, his hope, his strength, his courage, his decision and his victory over the world. When the apostles made request about faith they did wisely and well.

Faith is a grace which admits of degrees. It does not come to full strength and perfection as soon as it is planted in the heart by the Holy Ghost. There is 'little' faith and 'great' faith; there is 'weak' faith and 'strong' faith: both are spoken of in the Scriptures; both are to be seen in the experience of God's people. The more faith a Christian has, the more happy, holy and useful will he be. To promote the growth and progress of faith should be the daily prayer and endeavour of all who love life. When the apostles, said, 'Increase our faith', they did well.

If we have any faith let us pray for more of it. It is a bad sign of a man's spiritual state when he is satisfied to live on old stock, and does not hunger and thirst after growth in grace. Let a prayer for more faith form part of our daily devotions. Let us covet earnestly the best gifts. We are not to despise 'the day of small things' in a brother's soul, but we are not to be content with it in our own.

March 31

*I tell you that he will avenge them speedily. Nevertheless when the Son
of man cometh, shall he find faith on the earth?*
Luke 18:8

True faith will be found very scarce at the end of the
world.

The Lord Jesus shows this by asking a very solemn question:
'when the Son of man cometh, shall he find faith on the earth?'

The question before us is a very humbling one. It shows the
uselessness of expecting that all the world will be converted before
Christ comes again. It shows the foolishness of supposing that all persons
are 'good', and that though differing in outward matters, they are all
right at heart, and all going to heaven. Such notions find no countenance
in the text before us.

Where is the use, after all, of ignoring facts under our own eyes:
facts in the world, facts in the churches, facts in the congregations we
belong to, facts by our own doors and firesides? Where is faith to be
seen?

How many around us really believe what the Bible contains? How
many live as if they believed that Christ died for them, and that there is
a judgment, a heaven and a hell? These are most painful and serious
inquiries. But they demand and deserve an answer.

Have we faith ourselves? If we have, let us bless God for it. It is a
great thing to believe all the Bible. It is a matter for daily thankfulness if
we feel our sins, and really trust in Jesus. We may be weak, frail, erring,
shortcoming sinners: but do we believe? That is the grand question. If
we believe, we shall be saved. But he that believeth not, shall not see
life, and shall die in his sins (John 3:36; 8:24).

APRIL

April 1

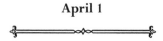

But as many as received him, to them gave he power to become the sons
of God, even to them that believe on his name.
John 1:12

The vast privileges of all who receive Christ, and believe
on Him.

We are told that 'as many as received him, to them gave he power
to become the sons of God, even to them that believe on his name'.

Christ will never be without some servants. If the vast majority of
the Jews did not receive Him as the Messiah, there were, at any rate, a
few who did. To them He gave the privilege of being God's children.
He adopted them as members of His Father's family. He reckoned them
His own brethren and sisters, bone of His bone, and flesh of His flesh.
He conferred on them a dignity which was ample recompense for the
cross which they had to carry for His sake. He made them sons and
daughters of the Lord Almighty.

Privileges like these, be it remembered, are the possession of all, in
every age, who receive Christ by faith, and follow Him as their Saviour.
They are 'sons of God through faith in Christ Jesus' (Gal. 3:26). They
are born again by a new and heavenly birth, and adopted into the family
of the King of kings. Few in number, and despised by the world as they
are, they are cared for with infinite love by a Father in heaven, who, for
His Son's sake, is well pleased with them. In time He provides them
with everything that is for their good. In eternity He will give them a
crown of glory that fadeth not away. These are great things! But faith in
Christ gives men an ample title to them. Good masters care for their
servants, and Christ cares for His.

Are we ourselves sons of God? Have we been born again? Have we
the marks that always accompany the new birth – sense of sin, faith in
Jesus, love of others, righteous living, separation from the world? Let
us never be content till we can give a satisfactory answer to these
questions.

Do we desire to be sons of God? Then let us 'receive Christ' as our
Saviour, and believe on Him with the heart. To everyone that so receives
Him, He will give the privilege of becoming a son of God.

April 2

When therefore he was risen from the dead, his disciples remembered
that he had said this unto them; and they believed the Scripture,
and the word which Jesus had said.
John 2:22

How men may remember words of religious truth long after they are spoken, and may one day see a meaning in them which at first they did not see.

We are told that our Lord said to the Jews, 'Destroy this temple, and in three days I will raise it up'. St John informs us distinctly that 'he spake of the temple of his body', that He referred to His own resurrection. Yet the meaning of the sentence was not understood by our Lord's disciples at the time that it was spoken. It was not till 'he was risen from the dead', three years after the events here described, that the full significance of the sentence flashed on their hearts. For three years it was a dark and useless saying to them. For three years it lay sleeping in their minds, like a seed in a tomb, and bore no fruit. But at the end of that time the darkness passed away. They saw the application of their Master's words, and as they saw it were confirmed in their faith. 'They remembered that he had said this', and as they remembered 'they believed'.

It is a comfortable and cheering thought, that the same kind of thing that happened to the disciples is often going on at the present day. The sermons that are preached to apparently heedless ears in churches, are not all lost and thrown away. The instruction that is given in schools and pastoral visits, is not all wasted and forgotten. The texts that are taught by parents to children are not all taught in vain. There is often a resurrection of sermons, and texts, and instruction, after an interval of many years. The good seed sometimes springs up after he that sowed it has been long dead and gone. Let preachers go on preaching, and teachers go on teaching, and parents go on training up children in the way they should go. Let them sow the good seed of Bible truth in faith and patience. Their labour is not in vain in the Lord. Their words are remembered far more than they think, and will yet spring up 'after many days' (1 Cor. 15:58; Eccles. 11:1).

April 3

The same came to Jesus by night, and said unto him, Rabbi, we know
that thou art a teacher come from God: for no man can do these
miracles that thou doest, except God be with him.
John 3:2

What a weak and feeble beginning a man may make in religion, and yet finally prove a strong Christian. We are told of a certain Pharisee, named Nicodemus, who, feeling concerned about his soul, 'came to Jesus by night'.

There can be little doubt that Nicodemus acted as he did on this occasion from the fear of man. He was afraid of what man would think, or say, or do, if his visit to Jesus was known. He came 'by night', because he had not faith and courage enough to come by day. And yet there came a time afterwards when this very Nicodemus took our Lord's part in open day in the council of the Jews. 'Doth our law judge any man,' He said, 'before it hear him, and know what he doeth?' (John 7:51). Nor was this all. There came a time when this very Nicodemus was one of the only two men who did honour to our Lord's dead body. He helped Joseph of Arimathea to bury Jesus, when even the apostles had forsaken their Master and fled. His last things were more than his first. Though he began ill, he ended well.

The history of Nicodemus is meant to teach us that we should never despise 'the day of small things' in religion (Zech. 4:10). We must not set down a man as having no grace, because his first steps towards God are timid and wavering, and the first movements of his soul are uncertain, hesitating and stamped with much imperfection. We must remember our Lord's reception of Nicodemus. He did not break the bruised reed, or quench the smoking flax, which He saw before Him (Matt. 12:20). Like Him, let us take inquirers by the hand, and deal with them gently and lovingly. In everything there must be a beginning. It is not those who make the most flaming profession of religion at first, who endure the longest and prove the most steadfast.

April 4

That whosoever believeth in him should not perish,
but have eternal life.
John 3:15

The peculiar plan by which the love of God has provided salvation for sinners.

That plan is the atoning death of Christ on the cross. Our Lord says to Nicodemus, 'as Moses lifted up the serpent in the wilderness, even so must the Son of man be lifted up: That whosoever believeth in him should not perish, but have eternal life.'

By being 'lifted up', our Lord meant nothing less than His own death upon the cross. That death, He would have us know, was appointed by God to be 'the life of the world' (John 6:51). It was ordained from all eternity to be the great propitiation and satisfaction for man's sin. It was the payment, by an almighty Substitute and Representative, of man's enormous debt to God. When Christ died upon the cross, our many sins were laid upon Him. He was made 'sin' for us. He was made 'a curse' for us (2 Cor. 5:21; Gal. 3:13). By His death He purchased pardon and complete redemption for sinners. The brazen serpent, lifted up in the camp of Israel, brought health and cure within the reach of all who were bitten by serpents. Christ crucified, in like manner, brought eternal life within reach of lost mankind. Christ has been lifted up on the cross, and man looking to Him by faith may be saved.

The truth before us is the very foundation-stone of the Christian religion. Christ's death is the Christian's life. Christ's cross is the Christian's title to heaven. Christ 'lifted up' and put to shame on Calvary is the ladder by which Christians 'enter into the holiest', and are at length landed in glory. It is true that we are sinners; but Christ has suffered for us. It is true that we deserve death; but Christ died for us. It is true that we are guilty debtors; but Christ has paid our debts with His own blood. This is the real gospel! This is the good news!

April 5

For God so loved the world, that he gave his only begotten Son,
that whosoever believeth in him should not perish, but have everlasting life.
John 3:16

The way in which the benefits of Christ's death are made our own.

That way is simply to put faith and trust in Christ. Faith is the same thing as believing. Three times our Lord repeats this glorious truth to Nicodemus. Twice He proclaims that 'whosoever believeth' shall not perish. Once He says, 'He that believeth on' the Son of God 'is not condemned'. Faith in the Lord Jesus is the very key of salvation. He that has it has life, and he that has it not has not life. Nothing whatever beside this faith is necessary to our complete justification; but nothing whatever, except this faith, will give us an interest in Christ. We may fast and mourn for sin, and do many things that are right, and use religious ordinances, and give all our goods to feed the poor, and yet remain unpardoned, and lose our souls. But if we will only come to Christ as guilty sinners, and believe on Him, our sins shall at once be forgiven, and our iniquities shall be entirely put away. Without faith there is no salvation; but through faith in Jesus, the vilest sinner may be saved.

If we would have a peaceful conscience in our religion, let us see that our views of saving faith are distinct and clear. Let us beware of supposing that justifying faith is anything more than a sinner's simple trust in a Saviour, the grasp of a drowning man on the hand held out for his relief. Let us beware of mingling anything else with faith in the matter of justification. Here we must always remember faith stands entirely alone. A justified man, no doubt, will always be a holy man. True believing will always be accompanied by godly living. But that which gives a man an interest in Christ, is not his living, but his faith. If we would know whether our faith is genuine, we do well to ask ourselves how we are living. But if we would know whether we are justified by Christ, there is but one question to be asked. That question is, 'Do we believe?'

April 6

Jesus answered and said unto them, This is the work of God,
that ye believe on him whom he hath sent.
John 6:29

T he high honour Christ puts on faith in Himself. The Jews had asked Him, 'What shall we do, that we might work the works of God?' In reply He says, 'This is the work of God, that ye believe on him whom he hath sent'. A truly striking and remarkable expression! If any two things are put in strong contrast, in the New Testament they are faith and works. Not working, but believing, – not of works but through faith – are words familiar to all careful Bible-readers. Yet here the great Head of the Church declares that believing on Him is the highest and greatest of all 'works'! It is 'the work of God'.

Doubtless our Lord did not mean that there is anything meritorious in believing. Man's faith, at the very best, is feeble and defective. Regarded as a 'work', it cannot stand the severity of God's judgment, deserve pardon or purchase heaven. But our Lord did mean that faith in Himself, as the only Saviour, is the first act of the soul which God requires at a sinner's hands. Till a man believes on Jesus, and rests on Jesus as a lost sinner, he is nothing. Our Lord did mean that faith in Himself is that act of the soul which specially pleases God. When the Father sees a sinner casting aside his own righteousness, and simply trusting in His dear Son, He is well pleased. Without such faith it is impossible to please God. Our Lord did mean that faith in Himself is the root of all saving religion. There is no life in a man till he believes. Above all, our Lord did mean that faith in Himself is the hardest of all spiritual acts to the natural man. Did the Jews want something to do in religion? Let them know that the greatest thing they had to do was to cast aside their pride, confess their guilt and need, and humbly believe.

April 7

Then came Peter to him, and said, Lord, how oft shall my brother sin
against me, and I forgive him? till seven times?
Matthew 18:21

The Lord Jesus lays it down as a general rule, that we ought to forgive others to the uttermost.

Peter put the question, 'how oft shall my brother sin against me, and I forgive him? till seven times?' He received for answer, 'I say not unto thee, Until seven times: but Until seventy times seven'.

The rule here laid down must of course be interpreted with sober-minded qualification. Our Lord does not mean that offences against the law of the land and good order of society, are to be passed over in silence; He does not mean that we are to allow people to commit thefts and assaults with impunity: all that He means is, that we are to study a general spirit of mercy and forgivingness towards our brethren. We are to bear much, and to put up with much, rather than quarrel; we are to look over much, rather than have any strife; we are to lay aside everything like malice, strife, revenge and retaliation. Such feelings are only fit for heathens: they are utterly unworthy of a disciple of Christ.

What a happy world it would be if this rule of our Lord's was more known and better obeyed! How many of the miseries of mankind are occasioned by disputes, quarrels, lawsuits and an obstinate tenacity about what men call 'their rights'! How many of them might be altogether avoided, if men were more willing to forgive, and more desirous for peace! Let us never forget that a fire cannot go on burning without fuel: just in the same way it takes two to make a quarrel. Let us each resolve, by God's grace, that of these two we will never be one. Let us resolve to return good for evil, and blessing for cursing, and so to melt down enmity, and change our foes into friends (Rom. 12:20). It was a fine feature in Archbishop Cranmer's character, that if you did him an injury he was sure to be your friend.

April 8

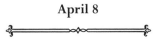

Verily I say unto you, All sins shall be forgiven unto the sons of men,
and blasphemies wherewith soever they shall blaspheme …
Mark 3:28

What a glorious declaration our Lord makes in these verses about the forgiveness of sins.

He says, 'All sins shall be forgiven unto the sons of men, and blasphemies wherewith soever they shall blaspheme'.

These words fall lightly on the ears of many persons. They see no particular beauty in them. But to the man who is alive to his own sinfulness and deeply sensible of his need of mercy, these words are sweet and precious. 'All sins shall be forgiven.' The sins of youth and age – the sins of head, and hand, and tongue, and imagination – the sins against all God's commandments – the sins of persecutors, like Saul – the sins of idolaters, like Manasseh – the sins of open enemies of Christ, like the Jews who crucified Him – the sins of backsliders from Christ, like Peter – all, all may be forgiven. The blood of Christ can cleanse all away. The righteousness of Christ can cover all, and hide all from God's eyes.

The doctrine here laid down is the crown and glory of the gospel. The very first thing it proposes to man is free pardon, full forgiveness, complete remission, without money and without pride. '[T]hrough this man is preached unto you the forgiveness of sins: and by him all that believe are justified from all things' (Acts 13:38-39).

Let us lay hold on this doctrine without delay, if we never received it before. It is for us, as well as for others. We too, this very day, if we come to Christ, may be completely forgiven. 'Though your sins be as scarlet, they shall be as white as snow' (Isa. 1:18).

Let us cleave firmly to this doctrine, if we have received it already. We may sometimes feel faint, and unworthy, and cast down. But if we have really come to Jesus by faith, our sins are clean forgiven. They are cast behind God's back, blotted out of the book of His remembrance, sunk into the depths of the sea. Let us believe and not be afraid.

April 9

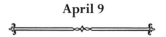

And when ye stand praying, forgive, if ye have ought against any: that
your Father also which is in heaven may forgive you your trespasses.
Mark 11:25

The absolute necessity of a forgiving spirit towards others.

This lesson is here taught us in a striking way. There is no immediate connection between the importance of faith, of which our Lord has just been speaking, and the subject of forgiving injuries. But the connecting link is prayer. First we are told that faith is essential to the success of our prayers. But then it is added, no prayer can be heard which does not come from a forgiving heart. 'And when ye stand praying, forgive, if ye have ought against any: that your Father also which is in heaven may forgive you your trespasses.'

The value of our prayers, we can all understand, depends exceedingly on the state of mind in which we offer them. But the point before us is one which receives far less attention than it deserves. Our prayers must not only be earnest, fervent, and sincere, and in the name of Christ. They must contain one more ingredient besides. They must come from a forgiving heart. We have no right to look for mercy if we are not ready to extend mercy to our brethren. We cannot really feel the sinfulness of the sins we ask to have pardoned if we cherish malice towards our fellow men. We must have the heart of a brother toward our neighbour on earth if we wish God to be our Father in heaven. We must not flatter ourselves that we have the Spirit of adoption if we cannot bear and forbear.

Let us leave this passage with serious self-inquiry. Do we know what it is to be of a forgiving spirit? Can we look over the injuries that we receive from time to time in this evil world? Can we pass over transgression and pardon an offence? If not, where is our Christianity? If not, why should we wonder that our souls do not prosper? Let us resolve to amend our ways in this matter. Let us determine by God's grace to forgive, even as we hope to be forgiven. This is the nearest approach we can make to the mind of Christ Jesus.

April 10

―――――◆―――――

Simon answered and said, I suppose that he, to whom he forgave most.
And he said unto him, Thou hast rightly judged.
Luke 7:43

A sense of having our sins forgiven is the mainspring and lifeblood of love to Christ.

This, beyond doubt, was the lesson which our Lord wished Simon the Pharisee to learn, when He told him the story of the two debtors. One owed his creditor 'five hundred pence, and the other fifty': both had 'nothing to pay', and both were forgiven freely. And then came the searching question: 'which of them will love him most?' Here was the true explanation, our Lord told Simon, of the deep love which the penitent woman before Him had displayed. Her many tears, her deep affection, her public reverence, her action in anointing His feet, were all traceable to one cause. She had been much forgiven, and so she loved much. Her love was the effect of her forgiveness, not the cause – the consequence of her forgiveness, not the condition – the result of her forgiveness, not the reason – the fruit of her forgiveness, not the root. Would the Pharisee know why this woman showed so much love? It was because she felt much forgiven. Would he know why he himself had shown his guest so little love? It was because he felt under no obligation – had no consciousness of having obtained forgiveness – had no sense of debt to Christ.

For ever let the mighty principle laid down by our Lord in this passage, abide in our memories, and sink down into our hearts. It is one of the great cornerstones of the whole gospel. It is one of the master-keys to unlock the secrets of the kingdom of God. The only way to make men holy, is to teach and preach free and full forgiveness through Jesus Christ. The secret of being holy ourselves, is to know and feel that Christ has pardoned our sins. Peace with God is the only root that will bear the fruit of holiness. Forgiveness must go before sanctification. We shall do nothing till we are reconciled to God. This is the first step in religion. We must work from life and not for life. Our best works before we are justified are little better than splendid sins. We must live by faith in the Son of God, and then, and not till then, we shall walk in His ways.

April 11

Take heed to yourselves: If thy brother trespass against thee,
rebuke him; and if he repent, forgive him.
Luke 17:3

The great importance of a forgiving spirit.
The Lord Jesus says, 'If thy brother trespass against thee, rebuke him; and if he repent, forgive him. And if he trespass against thee seven times in a day, and seven times in a day turn again to thee, saying, I repent; thou shalt forgive him.'

There are few Christian duties which are so frequently and strongly dwelt upon in the New Testament as this of forgiving injuries. It fills a prominent place in the Lord's Prayer. The only profession we make in all that prayer, is that of forgiving 'those who trespass against us'. It is a test of being forgiven ourselves. The man who cannot forgive his neighbour the few trifling offences he may have committed against him, can know nothing experimentally of that free and full pardon which is offered us by Christ (Matt. 18:35; Eph. 4:32). Not least, it is one leading mark of the indwelling of the Holy Ghost. The presence of the Spirit in the heart may always be known by the fruits He causes to be brought forth in the life. Those fruits are both active and passive. The man who has not learned to bear and forbear, to put up with much and look over much, is not born of the Spirit (1 John 2:14; Matt. 5:44, 45).

The doctrine laid down by our Lord in this place is deeply humbling. It shows most plainly the wide contrariety which exists between the ways of the world and the gospel of Christ. Who does not know that pride, and haughtiness, and high-mindedness, and readiness to take offence, and implacable determination never to forget and never to forgive, are common among baptized men and women? Thousands will go to the Lord's table, and even profess to love the gospel, who fire up in a moment at the least appearance of what they call 'offensive' conduct, and make a quarrel out of the merest trifles.

April 12

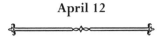

And after six days Jesus taketh with him Peter, and James, and John,
and leadeth them up into an high mountain apart by themselves:
and he was transfigured before them.
Mark 9:2

The marvellous vision they contain of the glory which Christ and His people shall have at His second coming. There can be no doubt that this was one of the principal purposes of the transfiguration. It was meant to teach the disciples, that though their Lord was lowly and poor in appearance now, He would one day appear in such royal majesty as became the Son of God. It was meant to teach them, that when their Master came the second time, His saints, like Moses and Elias, would appear with Him. It was meant to remind them, that though reviled and persecuted now, because they belonged to Christ, they would one day be clothed with honour, and be partakers of their Master's glory.

We have reason to thank God for this vision. We are often tempted to give up Christ's service, because of the cross and affliction which it entails. We see few with us, and many against us. We find our names cast out as evil, and all manner of evil said of us, because we believe and love the gospel. Year after year we see our companions in Christ's service removed by death, and we feel as if we knew little about them, except that they are gone to an unknown world, and that we are left alone. All these things are trying to flesh and blood. No wonder that the faith of believers sometimes languishes, and their eyes fail while they look for their hope.

Let us see in the story of the transfiguration, a remedy for such doubting thoughts as these. The vision of the holy mount is a gracious pledge that glorious things are in store for the people of God. Their crucified Saviour shall come again in power and great glory. His saints shall all come with Him, and are in safekeeping until that happy day. We may wait patiently. 'When Christ, who is our life, shall appear, then shall ye also appear with him in glory' (Col. 3:4).

April 13

And if I go and prepare a place for you, I will come again, and receive
you unto myself; that where I am, there ye may be also.
John 14:3

A solid ground for expecting good things to come. The evil heart of unbelief within us is apt to rob us of our comfort about heaven. 'We wish we could think it was all true.' – 'We fear we shall never be admitted into heaven.' – Let us hear what Jesus says to encourage us.

One cheering word is this – 'I go and prepare a place for you'. Heaven is a prepared place for a prepared people: a place which we shall find Christ Himself has made ready for true Christians. He has prepared it by procuring a right for every sinner who believes to enter in. None can stop us, and say we have no business there. He has prepared it by going before us as our Head and Representative, and taking possession of it for all the members of His mystical body. As our Forerunner He has marched in, leading captivity captive, and has planted His banner in the land of glory. He has prepared it by carrying our names with Him as our High Priest into the holy of holies, and making angels ready to receive us. They that enter heaven will find they are neither unknown nor unexpected.

Another cheering word is this: 'I will come again, and receive you unto myself'. Christ will not wait for believers to come up to Him, but will come down to them, to raise them from their graves and escort them to their heavenly home. As Joseph came to meet Jacob, so will Jesus come to call His people together and guide them to their inheritance. The second advent ought never to be forgotten. Great is the blessedness of looking back to Christ coming the first time to suffer for us, but no less great is the comfort of looking forward to Christ coming the second time, to raise and reward His saints (Heb. 9:25-28).

How much they miss who live in a dying world and yet know nothing of God as their Father and Christ as their Saviour! How much they possess who live the life of faith in the Son of God, and believe in Jesus!

April 14

*Father, I will that they also, whom thou hast given me, be with me
where I am; that they may behold my glory, which thou hast given me:
for thou lovedst me before the foundation of the world.*
John 17:24

Jesus prays that His people may at last be with Him and behold His glory.

'I will', He says, that those 'whom Thou hast given Me, be with Me where I am; that they may behold my glory ...'

This is a singularly beautiful and touching conclusion to our Lord's remarkable prayer. We may well believe that it was meant to cheer and comfort those who heard it, and strengthen them for the parting scene which was fast drawing near. But for all who read it even now, this part of His prayer is full of sweet and unspeakable comfort.

We do not see Christ now. We read of Him, hear of Him, believe in Him and rest our souls in His finished work. But even the best of us, at our best, walk by faith and not by sight, and our poor halting faith often makes us walk very feebly in the way to heaven. There shall be an end of all this state of things one day. We shall at length see Christ as He is, and know as we have been known. We shall behold Him face to face, and not through a glass darkly. We shall actually be in His presence and company, and go out no more. If faith has been pleasant, much more will certainly be. No wonder that when St Paul has written, 'Shall we ever be with the Lord', he adds, 'comfort one another with these words' (1 Thess. 4:17, 18).

We know little of heaven now. Our thoughts are all confounded, when we try to form an idea of a future state in which pardoned sinners shall be perfectly happy. '[I]t doth not yet appear what we shall be' (1 John 3:2). But we may rest ourselves on the blessed thought, that after death we shall be 'with Christ'. Whether before the resurrection in paradise, or after the resurrection in final glory, the prospect is still the same. True Christians shall be 'with Christ'. We need no more information. Where that blessed Person is who was born for us, died for us and rose again, there can be no lack of anything. David might well say 'in Thy presence is fullness of joy; at thy right hand there are pleasures for evermore' (Ps. 16:11).

April 15

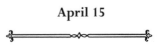

And after these things he went forth, and saw a publican, named Levi,
sitting at the receipt of custom: and he said unto him, Follow me.
Luke 5:27

The power of Christ's calling grace.

We read that our Lord called a publican named Levi to become one of His disciples. This man belonged to a class who were a very proverb for wickedness among the Jews. Yet even to him our Lord says, 'Follow me'. We read furthermore, that such mighty influence on Levi's heart accompanied our Lord's words, that although 'sitting at the receipt of custom', when called, he at once 'left all, rose up, and followed' Christ, and became a disciple.

We must never despair of anyone's salvation, so long as he lives, after reading a case like this. We must never say of anyone that he is too wicked, or too hardened, or too worldly to become a Christian. No sins are too many, or too bad, to be forgiven. No heart is too hard or too worldly, to be changed. He who called Levi still lives, and is the same that He was eighteen hundred years ago. With Christ nothing is impossible.

How is it with ourselves. This, after all, is the grand question. Are we waiting, and delaying, and hanging back, under the idea that the cross is too heavy, and that we can never serve Christ? Let us cast such thoughts away at once and for ever. Let us believe that Christ can enable us by His Spirit to give up all, and come out from the world. Let us remember that He who called Levi never changes. Let us take up the cross boldly, and go forward.

We can easily imagine that Levi's conversion was a cause of grief to his worldly friends. They saw him giving up a profitable calling, to follow a new teacher from Nazareth! They doubtless regarded his conduct as a grievous piece of folly, and an occasion for sorrow rather than joy. They only looked at his temporal losses by becoming a Christian. Of his spiritual gains they knew nothing. And there are many like them. There are always thousands of people who, if they hear of a relation being converted, consider it rather a misfortune. Instead of rejoicing, they only shake their heads and mourn.

April 16

And the lord said unto the servant, Go out into the highways and
hedges, and compel them to come in, that my house may be filled'.
Luke 14:23

God earnestly desires the salvation of souls, and would have all means used to procure acceptance for His gospel.
We read that when those who were first invited to the supper refused the invitation, 'the master of the house ... said to his servant, Go out quickly into the streets ... and bring in hither the poor, and the maimed, and the halt, and the blind'. We read that when this was done, and there was yet room, 'the lord said unto the servant, Go out into the highways and hedges, and compel them to come in, that my house may be filled'.

The meaning of these words can admit of little dispute. They surely justify us in asserting the exceeding love and compassion of God towards sinners. His long-suffering is inexhaustible. If some will not receive the truth, He will have others invited in their stead. His pity for the lost is no feigned and imaginary thing: He is infinitely willing to save souls.

Above all, the words justify every preacher and teacher of the gospel in employing all possible means to awaken sinners, and to turn them from their sins. If they will not come to us in public, we must visit them in private. If they will not attend our preaching in the congregation, we must be ready to preach from house to house. We must even not be ashamed to use a gentle violence. We must be instant in season, out of season (2 Tim. 4:2). We must deal with many an unconverted man as one half-asleep, half out of his mind and not fully conscious of the state he is in. We must press the gospel on his notice again and again. We must cry aloud and spare not. We must deal with him as we would with a man about to commit suicide. We must try to snatch him as a brand from the burning. We must say, 'I cannot, I will not, I dare not let you go on ruining your own soul'. The men of the world may not understand such earnest dealing; they may sneer at all zeal and fervour in religion as fanaticism; but the 'man of God' who desires to do the work of an evangelist, will heed little what the world says. He will remember the words of our parable. He will compel men to come in.

April 17

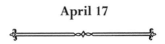

And he said, The things which are impossible with men are
possible with God.
Luke 18:27

How mighty is the power of God's grace.
We see this in the words which our Lord addressed to those who heard Him speaking of the rich man's danger. They said, 'Who then can be saved?' Our Lord's reply is broad and full: 'The things which are impossible with men are possible with God'. By grace a man may serve God, and reach heaven in any condition of life.

The Word of God contains many striking instances in illustration of this doctrine. Abraham, and David, and Hezekiah, and Jehoshaphat, and Josiah, and Job, and Daniel, were all great and rich; yet they all served God, and were saved: they all found grace sufficient for them, and overcame the temptations by which they were surrounded. Their Lord and Master still lives, and what He did for them He can do for others. He can give power to rich Christians to follow Christ in spite of their riches, as well as He did to rich Jews.

Let us beware of allowing ourselves to suppose that our own salvation is impossible, because of the hardness of our position. It is too often a suggestion of the devil and our own lazy hearts. We must not give way to it. It matters not where we live, so long as we are not following a sinful calling; it matters not what our income may be, whether we are burdened with riches or pinched with poverty: grace, and not place, is the hinge on which our salvation turns. Money will not keep us out of heaven if our hearts are right before God. Christ can make us more than conquerors; Christ can enable us to win our way through every difficulty. 'I can do all things', said St Paul, 'through Christ which strengtheneth me' (Phil. 4:13).

April 18

Then said the lord of the vineyard,What shall I do? I will send my
beloved son: it may be they will reverence him when they see him.
Luke 20:13

The amazing patience and long-suffering of God.
The conduct of the 'lord of the vineyard' is a vivid representation of God's dealings with man. It is a faithful picture of His merciful dealings with the Jewish Church. Prophet after prophet was sent to warn Israel of his danger; message after message was repeatedly sent, notwithstanding insults and injuries heaped on the messengers. It is a no less faithful picture of His gracious treatment of the Gentile Churches. For eighteen hundred years He has suffered their manners: they have repeatedly tried Him by false doctrines, superstitions and contempt of His word; yet He has repeatedly granted them seasons of refreshing, raised up for them holy ministers and mighty reformers, and not cut them off, notwithstanding all their persecutions. The Churches of Christ have no right to boast: they are debtors to God for innumerable mercies, no less than the Jews were in our Lord's time. They have not been dealt with according to their sins, nor rewarded according to their iniquities.

We should learn to be more thankful for God's mercy. We have probably little idea of the extent of our obligations to it, and of the number of gracious messages which the Lord of the vineyard is constantly sending to our souls. The last day will unfold to our wondering eyes a long list of unacknowledged kindnesses, of which while we lived we took no notice. Mercy we shall find was indeed God's darling attribute: 'he delighteth in mercy' (Micah 7:18). Mercies before conversion, mercies after conversion, mercies at every step on their journey on earth, will be revealed to the minds of saved saints, and make them ashamed of their own thanklessness. Sparing mercies, providential mercies, mercies in the way of warnings, mercies in the way of sudden visitations, will all be set forth in order before the minds of lost sinners, and confound them by the exhibition of their own hardness and unbelief. We shall all find that God was often speaking to us when we did not hear, and sending us messages which we did not regard.

April 19

No man can come to me, except the Father which hath sent me draw
him: and I will raise him up at the last day.
John 6:44

Man's natural helplessness and inability to repent or believe.

We find our Lord saying, 'No man can come unto me, except the Father which hath sent me draw him'. Until the Father draws the heart of man by His grace, man will not believe.

The solemn truth contained in these words is one that needs careful weighing. It is vain to deny that without the grace of God no-one ever can become a true Christian. We are spiritually dead, and have no power to give ourselves life. We need a new principle put in us from above. Facts prove it. Preachers see it. The Tenth Article of our own Church expressly declares it: 'The condition of man after the fall of Adam is such that he cannot turn and prepare himself, by his own natural strength and good work, to faith and calling upon God'. This witness is true.

But after all, of what does this inability of man consist? In what part of our inward nature does this impotence reside? Here is a point on which many mistakes arise. For ever let us remember that the will of man is the part of him which is in fault. His inability is not physical, but moral. It would not be true to say that a man has a real wish and desire to come to Christ, but no power to come. It would be far more true to say that a man has no power to come became he has no desire or wish. It is not true that he would come if he could. It is true that he could come if he would. The corrupt will – the secret disinclination – the want of heart, are the real causes of unbelief. It is here the mischief lies. The power that we want is a new will. It is precisely at this point that we need the 'drawing' of the Father. One thing at any rate is abundantly clear, and that is man's responsibility for his own soul. His inability to come to Christ does not make an end of his accountableness. Both things are equally true. If lost at last, it will prove to have been his own fault. His blood will be on his own head. Christ would have saved him but he would not be saved. He would not come to Christ, that he might have life.

April 20

*When he had heard therefore that he was sick, he abode two days still
in the same place where he was.*
John 11:6

Christ knows best at what time to do anything for His
people.

We read that when He had heard that Lazarus 'was sick, he
abode two days still in the same place where he was'. In fact, He
purposely delayed his journey, and did not come to Bethany till Lazarus
had been four days in the grave. No doubt He knew well what was
going on: but He never moved till the time came which He saw was
best. For the sake of the Church and the world, for the good of friends
and enemies, He kept away.

The children of God must constantly school their minds to learn
the great lesson now before us. Nothing so helps us to bear patiently
the trials of life as an abiding conviction of the perfect wisdom by which
everything around us is managed. Let us try to believe not only that all
that happens to us is well done, but that it is done in the best manner, by
the right instrument and at the right time. We are all naturally impatient
in the day of trial. We are apt to say, like Moses, when beloved ones are
sick, 'Heal her now, O God, I beseech thee' (Num. 12:13). We forget
that Christ is too wise a Physician to make any mistakes. It is the duty of
faith to say, 'My times are in Thy hand. Do with me as Thou wilt, how
Thou wilt, what Thou wilt, and when Thou wilt. Not my will, but Thine
be done.' The highest degree of faith is to be able to wait, sit still and
not complain.

Let us turn from the passage with a settled determination to trust
Christ entirely with all the concerns of this world, both public and
private. Let us believe that He by whom all things were made at first is
He who is managing all with perfect wisdom. The affairs of kingdoms,
families and private individuals, are all alike overruled by Him. He
chooses all the portions of His people. When we are sick, it is because
He knows it to be for our good: when He delays coming to help us it is
for the same wise reason. The hand that was nailed to the cross is too
wise and loving to smite without a needs-be, or to keep us waiting for
relief without a cause.

April 21

*Go ye therefore, and teach all nations, baptizing them in the name of
the Father, and of the Son, and of the Holy Ghost*
Matthew 28:19

The solemn mention of the blessed Trinity which our Lord makes in these verses.

He bids the apostles to baptize 'in the name of the Father, and of the Son, and of the Holy Ghost'.

This is one of those great plain texts which directly teach the mighty doctrine of the Trinity. It speaks of Father, Son and Holy Ghost, as three distinct Persons, and speaks of all three as coequal. Such as the Father is, such is the Son and such is the Holy Ghost. And yet these three are One.

This truth is a great mystery. Let it be enough to receive and believe it, and let us ever abstain from all attempts at explanation. It is childish folly to refuse assent to things that we do not understand. We are poor crawling worms of a day, and know little at our best about God and eternity: suffice it for us to receive the doctrine of the Trinity in unity, with humility and reverence, and to ask no vain questions. Let us believe that no sinful soul can be saved without the work of all three Persons in the blessed Trinity, and let us rejoice that Father, Son and Holy Ghost, who co-operated to make man, do also co-operate to save him. Here let us pause: we may receive practically what we cannot explain theoretically.

April 22

*After that he put his hands again upon his eyes, and made him look
up: and he was restored, and saw every man clearly.*
Mark 8:25

The manner in which the Spirit frequently works in the
conversion of souls.

We are all naturally blind and ignorant in the matters which
concern our souls. Conversion is an illumination, a change from darkness
to light, from blindness to seeing the kingdom of God. Yet few converted
people see things distinctly at first. The nature and proportion of
doctrines, practices and ordinances of the gospel are dimly seen by
them, and imperfectly understood. They are like the man before us,
who at first saw men as trees walking. Their vision is dazzled and
unaccustomed to the new world into which they have been introduced.
It is not till the work of the Spirit has become deeper and their
experience been somewhat matured, that they see all things clearly,
and give to each part of religion its proper place. This is the history of
thousands of God's children. They begin with seeing men as trees walking
– they end with seeing all clearly. Happy is he who has learned this
lesson well, and is humble and distrustful of his own judgment.

Finally, let us see in the gradual cure of this blind man, a striking
picture of the present position of Christ's believing people in the world,
compared with that which is to come. We see in part and know in part
in the present dispensation. We are like those that travel by night. We
know not the meaning of much that is passing around us. In the
providential dealings of God with His children, and in the conduct of
many of God's saints, we see much that we cannot understand, and
cannot alter. In short, we are like him that saw 'men as trees, walking'.

April 23

*And the angel answered and said unto her, The Holy Ghost shall come
upon thee, and the power of the Highest shall overshadow thee:
therefore also that holy thing which shall be born of thee shall be
called the Son of God.*

Luke 1:35

The prominent place assigned to the Holy Ghost in the
great mystery of the incarnation.

We find it written, 'The Holy Ghost shall come upon thee'. An
intelligent reader of the Bible will probably not fail to remember that
the honour here given to the Spirit is in precise harmony with the
teaching of Scripture in other places. In every step of the great work of
man's redemption we shall find special mention of the work of the
Holy Ghost. Did Jesus die to make atonement for our sins? It is written
that 'through the eternal Spirit [He] offered himself without spot to
God' (Heb. 9:14). Did He rise again for our justification? It is written
that He was 'quickened by the Spirit' (1 Pet. 3:18). Does He supply His
disciples with comfort between the time of His first and second advent?
It is written that the Comforter, whom He promised to send, is 'the
Spirit of truth' (John 14:17).

Let us take heed that we give the Holy Ghost the same place in our
personal religion which we find Him occupying in God's Word. Let us
remember that all that believers have, and are, and enjoy under the
gospel, they owe to the inward teaching of the Holy Spirit. The work of
each of the three Persons of the Trinity is equally and entirely needful
to the salvation of every saved soul. The election of God the Father, the
blood of God the Son and the sanctification of God the Spirit, ought
never to be separated in our Christianity.

April 24

And the Holy Ghost descended in a bodily shape like a dove upon him,
and a voice came from heaven, which said,
Thou art my beloved Son; in thee I am well pleased.
Luke 3:22

A remarkable proof of the doctrine of the Trinity. We have all the three Persons of the Godhead spoken of, as co-operating and acting at one time. God the Son begins the mighty work of His earthly ministry, by being baptized. God the Father solemnly accredits Him as the appointed Mediator, by a voice from heaven. God the Holy Ghost descends 'in a bodily shape like a dove' upon our Lord, and by so doing declares that this is He to whom the Father gives the Spirit without measure (John 3:34).

There is something deeply instructive, and deeply comforting in this revelation of the blessed Trinity, at this particular season of our Lord's earthly ministry. It shows us how mighty and powerful is the agency that is employed in the great business of our redemption. It is the common work of God the Father, God the Son and God the Holy Ghost. All three Persons in the Godhead are equally concerned in the deliverance of our souls from hell. The thought should cheer us, when disquieted and cast down. The thought should hearten and encourage us, when weary of the conflict with the world, the flesh and the devil. The enemies of our souls are mighty, but the Friends of our souls are mightier still. The whole power of the triune Jehovah is engaged upon our side. 'A threefold cord is not quickly broken' (Eccles. 4:12).

April 25

The wind bloweth where it listeth, and thou hearest the sound thereof,
but canst not tell whence it cometh, and whither it goeth:
so is every one that is born of the Spirit.
John 3:8

The instructive comparison which our Lord uses in explaining the new birth.

He saw Nicodemus perplexed and astonished by the things he had just heard. He graciously helped his wondering mind by an illustration drawn from the 'wind'. A more beautiful and fitting illustration of the work of the Spirit it is impossible to conceive.

There is much about the wind that is mysterious and inexplicable. Thou 'canst not tell', says our Lord, 'whence it cometh, and whither it goeth.' We cannot handle it with our hands, or see it with our eyes. When the wind blows, we cannot point out the exact spot where its breath first began to be felt, and the exact distance to which its influence shall extend. But we do not on that account deny its presence. It is just the same with the operations of the Spirit, in the new birth of man. They may be mysterious, sovereign and incomprehensible to us in many ways. But it is foolish to stumble at them because there is much about them that we cannot explain.

But whatever mystery there may be about the wind, its presence may always be known by its sound and effects. '[T]hou hearest the sound thereof,' says our Lord. When our ears hear it whistling in the windows, and our eyes see the clouds driving before it, we do not hesitate to say, 'There is wind.' It is just the same with the operations of the Holy Spirit in the new birth of man. Marvellous and incomprehensible as His work may be, it is work that can always be seen and known. The new birth is a thing that 'cannot be hid'. There will always be visible 'fruits of the Spirit' in everyone that is born of the Spirit.

April 26

Abide in me, and I in you. As the branch cannot bear fruit of itself,
except it abide in the vine; no more can ye, except ye abide in me.
John 15:4

The fruits of the Spirit are the only satisfactory evidence
of a man being a true Christian.

The disciple that abides in Christ, like a branch abiding in the
vine, will always bear fruit.

He that would know what the word 'fruit' means, need not wait
long for an answer. Repentance toward God, faith toward our Lord
Jesus Christ, holiness of life and conduct – these are what the New
Testament calls 'fruit'. These are the distinguishing marks of the man
who is a living branch of the true Vine. Where these things are wanting,
it is vain to talk of possessing 'dormant' grace and spiritual life. Where
there is no fruit there is no life. He that lacketh these things is 'dead
while [he] liveth' (1 Tim. 5:6).

True grace, we must not forget, is never idle. It never slumbers and
never sleeps. It is a vain notion to suppose that we are living members
of Christ, if the example of Christ is not to be seen in our characters
and lives. 'Fruit' is the only satisfactory evidence of saving union between
Christ and our souls. Where there is no fruit of the Spirit to be seen,
there is no vital religion in the heart. The Spirit of Life in Christ Jesus
will always make Himself known in the daily conduct of those in whom
He dwells. The Master Himself declares, 'every tree is known by his
own fruit' (Luke 6:44).

Just as the vine-dresser prunes and cuts back the branches of a fruitful
vine, in order to make them more fruitful, so does God purify and
sanctify believers by the circumstances of life in which He places them.
Trial, to speak plainly, is the instrument by which our Father in heaven
makes Christians more holy. By trial He calls out their passive graces,
and proves whether they can suffer His will as well as do it. By trial He
weans them from the world, draws them to Christ, drives them to the
Bible and prayer, shows them their own hearts, and makes them humble.
This is the process by which He 'purges' them, and makes them more
fruitful.

April 27

But when the Comforter is come, whom I will send unto you from the
Father, even the Spirit of truth, which proceedeth from the Father,
he shall testify of me ...
John 15:26

Our Lord speaks of the Holy Ghost.
He speaks of Him as a Person. He is 'the Comforter' who is to come; He is One 'sent' and 'proceeding'; He is One whose office it is to 'testify'. These are not words that can be used of a mere influence or inward feeling. So to interpret them is to contradict common sense, and to strain the meaning of plain language. Reason and fairness require us to understand that it is a personal Being who is here mentioned, even He whom we are justly taught to adore as the third Person in the blessed Trinity.

Again, our Lord speaks of the Holy Ghost as One who He 'will send unto you from the Father', and One 'who proceedeth from the Father'. These are deep sayings, no doubt, so deep that we have no line to fathom them. The mere fact that for centuries the Eastern and Western Churches of Christendom have been divided about their meaning, should teach us to handle them with modesty and reverence. One thing, at all events, is very clear and plain. There is a close and intimate connection between the Spirit, the Father and the Son. Why the Holy Ghost should be said to be sent by the Son, and to proceed from the Father, in this verse, we cannot tell. But we may quietly repose our minds in the thought expressed in an ancient creed, that 'In this Trinity none is afore or after other: none is greater or less than another'. 'Such as the Father is such is the Son, and such is the Holy Ghost.' Above all, we may rest in the comfortable truth that in the salvation of our souls all three Persons in the Trinity equally co-operate. It was God in Trinity who said, 'Let us create', and it is God in Trinity who says, 'Let us save'.

For ever let us take heed to our doctrine about the Holy Spirit. Let us make sure that we hold sound and scriptural views of His nature, His Person and His operations. A religion which entirely leaves Him out, and gives Him no place, is far from uncommon. Let us beware this religion is not ours.

April 28

Nevertheless I tell you the truth; It is expedient for you that I go away:
for if I go not away, the Comforter will not come unto you;
but if I depart, I will send him unto you.
John 16:7

A special reason why it was expedient for Him to go away from His disciples.

'[I]f I go not away,' He says, 'the Comforter will not come unto you.'

We can well suppose that our gracious Lord saw the minds of His disciples crushed at the idea of His leaving them. Little as they realized His full meaning, on this, as well as on other occasions, they evidently had a vague notion that they were about to be left, like orphans, in a cold and unkind world, by their almighty Friend. Their hearts quailed and shrunk back at the thought. Most graciously does our Lord cheer them by words of deep and mysterious meaning. He tells them that His departure, however painful it might seem, was not an evil, but a good. They would actually find it was not a loss, but a gain. His bodily absence would be more useful than His presence.

It is vain to deny that this is a somewhat dark saying. It seems at first sight hard to understand how in any sense it could be good that Christ should go away from His disciples. Yet a little reflection may show us that, like all our Lord's sayings, this remarkable utterance was wise, and right, and true. The following points, at any rate, deserve attentive consideration.

If Christ had not died, risen again and ascended up into heaven, it is plain that the Holy Ghost could not have come down with special power on the day of Pentecost, and bestowed His manifold gifts on the Church. Mysterious as it may be, there was a connection, in the eternal counsels of God, between the ascension of Christ and the outpouring of the Spirit.

April 29

Howbeit when he, the Spirit of truth, is come, he will guide you into all truth: for he shall not speak of himself; but whatsoever he shall hear, that shall he speak: and he will shew you things to come.
John 16:13

What the Holy Ghost would do for the whole of mankind, both Gentiles as well as Jews. He would reprove in every part of the earth the current ideas of men about sin, righteousness and judgment, and convince people of some far higher ideas on these points than they had before acknowledged. He would make men see more clearly the nature of sin, the need of righteousness, the certainty of judgment. In a word, He would insensibly be an Advocate and convincing Pleader for God throughout the whole world, and raise up a standard of morality, purity and knowledge, of which formerly men had no conception.

That the Holy Ghost actually did so in every part of the earth, after the day of Pentecost, is a simple matter of fact. The unlearned and lowly Jews, whom He sent forth and strengthened to preach the gospel after our Lord's ascension, 'turned the world upside down' (Acts 17:6), and in two or three centuries altered the habits, tastes and practices of the whole civilized world. The power of the devil received a decided check. Even infidels dare not deny that the doctrines of Christianity had an enormous effect on men's ways, lives and opinions, when they were first preached, and that there were no special graces of eloquence in the preachers that can account for it. In truth, the world was 'reproved and convinced', in spite of itself; and even those who did not become believers became better men. Surely this also was partly what our Lord had in view when He said to His disciples, 'When the Holy Ghost comes, He shall convince the world of sin, and righteousness, and judgment'.

Let us leave the whole passage, deep and difficult as it is, with a thankful remembrance of one comfortable promise which it contains. '[T]he Spirit of truth', says our Lord to His weak and half-informed followers, shall 'guide you into all truth.' That promise was for our sakes, no doubt, as well as for theirs. Whatever we need to know for our present peace and sanctification, the Holy Ghost is ready to teach us.

April 30

And I will pray the Father, and he shall give you another Comforter,
that he may abide with you for ever ...
John 14:16

A striking promise about the Holy Ghost.
This is the first time that the Holy Ghost is mentioned as Christ's special gift to His people. Of course we are not to suppose that He did not dwell in the hearts of all the Old Testament saints. But He was given with peculiar influence and power to believers when the New Testament dispensation came in, and this is the special promise of the passage before us. We shall find it useful, therefore, to observe closely the things that are here said about Him.

The Holy Ghost is spoken of as 'a Person'. To apply the language before us to a mere influence or inward feeling, is an unreasonable strain of words.

The Holy Ghost is called 'the Spirit of truth'. It is His special office to apply truth to the hearts of Christians, to guide them into all truth, and to sanctify them by the truth.

The Holy Ghost is said to be one whom the world cannot receive and does not know. His operations are in the strongest sense 'foolishness to the natural man' (1 Cor. 2:14). The inward feelings of conviction, repentance, faith, hope, fear and love, which He always produces, are precisely that part of religion which the world cannot understand.

The Holy Ghost is said to 'dwell in' believers, and to be known of them. They know the feelings that He creates, and the fruits that He produces, though they may not be able to explain them, or see at first whence they come. But they all are what they are – new men, new creatures, light and salt in the earth, compared to the worldly, by the indwelling of the Holy Ghost.

The Holy Ghost is given to the Church of the elect, 'to abide with them' until Christ comes the second time. He is intended to supply all the need of believers, and to fill up all that is wanting while Christ's visible presence is removed. He is sent to abide with and help them until Christ returns.

MAY

May 1

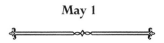

And when he had said this, he breathed on them, and saith unto them,
Receive ye the Holy Ghost.
John 20:22

The remarkable commission which our Lord conferred upon His eleven apostles.

We are told that He said, 'as my Father hath sent me, even so send I you. And when he had said this, he breathed on them, and saith unto them, Receive ye the Holy Ghost: Whose soever sins ye remit, they are remitted unto them; and whose soever sins ye retain, they are retained.' It is vain to deny that the true sense of these solemn words has been for centuries a subject of controversy and dispute. It is useless perhaps to expect that the controversy will ever be closed. The utmost that we can hope to do with the passage is to supply a probable exposition.

It seems then highly probable that our Lord in this place solemnly commissioned His apostles to go into all the world, and preach the gospel as He had preached it. He also conferred on them the power of declaring with peculiar authority whose sins were forgiven, and whose sins were not forgiven. That this is precisely what the apostles did is a simple matter of fact, which anyone may verify for himself by reading the book of Acts. When Peter proclaimed to the Jews, 'Repent ye therefore, and be converted', and when Paul declared at Antioch of Iconium, 'to you is the word of this salvation sent' – 'through this man is preached unto you the forgiveness of sins: And by him all that believe are justified', they were doing what this passage commissioned the apostles to do. They were opening with authority the door of salvation, and inviting with authority all sinners to enter in by it and be saved (Acts 3:19; 13:26-38).

No higher honour can be imagined than that of being Christ's ambassadors, and proclaiming in Christ's name the forgiveness of sins to a lost world. To treat ministers as being in any sense mediators between God and man, is to rob Christ of His prerogative, to hide saving truth from sinners and to exalt ordained men to a position which they are totally unqualified to fill.

May 2

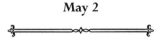

For he said unto him, Come out of the man, thou unclean spirit.
Mark 5:8

How complete is our Lord's power and authority over the devil.

We see it in the cry of the unclean spirit, 'I adjure thee by God, that thou torment me not.' We see it in the command, 'Come out of the man, thou unclean spirit', and the immediate obedience that followed. We see it in the blessed change that at once took place in him that was possessed: he was found 'sitting, and clothed, and in his right mind'. We see it in the petition of all the devils, 'Send us into the swine', confessing their consciousness that they could do nothing without leave. All these things show that one mightier than Satan was there. Strong as the great enemy of man was, he was in the presence of One stronger than he. Numerous as his hosts were, he was confronted with One who could command more than twelve legions of angels. 'Where the word of a king is, there is power' (Eccles. 8:4).

The truth here taught is full of strong consolation for all true Christians. We live in a world full of difficulties and snares. We are ourselves weak and compassed with infirmity. The awful thought that we have a mighty spiritual enemy ever near us, subtle, powerful and malicious as Satan is, might well disquiet us, and cast us down. But, thanks to be unto God, we have in Jesus an almighty Friend, who is 'able to save us to the uttermost'. He has already triumphed over Satan on the cross. He will ever triumph over him in the hearts of all believers, and intercede for them that their faith fail not. And He will finally triumph over Satan completely, when He shall come forth at the second advent, and bind him in the bottomless pit.

And now, are we ourselves delivered from Satan's power? This, after all, is the grand question that concerns our souls. He still reigns and rules in the hearts of all who are children of disobedience (Eph. 2:3). He is still a king over the ungodly. Have we, by grace, broken his bonds, and escaped his hand? Have we really renounced him and all his works? Do we daily resist him and flee? Do we put on the whole armour of God and stand against his wiles?

May 3

And on the morrow, when they were come from Bethany, he was hungry...
Mark 11:12

One of the many proofs that our Lord Jesus Christ was really a man.

We read that 'he was hungry'. He had a nature and bodily constitution like our own in all things, sin only excepted. He could weep and rejoice and suffer pain. He could be weary and need rest. He could be thirsty and need drink. He could be hungry and need food. Expressions like this should teach us the condescension of Christ. How wonderful they are when we reflect upon them! He who is the eternal God – He who made the world and all that it contains – He from whose hand the fruits of the earth, the fish of the sea, the fowls of the air, the beasts of the field, all had their beginning – He, even He was pleased to suffer hunger, when He came into the world to save sinners. This is a great mystery. Kindness and love like this pass man's understanding. No wonder that St Paul speaks of the 'unsearchable riches of Christ' (Eph. 3:8).

Expressions like this should teach us Christ's power to sympathize with His believing people on earth. He knows their sorrows by experience. He can be touched with the feeling of their infirmities. He has had experience of a body and its daily wants. He has suffered Himself the severe sufferings that the body of man is liable to. He has tasted pain, and weakness, and weariness, and hunger, and thirst. When we tell Him of these things in our prayers, He knows what we mean, and is no stranger to our troubles. Surely this is just the Saviour and Friend that poor, aching, groaning, human nature requires!

May 4

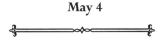

But he held his peace, and answered nothing.
Again the high priest asked him, and said unto him,
Art thou the Christ, the Son of the Blessed?
Mark 14:61

W**hat distinct testimony our Lord bore to His own Messiahship and second advent in glory.**

The high priest asks Him the solemn question, 'Art thou the Christ, the Son of the Blessed?' He receives at once the emphatic reply, 'I am: and ye shall see the Son of man sitting on the right hand of power, and coming in the clouds of heaven'.

These words of our Lord ought always to be had in remembrance. The Jews could never say after these words, that they were not clearly told that Jesus of Nazareth was the Christ of God. Before the great council of their priests and elders, He declared, 'I am' the Christ. The Jews could never say after these words, that He was so lowly and poor a person, that He was not worthy to be believed. He warned them plainly that His glory and greatness was all yet to come. They were only deferred and postponed till His second advent. They would yet see Him in royal power and majesty, 'sitting on the right hand of power', coming in the clouds of heaven, a Judge, Conqueror and a King. If Israel was unbelieving, it was not because Israel was not told what to believe.

Let us leave the passage with a deep sense of the reality and certainty of our Lord Jesus Christ's second coming. Once more at the very end of His ministry, and in the face of His deadly enemies, we find Him asserting the mighty truth that He will come again to judge the world. Let it be one of the leading truths in our own personal Christianity. Let us live in the daily recollection that our Saviour is one day coming back to this world. Let the Christ in whom we believe, be not only the Christ who died for us and rose again – the Christ who lives for us and intercedes – but the Christ who will one day return in glory, to gather together and reward His people, and to punish fearfully all His enemies.

May 5

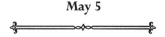

And when eight days were accomplished for the circumcising of the child, his name was called JESUS, which was so named of the angel before he was conceived in the womb.

Luke 2:21

The name by which our Lord was called, by God's special command.

'[H]is name was called JESUS, which was so named of the angel before he was conceived in the womb'.

The word Jesus means simply 'Saviour'. It is the same word as 'Joshua' in the Old Testament. Very striking and instructive is the selection of this name. The Son of God came down from heaven to be not only the Saviour, but the King, the Lawgiver, the Prophet, the Priest, the Judge of fallen man. Had He chosen any one of these titles, He would only have chosen that which was His own. But He passed by them all. He selects a name which speaks of mercy, grace, help and deliverance for a lost world. It is as a Deliverer and Redeemer that He desires principally to be known.

Let us often ask ourselves what our own hearts know of the Son of God. Is He our Jesus, our Saviour? This is the question on which our salvation turns. Let it not content us to know Christ as One who wrought mighty miracles, and spake as never man spake, or to know Him as One who is very God, and will one day judge the world. Let us see that we know Him experimentally, as our Deliverer from the guilt and power of sin, and our Redeemer from Satan's bondage. Let us strive to be able to say, 'This is my Friend: I was dead, and He gave me life: I was a prisoner and He set me free.' Precious indeed is this name of Jesus to all true believers! It is 'as ointment poured forth' (Cant. 1:3). It restores them when conscience troubled. It comforts them when cast down. It smooths their pillows in sickness. It supports them in the hour of death. 'The name of the LORD is a strong tower: the righteous runneth into it, and is safe' (Prov. 18:10).

May 6

And it came to pass, as he was alone praying, his disciples were with
him: and he asked them, saying, Whom say the people that I am?
Luke 9:18

The variety of opinions about our Lord Jesus Christ, which prevailed during His earthly ministry.

We are told that some said that He was John the Baptist; some that He was Elias; and some that one of the old prophets was risen again. One common remark applies to all these opinions. All were agreed that our Lord's doctrine was not like that of the scribes and Pharisees. All saw in Him a bold witness against the evil that was in the world.

Let it never surprise us to find the same variety of opinions about Christ and His gospel in our own times. God's truth disturbs the spiritual laziness of men. It obliges them to think. It makes them begin to talk, and reason, and speculate, and invent theories to account for its spread in some quarters, and its rejection in others. Thousands in every age of the Church spend their lives in this way, and never come to the point of drawing near to God. They satisfy themselves with a miserable round of gossip about this preacher's sermons, or that writer's opinions. They think 'this man goes too far', and 'that man does not go far enough'.

Some doctrines they approve, and others they disapprove. Some teachers they call 'sound', and others they call 'unsound'. They cannot quite make up their own minds what is true, or what is right. Year rolls on after year, and finds them in the same state – talking, criticising, fault-finding, speculating, but never getting any further – hovering like the moth round religion, but never settling down like the bee, to feed on its treasures. They never boldly lay hold of Christ. They never set themselves heartily to the great business of serving God. They never take up the cross, and become thorough Christians. And at last, after all their talking, they die in their sins, unprepared to meet God.

Let us not be content with a religion of this kind. It will not save us to talk and speculate, and bandy opinions about the gospel. The Christianity that saves, is a thing personally grasped, personally experienced, personally felt and personally possessed.

May 7

And as he spake, a certain Pharisee besought him to dine with him:
and he went in, and sat down to meat.
Luke 11:37

Our Lord Jesus Christ's readiness, when needful, to go into the company of the unconverted.

We read that 'a certain Pharisee besought him to dine with him'. The man was evidently not one of our Lord's disciples. Yet we are told that Jesus 'went in, and sat down to meat'.

The conduct of our Lord on this occasion, as on others, is meant to be an example to all Christians. Christ is our pattern as well as our propitiation. There are evidently times and occasions when the servant of Christ must mix with the ungodly and the children of this world. There may be seasons when it may be a duty to hold social intercourse with them, to accept their invitations and sit down at their tables. Nothing, of course, must induce the Christian to be a partaker in the sins or frivolous amusements of the world. But he must not be uncourteous. He must not entirely withdraw himself from the society of the unconverted, and become a hermit or an ascetic. He must remember that good may be done in the private room as well as in the pulpit.

One qualification however should never be forgotten when we act upon our Lord's example in this matter. Let us take heed that we go down into the company of the unconverted in the same spirit in which Christ went. Let us remember His boldness in speaking of the things of God. He was always 'about His Father's business'. Let us remember His faithfulness in rebuking sin. He spared not even the sins of those that entertained Him, when His attention was publicly called to them. Let us go into company in the same frame of mind, and our souls will take no harm. If we feel that we dare not imitate Christ in the company which we are invited to join, we may be sure that we had better stay at home.

May 8

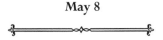

But I have a baptism to be baptized with; and how am I straitened till
it be accomplished!
Luke 12:50

How thoroughly the heart of Christ was set on finishing the work which He came into the world to do.

He says, 'I have a baptism to be baptized with' – a baptism of suffering, of wounds, of agony, of blood and of death. Yet none of these things moved Him. He adds, 'how am I straitened till [this baptism is] accomplished!' The prospect of coming trouble did not deter Him for a moment: He was ready and willing to endure all things in order to provide eternal redemption for His people. Zeal for the cause He had taken in hand was like burning fire within Him. To advance His Father's glory, to open the door of life to a lost world, to provide a fountain for all sin and uncleanness by the sacrifice of Himself, were continually the uppermost thoughts of His mind. He was pressed in spirit till this mighty work was finished.

For ever let us bear in mind that all Christ's sufferings on our behalf were endured willingly, voluntarily and of His own free choice. They were not submitted to patiently merely because He could not avoid them: they were not borne without a murmur merely because He could not escape them. He lived a humble life for thirty-three years because He loved to do so. He died a death of agony with a willing and a ready mind. Both in life and death He was carrying out the eternal counsel whereby God was to be glorified and sinners were to be saved. He carried it out with all His heart, mighty as the struggle was which it entailed on His flesh and blood. He delighted to do God's will. He was straitened till it was accomplished.

Let us not doubt that the heart of Christ in heaven is the same that it was when He was upon earth. He feels as deep an interest now about the salvation of sinners as He did formerly about dying in their stead. Jesus never changes: He is the same yesterday, and today, and forever. It is a certain fact, if men would only believe it, that Christ is far more willing to save us than we are to be saved.

May 9

David therefore calleth him Lord, how is he then his son?
Luke 20:44

What striking testimony to Christ's divinity the book of Psalms contains.

We read that after patiently replying to the attacks of His enemies, our Lord in turn propounds a question to them: He asks them to explain an expression in the hundred and tenth Psalm, where David speaks of the Messiah as his Lord. To this question the scribes could find no answer. They did not see the mighty truth, that Messiah was to be God as well as man, and that while as man He was to be David's son, as God He was to be David's Lord. Their ignorance of Scripture was thus exposed before all the people. Professing themselves to be instructors of others, and possessors of the key of knowledge, they were proved unable to explain what their own Scriptures contained. We may well believe that of all the defeats which our Lord's malicious enemies met with, none galled them more than this. Nothing so mortifies the pride of man, as to be publicly proved ignorant of that which he fancies is his own peculiar department of knowledge.

We have probably little idea how much deep truth is contained in the book of Psalms. No part of the Bible perhaps is better known in the letter, and none so little understood in the spirit. We err greatly if we suppose that it is nothing but a record of David's feelings, of David's experience, David's praises and David's prayers. The hand that held the pen was generally David's: but the subject-matter was often something far deeper and higher than the history of the son of Jesse. The book of Psalms, in a word, is a book full of Christ: Christ suffering, Christ in humiliation, Christ dying, Christ rising again, Christ coming the second time, Christ reigning over all. Both the advents are here. The advent in suffering, to bear the cross – the advent in power, to wear the crown. Both the kingdoms are here: the kingdom of grace during which the elect are gathered – the kingdom of glory, when every tongue shall confess that Jesus is Lord. Let us say to ourselves as we read, 'A greater than David is here.'

May 10

Then said they all, Art thou then the Son of God?
And he said unto them, Ye say that I am.
Luke 22:70

What a full and bold confession our Lord makes of His own Messiahship and divinity.

We read that in reply to this question of His enemies, 'Art thou then the Son of God?' He said unto them, 'Ye say that I am'. The meaning of this short sentence may not be clear at first sight to an English reader. It signifies in other words, 'Ye speak the truth: I am, as ye say, the Son of God'.

Our Lord's confession deprived His enemies of all excuse for unbelief. The Jews can never plead that our Lord left their forefathers in ignorance of His mission, and kept them in doubt and suspense. Here we see our Lord telling them plainly who He was, and telling them in words which would convey even more to a Jewish mind than they do to ours; and yet the confession had not the least good effect upon the Jews! Their hearts were hardened by prejudice; their minds were darkened by judicial blindness; the veil was over the eyes of their inward man: they heard our Lord's confession unmoved, and only plunged deeper into the most awful sin.

The bold confession of our Master upon this occasion, is intended to be an example to all His believing people. Like Him, we must not shrink from speaking out when occasion requires our testimony. The fear of man, and the presence of a multitude, must not make us hold our peace (Job 31:34). We need not blow a trumpet before us, and go out of our way, to proclaim our own religion; opportunities are sure to occur in the daily path of duty, when, like St Paul onboard ship, we may show whose we are and whom we serve (Acts 27:23). At such opportunities, if we have the mind of Christ, let us not be afraid to show our colours. A confessing Master loves bold, uncompromising and confessing disciples: them that honour Him by an outspoken, courageous testimony, He will honour, because they are walking in His steps. 'Whosoever therefore', He says, 'shall confess Me before men, him will I confess also before my Father which is in heaven' (Matt. 10:32).

May 11

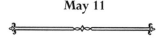

And when Jesus had cried with a loud voice, he said,
Father, into thy hands I commend my spirit:
and having said thus, he gave up the ghost.
Luke 23:46

The remarkable words which our Lord spoke when He died.

We read that when He had cried with a loud voice, He said, 'Father, into thy hands I commend my spirit: and having said thus, he gave up the ghost'.

There is a depth of meaning, no doubt, in these words, which we have no line to fathom. There was something mysterious about our Lord's death, which made it unlike the death of any mere man. He who spoke the words before us, we must carefully remember, was God as well as man: His divine and human nature were inseparably united. His divine nature of course could not die. He says Himself, 'I lay down my life, that I might take it again. No man taketh it from me, but I lay it down of myself. I have power to lay it down, and I have power to take it again' (John 10:17, 18). Christ died, not as we die when our hour is come – not because He was compelled and could not help dying, but voluntarily, and of His own free will.

There is a sense, however, in which our Lord's words supply a lesson to all true Christians: they show us the manner in which death should be met by all God's children; they afford an example which every believer should strive to follow. Like our Master, we should not be afraid to confront the king of terrors: we should regard him as a vanquished enemy, whose sting has been taken away by Christ's death; we should think of him as a foe who can hurt the body for a little season, but after that has no more that he can do; we should await his approaches with calmness and patience, and believe that when flesh fails, our soul will be in good keeping. This was the mind of dying Stephen: 'Lord Jesus,' he said, 'receive my spirit'. This was the mind of Paul the aged, when the time of his departure was at hand. He says 'I know whom I have believed, and am persuaded that he is able to keep that which I have committed to him against that day' (Acts 7:59; 2 Tim. 1:12).

May 12

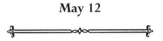

For the law was given by Moses, but grace and truth came by Jesus Christ.
John 1:17

The vast superiority of Christ to Moses, and of the gospel to the law.

It is written that 'the law was given by Moses, but grace and truth came by Jesus Christ'.

Moses was employed by God 'as a servant', to convey to Israel the moral and ceremonial law (Heb. 3:5). As a servant, he was faithful to Him who appointed him, but he was only a servant. The moral law, which he brought down from Mount Sinai, was holy, and just, and good. But it could not justify. It had no healing power. It could wound, but it could not bind up. It 'worked wrath' (Rom. 4:15). It pronounced a curse against any imperfect obedience. The ceremonial law, which he was commanded to impose on Israel, was full of deep meaning and typical instruction. Its ordinances and ceremonies made it an excellent schoolmaster to guide men toward Christ (Gal. 3:24). But the ceremonial law was only a schoolmaster. It could not make him that kept it perfect, as pertaining to the conscience (Heb. 9:9). It laid a grievous yoke on men's hearts, which they were not able to bear. It was a ministration of death and condemnation (2 Cor. 3:7-9). The light which men got from Moses and the law was at best only starlight compared to noonday.

Christ, on the other hand, came into the world 'as a Son', with the keys of God's treasury of grace and truth entirely in His hands (Heb. 3:6). Grace came by Him, when He made fully known God's gracious plan of salvation, by faith in His own blood, and opened the fountain of mercy to all the world. Truth came by Him, when He fulfilled in His own Person the types of the Old Testament, and revealed Himself as the true Sacrifice, the true mercy-seat and the true Priest. No doubt there was much of 'grace and truth' under the law of Moses. But the whole of God's grace, and the whole truth about redemption, were never known until Jesus came into the world, and died for sinners.

May 13

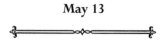

*The next day John seeth Jesus coming unto him, and saith, B
ehold the Lamb of God, which taketh away the sin of the world.*
John 1:29

The peculiar work which John the Baptist describes Christ as doing.

He says that He 'taketh away the sin of the world'. Christ is a Saviour. He did not come on earth to be a conqueror, or a philosopher, or a mere teacher of morality. He came to save sinners. He came to do that which man could never do for himself – to do that which money and learning can never obtain – to do that which is essential to man's real happiness – He came to take away sin.

Christ is a complete Saviour. He taketh away sin. He did not merely make vague proclamations of pardon, mercy and forgiveness. He 'took' our sins upon Himself, and carried them away. He allowed them to be laid upon Himself, and bore them 'in his own body on the tree' (1 Pet. 2:24). The sins of everyone that believes on Jesus are made as though they had never been sinned at all. The Lamb of God has taken them clean away.

Christ is an almighty Saviour, and a Saviour for all mankind. He 'taketh away the sin of the world'. He did not die for the Jews only, but for the Gentile as well as the Jew. He did not suffer for a few persons only, but for all mankind. The payment that He made on the cross was more than enough to make satisfaction for the debts of all. The blood that He shed was precious enough to wash away the sins of all. His atonement on the cross was sufficient for all mankind, though efficient only to them that believe. The sin that He took up and bore on the cross was the sin of the whole world.

Last, but not least, Christ is a perpetual and unwearied Saviour. He 'taketh away' sin. He is daily taking it away from everyone that believes on Him –daily purging, daily cleansing, daily washing the souls of His people, daily granting and applying fresh supplies of mercy. He did not cease to work for His saints, when He died for them on the cross. He lives in heaven as a Priest, to present His sacrifice continually before God. In grace as well as providence, Christ worketh still. He is ever taking away sin.

May 14

Now Jacob's well was there. Jesus therefore, being wearied with his journey,
sat thus on the well: and it was about the sixth hour.
John 4:6

What is said about our Lord's human nature.
We read that Jesus was 'wearied with his journey'. We learn
from this, as well as many other expressions in the Gospels,
that our Lord had a body exactly like our own. When the Word became
flesh, He took on Him a nature like our own in all things, sin only
excepted. Like ourselves, He grew from infancy to youth, and from
youth to man's estate. Like ourselves, He hungered, thirsted, felt pain
and needed sleep. He was liable to every sinless infirmity to which we
are liable. In all things His body was framed like our own.

The truth before us is full of comfort for all who are true Christians.
He to whom sinners are bid to come for pardon and peace, is One who
is Man as well as God. He had a real human nature when He was upon
earth. He took a real human nature with Him, when He ascended up
into heaven. We have at the right hand of God a High Priest who can be
touched with the feeling of our infirmities, because He has suffered
Himself being tempted. When we cry to Him in the hour of bodily pain
and weakness, He knows well what we mean. When our prayers and
praises are feeble through bodily weariness, He can understand our
condition. He knows our frame. He has learned by experience what it
is to be a man. To say that the Virgin Mary, or any one else, can feel
more sympathy for us than Christ, is ignorance no less than blasphemy.
The man Christ Jesus can enter fully into everything that belongs to
man's condition. The poor, the sick and the suffering, have in heaven
One who is not only an almighty Saviour, but a most feeling Friend.

The servant of Christ should grasp firmly this great truth, that there
are two perfect and complete natures in the one Person whom he serves.
The Lord Jesus, in whom the gospel bids us believe, is, without doubt,
almighty God – equal to the Father in all things, and able to save to the
uttermost all those that come unto God by Him. But that same Jesus is
no less certainly perfect man – able to sympathize with man in all his
bodily sufferings, and acquainted by experience with all that man's body
has to endure.

May 15

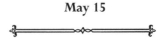

When Jesus therefore perceived that they would come and take him by force,
to make him a king, he departed again into a mountain himself alone.
John 6:15

O ur Lord Jesus Christ's humility.
We are told that, after feeding the multitude, He 'perceived
that they would come and take him by force to make him a
king'. At once He departed, and left them. He wanted no such honours
as these. He had come, 'not to be ministered unto, but to minister, and
to give his life a ransom for many' (Matt. 20:28)

We see the same spirit and frame of mind all through our Lord's
earthly ministry. From His cradle to His grave He was 'clothed with
humility' (1 Pet. 5:5). He was born of a poor woman, and spent the
first thirty years of His life in a carpenter's house at Nazareth. He was
followed by poor companions, many of them no better than fishermen.
He was poor in His manner of living: 'The foxes have holes, and the
birds of the air have nests; but the Son of man hath not where to lay his
head' (Matt. 8:20). When He went on the Sea of Galilee, it was in a
borrowed boat; when He rode into Jerusalem, it was on a borrowed
ass; when He was buried, it was in a borrowed tomb. '[T]hough he was
rich, yet for [our] sakes he became poor' (2 Cor. 8:9).

The example is one which ought to be far more remembered than
it is. How common are pride, and ambition, and high-mindedness! How
rare are humility and lowly-mindedness! How few ever refuse greatness
when offered to them! How many are continually seeking great things
for themselves, and forgetting the injunction, 'seek them not' (Jer. 45:5).
Surely it was not for nothing that our Lord, after washing the disciples'
feet, said, 'I have given you an example, that ye should do as I have
done' (John 13:15). There is little, it may be feared, of that feet-washing
spirit among Christians. But whether men will hear or forbear, humility
is the queen of graces. 'Tell me,' it has been said, 'how much humility a
man has, and I will tell you how much religion he has.' Humility is the
first step toward heaven, and the true way to honour. '[H]e that humbleth
himself shall be exalted' (Luke 18:14).

May 16

All that the Father giveth me shall come to me;
and him that cometh to me I will in no wise cast out.
John 6:37

A saying of Christ about those who come to Him.
We read that Jesus said, – 'him that cometh to me I will in no wise cast out'.

What does 'coming' mean? It means that movement of the soul which takes place when a man, feeling his sins, and finding out that he cannot save himself, hears of Christ, applies to Christ, trusts in Christ, lays hold on Christ and leans all his weight on Christ for salvation. When this happens, a man is said, in Scripture language, to 'come' to Christ.

What did our Lord mean by saying, 'I will in no wise cast him out'? He meant that He will not refuse to save anyone who comes to Him, no matter what he may have been. His past sins may have been very great. His present weakness and infirmity may be very great. But does he come to Christ by faith? Then Christ will receive him graciously, pardon him freely, place him in the number of His dear children and give him everlasting life.

These are golden works indeed! They have smoothed down many a dying pillow, and calmed many a troubled conscience. Let them sink down deeply into our memories, and abide there continually. A day will come when flesh and heart shall fail, and the world can help us no more. Happy shall we be in that day, if the Spirit witnesses with our spirit that we have really come to Christ!

We are taught by these words that Christ has brought into the world a salvation open and free to everyone. Our Lord draws a picture of it from the story of the brazen serpent, by which bitten Israelites in the wilderness were healed. Everyone that chose to 'look' at the brazen serpent might live. Just in the same way, everyone who desires eternal life may 'look' at Christ by faith, and have it freely. There is no barrier, no limit, no restriction. The terms of the gospel are wide and simple. Everyone may 'look and live'.

May 17

Then spake Jesus again unto them, saying, I am the light of the world: he that followeth me shall not walk in darkness, but shall have the light of life.
John 8:12

What the Lord Jesus says of Himself.

He proclaims, 'I am the light of the world'.

These words imply that the world needs light, and is naturally in a dark condition. It is so in a moral and spiritual point of view: and it has been so for nearly six thousand years. In ancient Egypt, Greece and Rome, in modern England, France and Germany, the same report is true. The vast majority of men neither see nor understand the value of their souls, the true nature of God, nor the reality of a world to come! Notwithstanding all the discoveries of art and science, 'darkness shall cover the earth, and gross darkness the people' (Isa. 60:2).

For this state of things, the Lord Jesus Christ declares Himself to be the only remedy. He has risen, like the sun, to diffuse light, and life, and peace, and salvation, in the midst of a dark world. He invites all who want spiritual help and guidance to turn to Him, and take Him for their leader. What the sun is to the whole solar system – the centre of light, and heat, and life, and fertility – that He has come into the world to be to sinners.

Let this saying sink down into our hearts. It is weighty, and full of meaning. False lights on every side invite man's attention in the present day. Reason, philosophy, earnestness, liberalism, conscience and the voice of the Church, are all, in their various ways, crying loudly that they have got 'the light' to show us. Their advocates know not what they say. Wretched are those who believe their high professions! He only is the true Light who came into the world to save sinners, who died as our Substitute on the cross, and sits at God's right hand to be our Friend. '[I]n thy light we see shall light' (Ps. 36:9).

May 18

Then said Jesus unto them again,
Verily, verily, I say unto you, I am the door of the sheep.
John 10:7

A most instructive picture of Christ Himself.
He utters one of those golden sayings which ought to be dear
to all true Christians. They apply to people as well as to ministers.
'I am the door: by me if any man enter in, he shall be saved, and shall go
in and out, and find pasture.'

We are all by nature separate and far off from God. Sin, like a great
barrier-wall, rises between us and our Maker. The sense of guilt makes
us afraid of Him. The sense of His holiness keeps us at a distance from
Him. Born with a heart at enmity with God, we become more and
more alienated from Him by practice, the longer we live. The very first
questions in religion that must be answered, are these: 'How can I draw
near to God? How can I be justified? How can a sinner like me be
reconciled to my Maker?'

The Lord Jesus Christ has provided an answer to these mighty
questions. By His sacrifice for us on the cross, He has opened a way
through the great barrier, and provided pardon and peace for sinners.
He has 'suffered for sin, the just for the unjust, to bring us to God'. He
has opened a way into the holiest, through His blood, by which we may
draw near to God with boldness, and approach God without fear. And
now He is able to save to the uttermost all who come unto God by
Him. In the highest sense He is 'the door'. No one can 'come to the
Father' but by Him.

Let us take heed that we use this door, and do not merely stand
outside looking at it. It is a door free and open to the chief of sinners: 'if
any man enter in [by it], he shall be saved'. It is a door within which we
shall find a full and constant supply for every want of our souls. We
shall find that we can 'go in and out' and enjoy liberty and peace. The
day comes when this door will be shut forever, and men shall strive to
enter in, but not be able. Then let us make sure of the work of our own
salvation. Let us not stand tarrying without, and halting between two
opinions. Let us enter in and be saved.

May 19

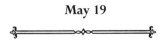

I am the good shepherd, and know my sheep, and am known of mine.
John 10:14

One of the principal offices which Jesus Christ fills for true Christians.

Twice over our Lord uses an expression which, to an Eastern hearer, would be singularly full of meaning. Twice over He says emphatically, 'I am the good shepherd'. It is a saying rich in consolation and instruction.

Like a good shepherd, Christ knows all His believing people. Their names, their families, their dwelling-places, their circumstances, their private history, their experience, their trials – with all these things Jesus is perfectly acquainted. There is not a thing about the least and lowest of them with which He is not familiar. The children of this world may not know Christians, and may count their lives folly: but the Good Shepherd knows them thoroughly, and, wonderful to say, though He knows them, does not despise them.

Like a good shepherd, Christ cares tenderly for all His believing people. He provides for all their wants in the wilderness of this world, and leads them by the right way to a city of habitation. He bears patiently with their many weaknesses and infirmities, and does not cast them off because they are wayward, erring, sick, footsore or lame. He guards and protects them against all their enemies, as Jacob did the flock of Laban; and of those that the Father has given Him He will have found at last to have lost none.

Like a good shepherd, Christ lays down His life for the sheep. He did it once for all, when He was crucified for them. When He saw that nothing could deliver them from hell and the devil but His blood, He willingly made His soul an offering for their sins. The merit of that death He is now presenting before the Father's throne. The sheep are saved for evermore, because the Good Shepherd died for them. This is indeed a love that passeth knowledge! 'Greater love hath no man than this, that a man lay down his life for his friends' (John 15:13).

May 20

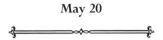

Jesus said unto her, I am the resurrection, and the life: he that
believeth in me, though he were dead, yet shall he live ...
John 11:25

The need of clear views of Christ's person, office and power.

This is a point which is forcibly brought out in the well-known sentence which our Lord addressed to Martha. In reply to her vague and faltering expression of belief in the resurrection at the last day, He proclaims the glorious truth, 'I am the resurrection, and the life'; 'I, even I, thy Master, am He that has the keys of life and death in His hands.' And then He presses on her once more that old lesson, which she had doubtless often heard, but never fully realized: 'he that believeth in me, though he were dead, yet shall he live: And whosoever liveth and believeth in me shall never die'.

There is matter here which deserves the close consideration of all true Christians. Many of them complain of want of sensible comfort in their religion. They do not feel the inward peace which they desire. Let them know that vague and indefinite views of Christ are too often the cause of all their perplexities. They must try to see more clearly the great object on which their faith rests. They must grasp more firmly His love and power toward them that believe, and the riches He has laid up for them even now in this world. We are many of us sadly like Martha. A little general knowledge of Christ as the only Saviour, is often all that we possess. But of the fullness that dwells in Him, of His resurrection, His priesthood, His intercession, His unfailing compassion, we have tasted little or nothing at all. They are things of which our Lord might well say to many, as He did to Martha, 'Believest thou this?'

Let us take shame to ourselves that we have named the name of Christ so long, and yet know so little about Him. What right have we to wonder that we feel so little sensible comfort in our Christianity? Our slight and imperfect knowledge of Christ is the true reason of our discomfort. Let the time past suffice us to have been lazy students in Christ's school: let the time to come find us more diligent in trying to 'know him, and the power of his resurrection' (Phil. 3:10).

May 21

Jesus saith unto him, I am the way, the truth, and the life:
no man cometh unto the Father, but by me.
John 14:6

What glorious names the Lord Jesus gives to Himself. He says, 'I am the way, the truth, and the life'. The fullness of these precious words can probably never be taken in by man. He that attempts to unfold them does little more than scratch the surface of a rich soil.

Christ is 'the way' – the way to heaven and peace with God. He is not only the guide, and teacher, and lawgiver, like Moses; He is Himself the door, the ladder and the road, through whom we must draw near to God. He has opened the way to the tree of life, which was closed when Adam and Eve fell, by the satisfaction He made for us on the cross. Through His blood we may draw near with boldness, and have access with confidence into God's presence (Eph. 3:12).

Christ is 'the truth' – the whole substance of true religion which the mind of man requires. Without Him the wisest heathen groped in gross darkness, and knew nothing rightly about God. Before He came even the Jews saw 'through a glass darkly', and discerned nothing distinctly under the type, figure and ceremonies of the Mosaic law. Christ is the whole truth, and meets and satisfies every desire of the human mind.

Christ is 'the life' – the sinner's title to eternal life and pardon, the believer's root of spiritual life and holiness, the surety of the Christian's resurrection life. He that believeth on Christ hath everlasting life. He that abideth in Him, as the branch abides in the vine, shall bring forth much fruit. He that believeth on Him, though he were dead, yet shall he live. The root of all life, for soul and for body, is Christ.

For ever let us grasp and hold fast to these truths. To use Christ daily as the way – to believe Christ daily as the truth, – to live on Christ daily as the life – this is to be a well-informed, a thoroughly furnished and an established Christian.

May 22

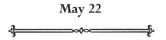

Jesus saith unto him, I am the way, the truth, and the life:
no man cometh unto the Father, but by me.
John 14:6

How expressly the Lord Jesus shuts out all ways of salvation but Himself.

'[N]o man', He declares, 'no man cometh unto the Father, but by me.'

It avails nothing that a man is clever, learned, highly gifted, amiable, charitable, kind-hearted and zealous about some sort of religion. All this will not save his soul, if he does not draw near to God by Christ's atonement, and make use of God's own Son as his Mediator and Saviour. God is so holy that all men are guilty and debtors in His sight. Sin is so sinful that no mortal man can make satisfaction for it. There must be a mediator, a ransom-payer, a redeemer, between ourselves and God, or else we can never be saved. There is only one door, one bridge, one ladder, between earth and heaven – the crucified Son of God. Whosoever will enter in by that door may be saved; but to him who refuses to use that door the Bible holds out no hope at all. '[W]ithout shedding of blood is no remission' (Heb. 9:22).

Let us beware, if we love life, of supposing that mere earnestness will take a man to heaven, though he know nothing of Christ. The idea is a deadly and ruinous error. Sincerity will never wipe away our sins. It is not true that every man will be saved by his own religion, no matter what he believes, provided he is diligent and sincere. We must not pretend to be wiser than God. Christ has said, and Christ will stand to it, 'no man cometh unto the Father, but by Me'.

May 23

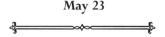

Peace I leave with you, my peace I give unto you: not as the world giveth,
give I unto you. Let not your heart be troubled, neither let it be afraid.
John 14:27

Christ's last legacy to His people.
We find him saying, 'Peace I leave with you, my peace I give unto you: not as the world giveth, give I unto you.'

Peace is Christ's peculiar gift to His people. He seldom gives them money, or worldly ease, or temporal prosperity. These are at best very questionable possessions. They often do more harm than good to the soul. They act as clogs and weights to our spiritual life. Inward peace of conscience, arising from a sense of pardoned sin and reconciliation with God, is a far greater blessing. This peace is the inheritance of all believers, whether high or low, rich or poor.

The peace which Christ gives He calls 'my peace'. It is specially His own to give, because He bought it by His own blood, purchased it by His own substitution and is appointed by the Father to dispense it to a perishing world. Just as Joseph was sealed and commissioned to give corn to the starving Egyptians, so is Christ specially sealed and commissioned, in the counsels of the eternal Trinity, to give peace to mankind (John 6:27).

The peace that Christ gives is not given as the world gives. What He gives the world cannot give at all, and what He gives is given neither unwillingly, nor sparingly, nor for a little time. Christ is far more willing to give than man is to receive. What He gives He gives to all eternity, and never takes away. He is ready to give abundantly 'above all that we ask or think'. '[O]pen thy mouth wide,' He says, 'and I will fill it' (Eph. 3:20; Ps. 81:10).

Who can wonder that a legacy like this should be backed by the renewed emphatic charge, 'Let not your heart be troubled, neither let it be afraid'? There is nothing lacking on Christ's part for our comfort, if we will only come to Him, believe and receive. The chief of sinners has no cause to be afraid. If we will only look by faith to the one true Saviour, there is medicine for every trouble of heart. Half our doubts and fears arise from dim perceptions of the real nature of Christ's gospel.

May 24

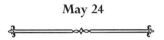

As thou hast given him power over all flesh, that he should give
eternal life to as many as thou hast given him.
John 17:2

What a glorious account they contain of our Lord Jesus Christ's office and dignity.

We read that the Father has 'given him power over all flesh, that he should give eternal life'. The keys of heaven are in Christ's hands. The salvation of every soul of mankind is at His disposal. We read, furthermore, that it 'is life eternal' to know the only true God, and Jesus Christ whom He has sent. The mere knowledge of God is not sufficient, and saves none. We must know the Son as well as the Father. God known without Christ is a Being whom we can only fear, and dare not approach. It is God 'in Christ, reconciling the world unto himself' (2 Cor. 5:19), who alone can give to the soul life and peace. We read, furthermore, that Christ has finished the work which the Father gave Him to do. He has finished the work of redemption, and wrought out a perfect righteousness for His people. Unlike the first Adam, who failed to do God's will and brought sin into the world, the Second Adam has done all, and left nothing undone that He came to do. Finally, we read that Christ had glory with the Father 'before the world was': unlike Moses and David, He existed from all eternity, long before He came into the world, and He shared glory with the Father, before He was made flesh and born of the Virgin Mary.

Each of these marvellous sayings contains matter which our weak minds have not power to comprehend fully. We must be content to admire and reverence what we cannot thoroughly grasp and explain. But one thing is abundantly clear: sayings like these can only be used of one who is very God. To no patriarch, or prophet, or king, or apostle, is any such language ever applied in the Bible. It belongs to none but God! For ever let us thank God that the hope of a Christian rests on such a solid foundation as a divine Saviour.

May 25

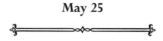

*Then said Jesus unto Peter, Put up thy sword into the sheath: the cup
which my Father hath given me, shall I not drink it?*
John 18:11

Our Lord's perfect submission to his Father's will. Once, in another place, we find Him saying, 'if it be possible, let this cup pass from me: nevertheless not as I will, but as thou wilt.' Again, in another place, we find Him saying, 'if this cup may not pass away from me except I drink it, thy will be done'. Here, however, we find even a higher pitch of cheerful acquiescence: 'The cup that my Father hath given Me, shall I not drink it?' (Matt. 26:39-42).

Let us see in this blessed frame of mind, a pattern for all who profess and call themselves Christians. Far as we may come short of the Master's standard, let this be the mark at which we continually aim. Determination to have our own way, and do only what we like, is one great source of unhappiness in the world. The habit of laying all our matters before God in prayer, and asking Him to choose our portion, is one chief secret of peace. He is the truly wise man who has learned to say at every stage of his journey, 'Give me what Thou wilt, place me where Thou wilt, do with me as Thou wilt; but not my will, but Thine be done.' This is the man who has the mind of Christ. By self-will Adam and Eve fell, and brought sin and misery into the world. Entire submission of will to the will of God is the best preparation for that heaven where God will be all.

May 26

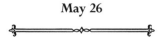

Pilate therefore went forth again, and saith unto them, Behold, I bring
him forth to you, that ye may know that I find no fault in him.
John 19:4

The first portrait in the picture is that of our Lord Jesus Christ Himself.

We see the Saviour of mankind scourged, crowned with thorns, mocked, smitten, rejected by His own people, unjustly condemned by a judge who saw no fault in Him and finally delivered up to a most painful death. Yet this was He who was the eternal Son of God whom the Father's countless angels delighted to honour! This was He who came into the world to save sinners, and after living a blameless life for thirty years, spent the last three years of His time on earth in going about doing good, and preaching the gospel. Surely the sun never shone on a more wondrous sight since the day of its creation!

Let us admire that love of Christ which, St Paul declares, 'passeth knowledge', and let us see an endless depth of meaning in the expression. There is no earthly love with which it can be compared, and no standard by which to measure it. It is a love that stands alone. Never let us forget, when we ponder this tale of suffering, that Jesus suffered for our sins, the Just for the unjust, that He was wounded for our transgressions and bruised for our iniquities, and that with His stripes we are healed.

Let us diligently follow the example of His patience in all the trials and afflictions of life, and especially in those which may be brought upon us by religion. When He was reviled, He reviled not again; when He suffered, He threatened not, but committed Himself to Him that judgeth righteously. Let us arm ourselves with the same mind. Let us consider Him who endured such contradiction of sinners without a murmur, and strive to glorify Him by suffering well, no less than by doing well.

May 27

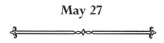

The Son of man shall send forth his angels, and they shall gather out
of his kingdom all things that offend, and them which do iniquity ...
Matthew 13:41

There is to be a day of separation between the godly and the ungodly members of the visible Church, at the end of the world. The present mixed state of things is not to be forever: the wheat and the tares are to be divided at last. The Lord Jesus shall 'send forth his angels' in the day of His second advent, and gather all professing Christians into two great companies. Those mighty reapers shall make no mistake: they shall discern with unerring judgment between the righteous and the wicked, and place every one in his own lot. The saints and faithful servants of Christ shall receive glory, honour and eternal life: the worldly, the ungodly, the careless and the unconverted shall be cast 'into a furnace of fire'.

There is something peculiarly solemn in this part of the parable. The meaning of it admits of no mistake: our Lord Himself explains it in words of singular clearness, as if He would impress it deeply on our minds. Well may He say at the conclusion, 'Who hath ears to hear, let him hear.'

Let the ungodly man tremble when he reads this parable: let him see in its fearful language his own certain doom, unless he repents and is converted; let him know that he is sowing misery for himself, if he goes on still in his neglect of God; let him reflect that his end will be to be gathered among the 'bundles of tares', and be burned. Surely such a prospect ought to make a man think! As Baxter truly says, 'We must not misinterpret God's patience with the ungodly.'

Let the believer in Christ take comfort when he reads this parable: let him see that there is happiness and safety prepared for him in the great and dreadful day of the Lord. The voice of the archangel and the trump of God will proclaim no terror for him: they will summon him to join what he has long desired to see – a perfect Church and a perfect communion of saints. How beautiful will the whole body of believers appear when finally separated from the wicked!

May 28

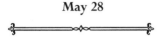

*And before him shall be gathered all nations: and he shall separate them one
from another, as a shepherd divideth his sheep from the goats ...*
Matthew 25:32

In what manner the judgment will be conducted in the last day.
We read of several striking particulars on this point: let us see what they are.

The last judgment will be a judgment according to evidence. The works of men are the witnesses which will be brought forward, and above all their works of charity. The question to be ascertained will not merely be what we said, but what we did: not merely what we professed, but what we practised. Our works unquestionably will not justify us: we are justified by faith without the deeds of the law; but the truth of our faith will be tested by our lives. Faith which hath not works is dead, being alone (Jas. 2:17).

The last judgment will be a judgment that will bring joy to all true believers. They will hear those precious words, 'Come, ye blessed of My Father, inherit the kingdom'; they will be owned and confessed by their Master before His Father and the holy angels; they shall find that the wages He gives to His faithful servants are nothing less than 'a kingdom'. The least, and lowest, and poorest of the family of God, shall have a crown of glory, and be a king!

The last judgment will be a judgment that will strikingly bring out the characters both of the lost and the saved. They on the right hand, who are Christ's sheep, will still be 'clothed with humility' (1 Pet. 5:5). They will marvel to hear any work of theirs brought forward and commended. They on the left hand, who are not Christ's, will still be blind and self-righteous. They will not be sensible of any neglect of Christ: 'Lord,' they say, 'when saw we Thee – and did not minister unto Thee?' Let this thought sink down into our hearts. Characters on earth will prove an everlasting possession in the world to come: with the same heart that men die, with that heart they will rise again.

May 29

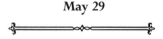

And these shall go away into everlasting punishment:
but the righteous into life eternal.
Matthew 25:46

What will be the final results of the judgment day. We are told this in words that ought never to be forgotten: 'The wicked shall go away into everlasting punishment: but the righteous into life eternal'.

The state of things after the judgment is changeless and without end. The misery of the lost, and the blessedness of the saved, are both alike for ever: let no man deceive us on this point. It is clearly revealed in Scripture: the eternity of God, and heaven, and hell, all stand on the same foundation. As surely as God is eternal, so surely is heaven an endless day without night, and hell an endless night without day.

Who shall describe the blessedness of eternal life? It passes the power of man to conceive: it can only be measured by contrast and comparison. An eternal rest, after warfare and conflict; the eternal company of saints, after buffeting with an evil world; an eternally glorious and painless body, after struggling with weakness and infirmity; and eternal sight of Jesus face to face, after only hearing and believing – all this is blessedness indeed. And yet the half of it remains untold.

Who shall describe the misery of eternal punishment? It is something utterly indescribable and inconceivable. The eternal pain of body; the eternal sting of an accusing conscience; the eternal society of none but the wicked, the devil and his angels; the eternal remembrance of opportunities neglected and Christ despised; the eternal prospect of a weary, hopeless future – all this is misery indeed: it is enough to make our ears tingle, and our blood run cold. And yet this picture is nothing compared to the reality.

Let us close these verses with serious self-inquiry. Let us ask ourselves on which side of Christ we are likely to be at the last day. Shall we be on the right hand, or shall we be on the left? Happy is he who never rests till he can give a satisfactory answer to this question.

May 30

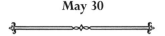

And it came to pass, that when he was returned, having received the
kingdom, then he commanded these servants to be called unto him, to
whom he had given the money, that he might know how much every
man had gained by trading.
Luke 19:15

The certain reckoning which awaits all professing Christians.

We are told that when the master returned, he 'commanded his servants to be called ... that he might know how much every man had gained.'

.There is a day coming when the Lord Jesus Christ shall judge His people, and give to everyone according to His works. The course of this world shall not always go on as it does now. Disorder, confusion, false profession and unpunished sin, shall not always cover the face of the earth: the great white throne shall be set up; the Judge of all shall sit upon it; the dead shall be raised from their graves; the living shall all be summoned to the bar; the books shall be opened. High and low, rich and poor, gentle and simple, all shall at length give account to God, and all shall receive an eternal sentence.

Let the thought of this judgment exercise an influence on our hearts and lives; let us wait patiently when we see wickedness triumphing in the earth. The time is short, there is One who sees and notes down all the ungodly are doing: 'there be higher than they' (Eccles. 5:8). Above all, let us live under an abiding sense that we shall stand one day at the judgment seat of Christ. Let us 'judge ourselves', that we be not condemned of the Lord. It is a weighty saying of St James: 'So speak ye, and so do, as they that shall be judged by the law of liberty' (1 Cor. 11:31; Jas. 2:12).

May 31

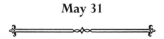

And another came, saying, Lord, behold, here is thy pound,
which I have kept laid up in a napkin …
Luke 19:20

The certain exposure of all unfaithful Christians at the last day.

We are told of one servant who had done nothing with his lord's money, but had 'laid it up in a napkin'. We are told of his useless arguments in his own defence, and of his final ruin, for not using the knowledge which he confessedly possessed. There can be no mistake as to the persons he represents; he represents the whole company of the ungodly; and his ruin represents their miserable end in the judgment day.

Let us never forget the end to which all ungodly people are coming. Sooner or later, the unbeliever and the impenitent will be put to shame before the whole world, stripped of the means of grace and hope of glory, and cast down to hell. There will be no escape at the last day: false profession and formality will fail to abide the fire of God's judgment; grace, and grace only, shall stand. Men will discover at last, that there is such a thing as 'the wrath of the Lamb'. The excuses with which so many content their consciences now shall prove unavailing at the bar of Christ, the most ignorant shall find that they had knowledge enough to be their condemnation. The possessors of buried talents and misused privileges will discover at last that it would have been good for them never to have been born.

These are solemn things. Who shall stand in the great day when the Master requires an account of 'His pounds'? The words of St Peter will form a fitting conclusion to the whole parable: 'seeing that ye look for such things, be diligent that ye may be found of him in peace, without spot, and blameless' (2 Pet. 3:14).

JUNE

June 1

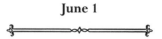

And as they were eating, Jesus took bread, and blessed it, and brake it,
and gave it to the disciples, and said, Take, eat; this is my body.
Matthew 26:26

The right meaning of our Lord's words, 'this is my body
... this is my blood'.

It is needless to say, that this question has divided the visible
Church of Christ. It has caused volumes of controversial theology to be
written: but we must not shrink from having decided opinions upon it,
because theologians have disputed and differed. Unsoundness on this
point has given rise to many deplorable superstitions.

The plain meaning of our Lord's words appears to be this: 'This
bread represents my body. This wine represents my blood.' He did not
mean that the bread He gave to His disciples was really and literally His
body; He did not mean that the wine He gave to His disciples was really
and literally His blood. Let us lay firm hold on this interpretation: it
may be supported by several grave reasons.

The conduct of the disciples at the Lord's Supper forbids us to believe
that the bread they received was Christ's body, and the wine they
received was Christ's blood. They were all Jews, taught from their infancy
to believe that it was sinful to eat flesh with the blood (Deut. 12:23-
25); yet there is nothing in the narrative to show that they were startled
by our Lord's words. They evidently perceived no change in the bread
and wine.

Our own senses at the present day forbid us to believe that there is
any change in the bread and wine in the Lord's Supper: our own taste
tells us that they are really and literally what they appear to be. Things
above our reason the Bible requires us to believe; but we are never bid
to believe that which contradicts our senses.

Our Lord speaks of Himself as the 'door' and the 'vine', and we
know that He is using emblems and figures when He so speaks: there is
therefore no inconsistency in supposing that He used figurative language
when He appointed the Lord's Supper; and we have the more right to
say so when we remember the grave objections which stand in the way
of a literal view of His words.

June 2

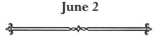

But I say unto you, I will not drink henceforth of this fruit of the vine,
until that day when I drink it new with you in my Father's kingdom.
Matthew 26:29

The purpose and object for which the Lord's Supper was appointed.

This is a subject again on which great darkness prevails. The ordinance of the Lord's Supper has been regarded as something mysterious and past understanding: immense harm has been done to Christianity by the vague and high-flown language in which many writers have indulged in treating of the sacrament; there is certainly nothing to warrant such language in the account of its original institution. The more simple our views of its purpose, the more scriptural they are likely to be.

The Lord's Supper is not a sacrifice. There is no oblation in it – no offering up of anything but our prayers, praises and thanksgivings. From the day that Jesus died there needed no more offering for sin: by one offering He perfected for ever them that are sanctified (Heb. 10:14). Priests, altars and sacrifices, all ceased to be necessary, when the Lamb of God offered up Himself. Their office came to an end: their work was done.

The Lord's Supper has no power to confer benefit on those who come to it, if they do not come to it with faith. The mere formal act of eating the bread and drinking the wine is utterly unprofitable, unless it is done with a right heart. It is eminently an ordinance for the living soul, not for the dead, for the converted, not for the unconverted.

The Lord's Supper was ordained for a continual remembrance of the sacrifice of Christ's death, until He comes again. The benefits it confers are spiritual, not physical: its effects must be looked for in our inward man. It was intended to remind us, by the visible, tangible emblems of bread and wine, that the offering of Christ's body and blood for us on the cross is the only atonement for sin, and the life of the believer's soul; it was meant to help our poor weak faith to closer fellowship with our crucified Saviour, and to assist us in spiritually feeding on Christ's body and blood.

June 3

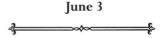

And as they sat and did eat, Jesus said, Verily I say unto you,
One of you which eateth with me shall betray me.
Mark 14:18

Self-examination should precede the reception of the Lord's Supper.

We cannot doubt that this was one object of our Lord's solemn warning, 'One of you which eateth with me shall betray me'. He meant to stir up in the minds of His disciples those very searchings of heart which are here so touchingly recorded: 'they began to be sorrowful, and to say unto him one by one, Is it I? and another said, Is it I?' He meant to teach His whole Church throughout the world, that the time of drawing near to the Lord's table should be a time for diligent self-inquiry.

The benefit of the Lord's Supper depends entirely on the spirit and frame of mind in which we receive it. The bread which we there eat, and the wine which we there drink, have no power to do good to our souls, as medicine does good to our bodies, without the co-operation of our hearts and wills. They will not convey any blessing to us by virtue of the minister's consecration, if we do not receive them rightly, worthily and with faith. To assert, as some do, that the Lord's Supper must do good to all communicants, whatever be the state of mind in which they receive it, is a monstrous and unscriptural figment, and has given rise to gross and wicked superstition.

The state of mind which we should look for in ourselves, before going to the Lord's table, is well described in the Catechism of the Church of England. We ought to 'examine ourselves whether we repent truly of our former sins, whether we steadfastly purpose to lead a new life, whether we have a lively faith in God's mercy through Christ, and a thankful remembrance of His death, and whether we are in charity with all men.' If our conscience can answer these questions satisfactorily, we may receive the Lord's Supper without fear. More than this God does not require of any communicant. Less than this ought never to content us.

June 4

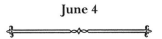

And he took bread, and gave thanks, and brake it, and gave unto them, saying,
This is my body which is given for you: this do in remembrance of me.
Luke 22:19

The principal object of the Lord's Supper was to remind Christians of Christ's death for sinners.
In appointing the Lord's Supper, Jesus distinctly tells His disciples that they were to do what they did, 'in remembrance of Him'. In one word the Lord's Supper is not a sacrifice: it is eminently a commemorative ordinance.

The bread that the believer eats at the Lord's table is intended to remind him of Christ's body given to death on the cross for his sins; the wine that he drinks is intended to remind him of Christ's blood shed to make atonement for his transgressions. The whole ordinance was meant to keep fresh in his memory the sacrifice of Christ on the cross, and the satisfaction which that sacrifice made for the sin of the world. The two elements of bread and wine were intended to preach Christ crucified as our substitute, under lively emblems; they were to be a visible sermon, appealing to the believer's senses, and teaching the old foundation truth of the gospel, that Christ's death on the cross is the life of man's soul.

We shall do well to keep steadily in view this simple view of the Lord's Supper. That a special blessing is attached to a worthy use of it, as well to the worthy use of every ordinance appointed by Christ, there is of course no doubt; but that there is any other means by which Christians can eat Christ's body and drink Christ's blood, excepting faith, we must always steadily deny. He that comes to the Lord's table with faith in Christ, may confidently expect to have his faith increased by receiving the bread and wine; but he that comes without faith has no right to expect a blessing. Empty he comes to the ordinance and empty he will go away.

We should cling firmly to the great principle laid down at its institution – that it is eminently a commemorative ordinance, and that reception of it, without faith and a thankful remembrance of Christ's death, can do us no good.

June 5

Then Jesus beholding him loved him, and said unto him, One thing thou
lackest: go thy way, sell whatsoever thou hast, and give to the poor, and thou
shalt have treasure in heaven: and come, take up the cross, and follow me.
Mark 10:21

The love of Christ towards sinners.

This is a truth which is brought out in the expression used by St Mark, when in his account of this man's story, he says that 'Jesus beholding him loved him'. That love, beyond doubt, was a love of pity and compassion. Our Lord beheld with pity the strange mixture of earnestness and ignorance which the case before Him presented. He saw with compassion a soul struggling with all the weakness and infirmity entailed by the fall; the conscience ill at ease and sensible that it wanted relief – the understanding sunk in darkness, and blinded as to the first principles of spiritual religion. Just as we look with sorrow at some noble ruin, roofless, and shattered, and unfit for man's use, yet showing many a mark of the skill with which it was designed and reared at first, so may we suppose that Jesus looked with tender concern at this man's soul.

We must never forget that Jesus feels love and compassion for the souls of the ungodly. Without controversy He feels a peculiar love for those who hear His voice and follow Him. They are His sheep, given to Him by the Father, and watched with a special care. They are His bride, joined to Him in an everlasting covenant, and dear to Him as part of Himself. But the heart of Jesus is a wide heart. He has abundance of pity, compassion and tender concern even for those who are following sin and the world. He who wept over unbelieving Jerusalem is still the same: He would still gather into His bosom the ignorant and self-righteous, the faithless and impenitent, if they were only willing to be gathered.

We may boldly tell the chief of sinners that Christ loves him (Matt. 23:37). Salvation is ready for the worst of men, if they will only come to Christ. If men are lost, it is not because Jesus does not love them, and is not ready to save. His own solemn words unravel the mystery: 'men loved darkness rather than light'. 'Ye will not come to me, that ye might have life' (John 3:19; 5:40).

June 6

And stood at his feet behind him weeping, and began to wash his feet
with tears, and did wipe them with the hairs of her head, and kissed
his feet, and anointed them with the ointment.
Luke 7:38

Grateful love is the secret of doing much for Christ. The penitent woman, in the story before us, showed far more honour to our Lord than the Pharisee had done. She 'stood at his feet behind him weeping'. She '[wash]ed his feet with tears'. She '[wipe]d them with the hairs of her head'. She 'kissed his feet, and anointed them with the [costly] ointment'. No stronger proofs of reverence and respect could she have given, and the secret of her giving such proofs, was love. She loved our Lord, and she thought nothing too much to do for Him. She felt deeply grateful to our Lord, and she thought no mark of gratitude too costly to bestow on Him.

More 'doing' for Christ is the universal demand of all the Churches. It is the one point on which all are agreed. All desire to see among Christians, more good works, more self-denial, more practical obedience to Christ's commands. But what will produce these things? Nothing, nothing but love. There never will be more done for Christ till there is more hearty love to Christ Himself. The fear of punishment, the desire of reward, the sense of duty, are all useful arguments, in their way, to persuade men to holiness. But they are all weak and powerless until a man loves Christ. Once let that mighty principle get hold of a man, and you will see his whole life changed.

Let us never forget this. However much the world may sneer at 'feelings' in religion, and however false or unhealthy religious feelings may sometimes be, the great truth still remains behind – that feeling is the secret of doing. The heart must be engaged for Christ, or the hands will soon hang down. The affections must be enlisted into His service, or our obedience will soon stand still. It will always be the loving workman who will do most in the Lord's vineyard.

June 7

But when Jesus heard it, he answered him, saying, Fear not:
believe only, and she shall be made whole.
Luke 8:50

Faith in Christ's love and power is the best remedy in time of trouble.

We are told that when Jesus heard the tidings that the ruler's daughter was dead, He said to him, 'Fear not: believe only, and she shall be made whole'. These words, no doubt, were spoken with immediate reference to the miracle our Lord was going to perform. But we need not doubt that they were also meant for the perpetual benefit of the Church of Christ. They were meant to reveal to us the grand secret of comfort in the hour of need. That secret is to exercise faith, to fall back on the thought of Christ's loving heart and mighty hand, in one word, to believe.

Let a petition for more faith form a part of all our daily prayers. As ever we would have peace, and calmness, and quietness of spirit, let us often say, 'Lord increase our faith.' A hundred painful things may happen to us every week in this evil world, of which our poor weak minds cannot see the reason. Without faith we shall be constantly disquieted and cast down. Nothing will make us cheerful and tranquil but an abiding sense of Christ's love, Christ's wisdom, Christ's care over us and Christ's providential management of all our affairs. Faith will not sink under the weight of evil tidings (Ps. 112:7). Faith can sit still and wait for better times. Faith can see light even in the darkest hour, and a needs-be for the heaviest trial. Faith can find room to build ebenezers under any circumstances, and can sing songs in the night in any condition. '[H]e that believeth shall not make haste.' 'Thou wilt keep him in perfect peace, whose mind is stayed on thee' (Isa. 28:16; 26:3). Once more let the lesson be graven on our minds. If we would travel comfortably through this world, we must 'believe'.

June 8

What man of you, having an hundred sheep, if he lose one of them,
doth not leave the ninety and nine in the wilderness, and go after that
which is lost, until he find it?
Luke 15:4

The remarkable figures under which our Lord describes His own love towards sinners.

We read that in reply to the taunting remark of His enemies He spoke three parables – the parables of the lost sheep, the lost piece of silver and the prodigal son. The two first of these parables are now before us. All three are meant to illustrate one and the same truth. They all throw strong light on Christ's willingness to save sinners.

Christ's love is an active, working love. Just as the shepherd did not sit still bewailing his lost sheep, and the woman did not sit still bewailing her lost money, so our blessed Lord did not sit still in heaven pitying sinners. He left the glory which He had with the Father, and humbled Himself to be made in the likeness of man. He came down into the world to seek and save that which was lost. He never rested till He had made atonement for our transgressions, brought in everlasting righteousness, provided eternal redemption and opened a door of life to all who are willing to be saved. Christ's love is a self-denying love. The shepherd brought his lost sheep home on his own shoulders rather than leave it in the wilderness. The woman lighted a candle, and swept the house, and searched diligently, and spared no pains, till she found her lost money. And just so did Christ not spare Himself when He undertook to save sinners: He 'endured the cross, despising the shame'; He 'lay down his life for his friends'. Greater love than this cannot be shown (Heb. 12:2; John 15:13).

Christ's love is a deep and mighty love. Just as the shepherd rejoiced to find his sheep, and the woman to find her money, so does the Lord Jesus rejoice to save sinners. It is a real pleasure to Him to pluck them as brands from the burning. It was His 'meat and drink', when upon earth, to finish the work which He came to do: He felt straitened in spirit till it was accomplished. It is still His delight to show mercy. He is far more willing to save sinners than sinners are to be saved.

June 9

And the Lord turned, and looked upon Peter. And Peter remembered the
word of the Lord, how he had said unto him,
Before the cock crow, thou shalt deny me thrice.

Luke 22:61

The infinite mercy of our Lord Jesus Christ.
This is a lesson which is brought out most forcibly by a fact which is only recorded in St Luke's Gospel. We are told that when Peter denied Christ the third time, and the cock crew, 'the Lord turned, and looked upon Peter'. Those words are deeply touching! Surrounded by blood thirsty and insulting enemies, in the full prospect of horrible outrages, an unjust trial and a painful death, the Lord Jesus yet found time to think kindly of His poor erring disciple: even then He would have Peter know He did not forget him. Sorrowfully no doubt, but not angrily, He 'turned and looked upon Peter'. There was deep meaning in that look. It was a sermon which Peter never forgot.

The love of Christ towards His people is a deep well which has no bottom. Let us never measure it by comparison with any kind of love of man or woman: it exceeds all other love, as far as the sun exceeds the rushlight. There is about it a mine of compassion, and patience, and readiness to forgive sin, of whose riches we have but a faint conception. Let us not be afraid to trust that love, when we first feel our sins: let us never be afraid to go on trusting it after we have once believed. No man need despair, however far he may have fallen, if he will only repent and turn to Christ. If the heart of Jesus was so gracious when He was prisoner in the judgment hall, we surely need not think it is less gracious when He sits in glory at the right hand of God.

June 10

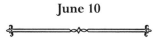

For God so loved the world, that he gave his only begotten Son, that whosoever
believeth in him should not perish, but have everlasting life.
John 3:16

T he original source from which man's salvation springs.
That source is the love of God the Father. Our Lord says to
Nicodemus, 'God so loved the world, that he gave his only
begotten Son, that whosoever believeth in him should not perish, but
have everlasting life'.

This wonderful verse has been justly called by Luther, 'The Bible in
miniature.' No part of it, perhaps, is so deeply important as the first
five words, 'God so loved the world'. The love here spoken of is not
that special love with which the Father regards His own elect, but that
mighty pity and compassion with which He regards the whole race of
mankind. Its object is not merely the little flock which He has given to
Christ from all eternity, but the 'world' of sinners, without any
exception. There is a deep sense in which God loves that world. All
whom He has created He regards with pity and compassion. Their sins
He cannot love; but He loves their souls. '[H]is tender mercies are over
all his works' (Ps. 145:9). Christ is God's gracious gift to the whole
world.

Let us take heed that our views of the love of God are sand well-
defined. The subject is one on which error abounds on either side. On
the one hand we must beware of vague and exaggerated opinions. We
must maintain firmly that God hates wickedness, and that the end of all
who persist in wickedness will be destruction. It is not true that God's
love is 'lower than hell'. It is not true that God so loved the world that
all mankind will be finally saved, but that He so loved the world as to
give His Son to be the Saviour of all who believe. His love is offered to
all men freely, fully, honestly and unreservedly, but it is only through
the one channel of Christ's redemption.

June 11

Now Jesus loved Martha, and her sister, and Lazarus.
John 11:5

Christ loves all who are true Christians.
We read that 'Jesus loved Martha, and her sister, and Lazarus'. The characters of these three good people seem to have been somewhat different. Of Martha, we are told in a certain place, that she was 'careful and troubled about many things,' while Mary 'sat at Jesus' feet, and heard His word'. Of Lazarus, we are told nothing distinctive at all. Yet all these were loved by the Lord Jesus. They all belonged to His family, and He loved them all.

We must carefully bear this in mind in forming our estimate of Christians. We must never forget that there are varieties in character, and that the grace of God does not cast all believers into one and the same mould. Admitting fully that the foundations of Christian character are always the same, and that all God's children repent, believe, are holy, prayerful and Scripture-loving, we must make allowances for wide varieties in their temperaments and habits of mind.

We must not undervalue others because they are not exactly like ourselves. The flowers in a garden may differ widely, and yet the gardener feels interest in all. The children of a family may be curiously unlike one another, and yet the parents care for all. It is just so with the Church of Christ. There are degrees of grace, and varieties of grace; but the least, the weakest, the feeblest disciples, are all loved by the Lord Jesus. Then let no believer's heart fail because of his infirmities; and, above all, let no believer dare to despise and undervalue a brother.

June 12

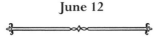

A new commandment I give unto you, That ye love one another; as I
have loved you, that ye also love one another.
John 13:34

What great importance our Lord Jesus attaches to the grace of brotherly love.

Almost as soon as the false apostle had left the faithful eleven, comes the injunction, 'love one another'. Immediately after the sad announcement that He would leave them soon, the commandment is given, 'love one another'. It is called a 'new' commandment, not because it had never been given before, but because it was to be more honoured, to occupy a higher position, to be backed by a higher example than it ever had been before. Above all, it was to be the test of Christianity before the world. 'By this shall all men know that ye are my disciples, if ye have love one to another.'

Let us take heed that this well-known Christian grace is not merely a notion in our heads, but a practice in our lives. Of all the commands of our Master there is none which is so much talked about and so little obeyed as this. Yet, if we mean anything when we profess to have charity and love toward all men, it ought to be seen in our tempers and our words, our bearing and our doing, our behaviour at home and abroad, our conduct in every relation of life. Specially it ought to show itself forth in all our dealing with other Christians. We should regard them as brethren and sisters, and delight to do anything to promote their happiness. We should abhor the idea of envy, malice and jealousy towards a member of Christ, and regard it as a downright sin. This is what our Lord meant when He told us to 'love one another'.

Christ's cause in the earth would prosper far more than it does if this simple law was more honoured. There is nothing that the world understands and values more than true charity. The very men who cannot comprehend doctrine, and know nothing of theology, can appreciate charity. It arrests their attention, and makes them think. For the world's sake, if for no other cause, let us follow after charity 'more and more' (1 Thess. 4:10).

June 13

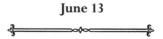

The first day of the week cometh Mary Magdalene early, when it was yet dark,
unto the sepulchre, and seeth the stone taken away from the sepulchre.
John 20:1

Those who love Christ most are those who have received most benefit from Him.

The first whom St John names among those who came to Christ's sepulchre, is Mary Magdalene. The history of this faithful woman, no doubt, is hidden in much obscurity. A vast amount of needless obloquy has been heaped upon her memory, as if she was once an habitual sinner against the seventh commandment. Yet there is literally no evidence whatever that she was anything of the kind! But we are distinctly told that she was one out of whom the Lord had cast 'seven devils' (Mark 16:9; Luke 8:2) – one who had been subject in a peculiar way to Satan's possession – and one whose gratitude to our Lord for deliverance was a gratitude that knew no bounds. In short, of all our Lord's followers on earth, none seem to have loved Him so much as Mary Magdalene. None felt that they owed so much to Christ. None felt so strongly that there was nothing too great to do for Christ. Hence, as Bishop Andrews beautifully puts it, 'She was last at His cross, and first at His grave. She stayed longest there, and was soonest here. She could not rest till she was up to seek Him. She sought Him while it was yet dark, even before she had light to seek Him by.' In a word, having received much, she loved much; and loving much, she did much, in order to prove the reality of her love.

How is it that many who profess and call themselves Christians, do so little for the Saviour whose name they bear? How is it that many, whose faith and grace it would be uncharitable to deny, work so little, give so little, say so little, take so little pains, to promote Christ's cause, and bring glory to Christ in the world? These questions admit of only one answer. It is a low sense of debt and obligation to Christ, which is the amount of the whole matter. Let us daily pray that we may see the sinfulness of sin, and the amazing grace of Christ, more clearly and distinctly.

June 14

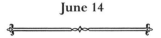

And he spake many things unto them in parables, saying,
Behold, a sower went forth to sow ...
Matthew 13:3

The work of the preacher resembles that of the sower. Like the sower, the preacher must sow good seed, if he wants to see fruit. He must sow the pure Word of God, and not the traditions of the Church, or the doctrines of men. Without this, his labour will be in vain. He may go to and fro, and seem to say much, and to work much in his weekly round of ministerial duty; but there will be no harvest of souls for heaven, no living results and no conversions.

Like the sower, the preacher must be diligent. He must spare no pains; he must use every possible means to make his work prosper; he must patiently 'sow beside all waters', and 'sow in hope'; he must be 'instant in season [and] out of season'; he must not be deterred by difficulties and discouragements: 'He that observeth the wind shall not sow'. No doubt his success does not entirely depend upon his labour and diligence; but without labour and diligence success will not be obtained (Isa. 32:20; 2 Tim. 4:2; Eccles. 11: 4).

Like the sower, the preacher cannot give life. He can scatter the seed committed to his charge, but he cannot command it to grow: he may offer the word of truth to a people, but he cannot make them receive it and bear fruit. To give life is God's solemn prerogative: 'It is the spirit that quickeneth'. God alone can 'giveth the increase' (John 6:63; 1 Cor. 3:7).

Let these things sink down into our hearts. It is no light thing to be a real minister of God's Word. To be an idle, formal workman in the Church is an easy business: to be a faithful sower is very hard. Preachers ought to be specially remembered in our prayers.

June 15

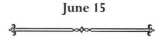

And he spake many things unto them in parables, saying,
Behold, a sower went forth to sow ...
Matthew 13:3

There are various ways of hearing the Word of God without benefit.

We may listen to a sermon with a heart like the hard 'wayside': careless, thoughtless and unconcerned. Christ crucified may be affectionately set before us, and we may hear of His sufferings with utter indifference, as a subject in which we have no interest. Fast as the words fall on our ears, the devil may pluck them away, and we may go home as if we have not heard a sermon at all. Alas, there are many such hearers! It is as true of them as of the idols of old, 'eyes have they, but they see not; They have ears, but they hear not' (Ps. 135:16, 17). Truth seems to have no more effect on their hearts than water on a stone.

We may listen to a sermon with pleasure, while the impression produced on us is only temporary and short-lived. Our hearts, like the 'stony ground', may yield a plentiful crop of warm feelings and good resolutions; but all this time there may be no deeply rooted work in our souls, and the first cold blast of opposition or temptation may cause our seeming religion to wither away. Alas, there are many such hearers! The mere love of sermons is no sign of grace. Thousands of baptized people are like the Jews of Ezekiel's day: 'thou art unto them as a very lovely song of one that hath a pleasant voice, and can play well on an instrument: for they hear thy words, but they do them not' (Ezek. 33:32).

We may listen to a sermon, and approve of every word it contains, and yet get no good from it, in consequence of the absorbing influence of this world. Alas, there are many such hearers! They know the truth well: they hope one day to be decided Christians; but they never come to the point of giving up all for Christ's sake. They never make up their minds to 'seek first the kingdom of God' – and so die in their sins.

June 16

And these are they which are sown on good ground; such as hear the
word, and receive it, and bring forth fruit, some thirtyfold, some sixty,
and some an hundred.
Mark 4:20

There are some hearers of the gospel whose hearts are like the good ground in a field.

These are they who really receive Christ's truth into the bottom of their hearts, believe it implicitly, and obey it thoroughly. In these the fruits of that truth will be seen – uniform, plain and unmistakable results in heart and life. Sin will be truly hated, mourned over, resisted and renounced. Christ will be truly loved, trusted in, followed and obeyed. Holiness will show itself in all their conversation, in humility, spiritual-mindedness, patience, meekness and charity. There will be something that can be seen. The true work of the Holy Ghost cannot be hid.

There will always be some persons in this state of soul, where the gospel is faithfully preached. Their numbers may very likely be few, compared to the worldly around them. Their experience and degree of spiritual attainment may differ widely, some bringing forth thirty, some sixty and some a hundredfold. But the fruit of the seed falling into good ground will always be of the same kind. There will always be visible repentance, visible faith in Christ and visible holiness of life. Without these things there is no saving religion.

And now let us ask ourselves: What are we? Under which class of hearers ought we to be ranked? With what kind of hearts do we hear the Word? Never, never may we forget that there are three ways of hearing without profit, and only one way of hearing aright! Never, never may we forget that there is only one infallible mark of being a right-hearted hearer! That mark is to bear fruit. To be without fruit, is to be on the way to hell.

June 17

And they went out, and preached that men should repent.
Mark 6:12

What was the doctrine which our Lord's apostles preached.

We read that 'they went out and preached that men should repent'.

The necessity of repentance may seem at first sight a very simple and elementary truth. And yet volumes might be written to show the fullness of the doctrine, and the suitableness of it to every age and time, and to every rank and class of mankind. It is inseparably connected with right views of God, of human nature, of sin, of Christ, of holiness and of heaven. All have sinned and come short of the glory of God. All need to be brought to a sense of their sins – to a sorrow for them – to a willingness to give them up – and to a hunger and thirst after pardon. All, in a word, need to be born again and to flee to Christ. This is repentance unto life. Nothing less than this is required for the salvation of any man. Nothing less than this ought to be pressed on men, by everyone who professes to teach Bible religion. We must bid men repent, if we would walk in the steps of the apostles, and when they have repented, we must bid them repent more and more to their last day.

Have we ourselves repented? This, after all, is the question that concerns us most. It is well to know what the apostles taught. It is well to be familiar with the whole system of Christian doctrine. But it is far better to know repentance by experience, and to feel it inwardly in our own hearts. May we never rest till we know and feel that we have repented! There are no impenitent people in the kingdom of heaven. All who enter in there have felt, mourned over, forsaken and sought pardon for sin. This must be our experience, if we hope to be saved.

June 18

The Spirit of the Lord is upon me, because he hath anointed me to preach the gospel to the poor; he hath sent me to heal the broken-hearted, to preach deliverance to the captives, and recovering of sight to the blind, to set at liberty them that are bruised ...

Luke 4:18

Whand a striking account our Lord gave to the congregation at Nazareth, of His own office and ministry.
We are told that He chose a passage from the book of Isaiah, in which the prophet foretold the nature of the work Messiah was to do when He came into the world. He read how it was foretold that He would 'preach the gospel to the poor' – how He would be sent to 'heal the brokenhearted', how He would 'preach deliverance to the captives ... sight to the blind ... liberty' to the bruised – and how He would 'proclaim that a year of jubilee to all the world had come'. And when our Lord had read this prophecy, He told the listening crowd around Him, that He Himself was the Messiah of whom these words were written, and that in Him and in His gospel the marvellous figures of the passage were about to be fulfilled.

We may well believe that there was a deep meaning in our Lord's selection of this special passage of Isaiah. He desired to impress on His Jewish hearers, the true character of the Messiah, whom He knew all Israel were then expecting. He well knew that they were looking for a mere temporal king, who would deliver them from Roman dominion, and make them once more first among the nations. Such expectations, He would have them understand, were premature and wrong. Messiah's kingdom at His first coming was to be a spiritual kingdom over hearts. His victories were not to be over worldly enemies, but over sin. His redemption was not to be from the power of Rome, but from the power of the devil and the world. It was in this way, and in no other way at present, that they must expect to see the words of Isaiah fulfilled.

June 19

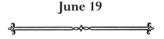

And he said unto them, I must preach the kingdom of God to other
cities also: for therefore am I sent.
Luke 4:43

The declaration of our Lord as to one of the objects of His coming into the world.

We read that He said, 'I must preach the kingdom of God to other cities also: for therefore am I sent.'

An expression like this ought to silence for ever the foolish remarks that are sometimes made against preaching. The mere fact that the eternal Son of God undertook the office of a preacher, should satisfy us that preaching is one of the most valuable means of grace. To speak of preaching, as some do, as a thing of less importance than reading public prayers or administering the sacraments, is, to say the least, to exhibit ignorance of Scripture. It is a striking circumstance in our Lord's history, that although He was almost incessantly preaching, we never read of His baptizing any person. The witness of John is distinct on this point: 'Jesus baptized not' (John 4:2).

Let us beware of despising preaching. In every age of the Church it has been God's principal instrument for the awakening of sinners and the edifying of saints. The days when there has been little or no preaching have been days when there has been little or no good done in the Church. Let us hear sermons in a prayerful and reverent frame of mind, and remember that they are the principal engines which Christ Himself employed, when He was upon earth. Not least, let us pray daily for a continual supply of faithful preachers of God's Word. According to the state of the pulpit will always be the state of a congregation and of a Church.

June 20

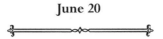

And he sent them to preach the kingdom of God, and to heal the sick.
Luke 9:2

One of the principal works which the apostles were commissioned to take up was preaching.
We read that our Lord 'sent them to preach the kingdom of God', and that they 'went through the towns, preaching the gospel'.

The importance of preaching, as a means of grace, might easily be gathered from this passage, even if it stood alone. But it is but one instance, among many, of the high value which the Bible everywhere sets upon preaching. It is, in fact, God's chosen instrument for doing good to souls. By it sinners are converted, inquirers led on and saints built up. A preaching ministry is absolutely essential to the health and prosperity of a visible Church. The pulpit is the place where the chief victories of the gospel have always been won, and no Church has ever done much for the advancement of true religion in which the pulpit has been neglected. Would we know whether a minister is a truly apostolical man? If he is, he will give the best of his attention to his sermons. He will labour and pray to make his preaching effective, and he will tell his congregation that he looks to preaching for the chief results on souls. The minister who exalts the sacraments, or forms of the Church, above preaching, may be zealous, earnest, conscientious and a respectable minister; but his zeal is not according to knowledge. He is not a follower of the apostles.

June 21

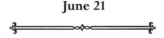

And whosoever will not receive you, when ye go out of that city,
shake off the very dust from your feet for a testimony against them.
Luke 9:5

Our Lord prepares His disciples to meet with unbelief and impenitence in those to whom they preached. He speaks of those 'who will not receive them' as a class which they must expect to see. He tells them how to behave, when not received, as if it was a state of things to which they must make up their mind.

All ministers of the gospel would do well to read carefully this portion of our Lord's instructions. All missionaries, and district visitors, and Sunday-school teachers, would do well to lay it to heart. Let them not be cast down if their work seems in vain, and their labour without profit. Let them remember that the very first preachers and teachers whom Jesus employed were sent forth with a distinct warning, that not all would believe. Let them work on patiently, and sow the good seed without fainting. Duties are theirs. Events are God's. Apostles may plant and water. The Holy Ghost alone can give spiritual life. The Lord Jesus knows what is in the heart of man. He does not despise His labourers because little of the seed they sow bears fruit. The harvest may be small. But every labourer shall be rewarded according to his work.

June 22

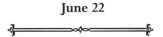

And heal the sick that are therein, and say unto them,
The kingdom of God is come nigh unto you.
Luke 10:9

The simplicity of the tidings which our Lord commanded some of His first messengers to proclaim. We read that they were commissioned to say, 'The kingdom of God is come nigh unto you'.

These words we should probably regard as the keynote to all that the seventy disciples said. We can hardly suppose that they said nothing else but this single sentence. The words no doubt implied far more to a Jewish hearer at the time when they were spoken, than they convey to our minds at the present day. To a well-instructed Israelite, they would sound like an announcement that the times of Messiah had come – that the long-promised Saviour was about to be revealed – that the 'desire of all nations' was about to appear (Hag. 2:7). All this is unquestionably true. Such an announcement suddenly made by seventy men, evidently convinced of the truth of what they said, travelling over a thickly peopled country, could hardly fail to draw attention and excite inquiry. But still the message is peculiarly and strikingly simple.

It may be doubted whether the modern way of teaching Christianity, as a general rule, is sufficiently simple. It is a certain fact that deep reasoning and elaborate arguments are not the weapons by which God is generally pleased to convert souls. Simple plain statements, boldly and solemnly made, and made in such a manner that they are evidently felt and believed by him who makes them, seem to have the most effect on hearts and consciences. Parents and teachers of the young, ministers and missionaries, Scripture-readers and district visitors, would all do well to remember this. We need not be so anxious as we often are about fencing, and proving, and demonstrating, and reasoning out the doctrines of the gospel. Not one soul in a hundred was ever brought to Christ in this fashion. We want more simple, plain, solemn, earnest, affectionate statements of simple gospel truths.

June 23

And that repentance and remission of sins should be preached in his
name among all nations, beginning at Jerusalem.
Luke 24:47

The first truths which the Lord Jesus bade His disciples preach after He left the world.

We read that 'repentance and remission of sins' were to be preached in His name among all nations.

'Repentance and remission of sins' are the first things which ought to be pressed on the attention of every man, woman and child throughout the world. All ought to be told the necessity of repentance. All are by nature desperately wicked: without repentance and conversion none can enter the kingdom of God. All ought to be told God's readiness to forgive everyone who believes on Christ. All are by nature guilty and condemned; but anyone may obtain by faith in Jesus, free, full and immediate pardon. All, not least, ought to be continually reminded that repentance and remission of sins are inseparably linked together. Not that our repentance can purchase our pardon: pardon is the free gift of God to the believer in Christ; but still it remains true, that a man impenitent is a man unforgiven.

He that desires to be a true Christian must be experimentally acquainted with repentance and remission of sins. These are the principal things in saving religion. To belong to a pure church, and hear the gospel, and receive the sacraments, are great privileges: but are we converted? Are we justified? If not, we are dead before God. Happy is that Christian who keeps these two points continually before his eyes! Repentance and remission are not mere elementary truths, and milk for babes; the highest standard of sanctity is nothing more than a continual growth in practical knowledge of these two points. The brightest saint is the man who has the most heart-searching sense of his own sinfulness, and the liveliest sense of his own complete acceptance in Christ.

June 24

And all bare him witness, and wondered at the gracious words which proceeded out of his mouth. And they said, Is not this Joseph's son?
Luke 4:22

What an instructive example we have in these verses of the manner in which religious teaching is often heard.

We are told that when our Lord had finished His sermon at Nazareth, His hearers 'bare him witness, and wondered at the gracious words which proceeded out of his mouth'. They could not find any flaw in the exposition of Scripture they had heard. They could not deny the beauty of the well-chosen language to which they had listened. 'Never man spake like this man.' But their hearts were utterly unmoved and unaffected. They were even full of envy and enmity against the Preacher. In short, there seems to have been no effect produced on them, except a little temporary feeling of admiration.

It is vain to conceal from ourselves that there are thousands of persons, in Christian churches, in little better state of mind than our Lord's hearers at Nazareth. There are thousands who listen regularly to the preaching of the gospel, and admire it while they listen. They do not dispute the truth of what they hear. They even feel a kind of intellectual pleasure in hearing a good and powerful sermon. But their religion never goes beyond this point. Their sermon-hearing does not prevent them living a life of thoughtlessness, worldliness and sin.

Let us often examine ourselves on this important point. Let us see what practical effect is produced in our hearts and lives by the preaching which we profess to like. Does it lead us to true repentance towards God, and lively faith towards our Lord Jesus Christ? Does it excite us to weekly efforts to cease from sin, and to resist the devil? These are the fruits which sermons ought to produce, if they are really doing us good. Without such fruit, a mere barren admiration is utterly worthless. It is no proof of grace. It will save no soul.

June 25

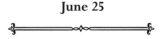

And all bare him witness, and wondered at the gracious words which
proceeded out of his mouth. And they said, Is not this Joseph's son?
Luke 4:22

How apt men are to despise the highest privileges, when they are familiar with them.

We see it in the conduct of the men of Nazareth when they had heard the Lord Jesus preach. They could find no fault in His sermon. They could point to no inconsistency in His past life and conversation. But because the Preacher had dwelt among them thirty years, and His face, and voice, and appearance were familiar to them, they would not receive His doctrine. They said to one another, 'Is not this Joseph's son?' Is it possible that one so well-known as this man can be the Christ? And they drew from our Lord's lips the solemn saying, 'No prophet is accepted in his own country'.

We shall do well to remember this lesson in the matter of ordinances and means of grace. We are always in danger of undervaluing them when we have them in abundance. We are apt to think lightly of the privilege of an open Bible, a preached gospel and the liberty of meeting together for public worship. We grow up in the midst of these things, and are accustomed to have them without trouble. And the consequence is that we often hold them very cheap, and underrate the extent of our mercies. Let us take heed to our own spirit in the use of sacred things. Often as we may read the Bible, let us never read it without deep reverence. Often as we hear the name of Christ, let us never forget that He is the One Mediator in whom is life. Even the manna that came down from heaven was at length scorned by Israel, as 'light bread' (Num. 21:5). It is an evil day with our souls, when Christ is in the midst of us, and yet, because of our familiarity with His name, is lightly esteemed.

June 26

And why beholdest thou the mote that is in thy brother's eye, but
perceivest not the beam that is in thine own eye?
Luke 6:41

Those who reprove the sins of others should strive to be of blameless life.

Our Lord teaches us this lesson by a practical saying. He shows the unreasonableness of a man finding fault with a 'mote', or trifling thing in a brother's eye, while he himself has a 'beam', or some large and formidable object sticking in his own eye.

The lesson must doubtless be received with suitable and scriptural qualifications. If no man is to teach or preach to others, until he himself is faultless, there could be no teaching or preaching in the world. The erring would never be corrected, and the wicked would never be reproved. To put such a sense as this on our Lord's words, brings them into collision with other plain passages of Scripture.

The main object of our Lord Jesus appears to be to impress on ministers and teachers the importance of consistency of life. The passage is a solemn warning not to contradict by our lives what we have said with our lips. The office of the preacher will never command attention, unless he practises what he preaches. Episcopal ordination, university degrees, high-sounding titles, a loud profession of doctrinal purity, will never procure respect for a minister's sermon, if his congregation sees him clinging to ungodly habits.

But there is much here which we shall all do well to remember. The lesson is one which many besides ministers should seriously consider. All heads of families and masters of households, all parents, all teachers of schools, all tutors, all managers of young people, should often think of the 'mote' and the 'beam'. All such should see in our Lord's words the mighty lesson, that nothing influences others so much as consistency. Let the lesson be treasured up and not forgotten.

June 27

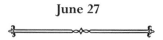

And he said unto them, Ye are they which justify yourselves before men;
but God knoweth your hearts: for that which is highly esteemed among
men is abomination in the sight of God.
Luke 16:15

How widely different is the estimate set on things by man from that which is set on things by God. Our Lord Jesus Christ declares this in a severe rebuke which He addresses to the covetous Pharisees who derided Him. He says, 'Ye are they which justify yourselves before men; but God knoweth your hearts: for that which is highly esteemed among men is abomination in the sight of God'.

The truth of this solemn saying appears on every side of us. We have only to look round the world and mark the things on which most men set their affections, in order to see it proved in a hundred ways. Riches and honours, and rank, and pleasure, are the chief objects for which the greater part of mankind are living: yet these are the very things which God declares to be 'vanity', and of the love of which He warns us to beware! Praying, and Bible-reading, and holy living, and repentance, and faith, and grace, and communion with God, are things for which few care at all: yet these are the very things which God in His Bible is ever urging on our attention! The disagreement is glaring, painful and appalling. What God calls good, that man calls evil: what God calls evil, that man calls good!

Whose words, after all, are true? Whose estimate is correct? Whose judgment will stand at the last day? By whose standard will all be tried, before they receive their eternal sentence? Before whose bar will the current opinions of the world be tested and weighed at last? These are the only questions which ought to influence our conduct; and to these questions the Bible returns a plain answer. The counsel of the Lord – it alone shall stand for ever. The word of Christ – it alone shall judge man at the last day. By that word let us live. By that word let us measure everything, and every person in this evil world. It matters nothing what man thinks: 'What saith the Lord?'

June 28

The officers answered, Never man spake like this man.
John 7:46

How eminent must have been our Lord's gifts, as a public Teacher of religion.

We are told that even the officers of the chief priests, who were sent to take Him, were struck and amazed. They were, of course, not likely to be prejudiced in His favour. Yet, even they reported, 'Never man spake like this man'.

Of the manner of our Lord's public speaking, we can of necessity form little idea. Action, and voice, and delivery are things that must be seen and heard to be appreciated. That our Lord's manner was peculiarly solemn, arresting and impressive, we need not doubt. It was probably something very unlike what the Jewish officers were accustomed to hear. There is much in what is said in another place: 'he taught them as one having authority, and not as the scribes' (Matt. 7:29).

Of the matter of our Lord's public speaking, we may form some conception from the discourses which are recorded in the four Gospels. The leading features of these discourses are plain and unmistakable. The world has never seen anything like them since the gift of speech was given to man. They often contain deep truths, which we have no line to fathom. But they often contain simple things, which even a child can understand. They are bold and outspoken in denouncing national and ecclesiastical sins, and yet they are wise and discreet in never giving needless offence. They are faithful and direct in their warnings, and yet loving and tender in their invitations. For a combination of power and simplicity, of courage and prudence, of faithfulness and tenderness, we may well say, 'Never man spake like this Man'!

It would be well for the Church of Christ if ministers and teachers of religion would strive more to speak after their Lord's pattern. Let them remember that fine bombastic language, and a sensational, theatrical style of address, are utterly unlike their Master. Let them realize that an eloquent simplicity is the highest attainment of public speaking. Of this their Master left them a glorious example.

June 29

And his fame went throughout all Syria: and they brought unto him
all sick people that were taken with divers diseases and torments, and
those which were possessed with devils, and those which were lunatick,
and those that had the palsy; and he healed them.
Matthew 4:24

The general character of the miracles by which our Lord confirmed His mission.

Here we are told of them in the mass; hereafter we shall find many of them described particularly: and what is their character? They were miracles of mercy and kindness. Our Lord 'went about doing good'.

These miracles are meant to teach us our Lord's power. He that could heal sick people with a touch, and cast out devils with a word, is 'able to save all them to the uttermost that come unto God by Him'. He is almighty.

These miracles are meant to be types and emblems of our Lord's skill as a spiritual physician. He, before whom no bodily disease proved incurable, is mighty to cure every ailment of our souls: there is no broken heart that He cannot heal; there is no wound of conscience that He cannot cure. Fallen, crushed, bruised, plague-stricken as we all are by sin, Jesus by His blood and Spirit can make us whole. Only let us apply to Him.

These miracles, not least, are intended to show us Christ's heart. He is a most compassionate Saviour: He rejected no-one who came to Him; He refused no-one, however loathsome and diseased; He had an ear to hear all, and a hand to help all, and a heart to feel for all. There is no kindness like His. His compassions fail not.

May we all remember that the Lord Jesus is 'the same yesterday, and to day, and for ever' (Heb. 13:8).

High in heaven at God's right hand, He is not in the least altered. He is just as able to save, just as willing to receive, just as ready to help, as He was eighteen hundred years ago. Should we have spread out our wants before Him then? Let us do the same now. He can 'heal all manner of sickness and all manner of disease.'

June 30

And Jesus put forth his hand, and touched him, saying, I will; be thou
clean. And immediately his leprosy was cleansed.
Matthew 8:3

How great is the power of our Lord Jesus Christ.
Leprosy is the most fearful disease by which man's body can be afflicted. He that has it is like one dead while he lives; it is a complaint regarded by physicians as incurable (2 Kgs. 5:7). Yet Jesus says 'be thou clean. And immediately his leprosy was cleansed'. To heal a person of the palsy without even seeing him, by only speaking a word, is to do that which our minds cannot even conceive: yet Jesus commands, and at once it is done. To give a woman prostrate with a fever, not merely relief, but strength to do work in an instant, would baffle the skill of all the physicians on earth: yet Jesus 'touched' Peter's wife's mother, and she arose, and ministered unto them. These are the doings of One that is almighty. There is no escape from the conclusion. This was 'the finger of God' (Exod. 8:19).

Behold here a broad foundation for the faith of a Christian! We are told in the gospel to come to Jesus, to believe on Jesus, to live the life of faith in Jesus; we are encouraged to lean on Him, to cast all our care on Him, to repose all the weight of our souls on Him. We may do so without fear: He can bear all; He is a strong rock: He is almighty. It was a fine saying of an old saint, 'My faith can sleep sound on no other pillow than Christ's omnipotence.' He can give life to the dead; He can give power to the weak; He can 'increase strength to them that have no might'. Let us trust Him and not be afraid. The world is full of snares: our hearts are weak. But with Jesus nothing is impossible.

JULY

July 1

Insomuch that the multitude wondered, when they saw the dumb to
speak, the maimed to be whole, the lame to walk, and the blind to see:
and they glorified the God of Israel.
Matthew 15:31

The marvellous ease and power with which our Lord healed all who were brought to Him.

We read that 'the multitude wondered, when they saw the dumb to speak, the maimed to be whole, the lame to walk, and the blind to see: and they glorified the God of Israel'.

Behold in these words a lively emblem of our Lord Jesus Christ's power to heal sin-diseased souls! There is no ailment of heart that He cannot cure. There is no form of spiritual complaint that He cannot overcome. The fever of lust, the palsy of the love of the world, the slow consumption of indolence and sloth, the heart disease of unbelief – all, all give way when He sends forth His Spirit on any one of the children of men. He can put a new song in a sinner's mouth, and make him speak with love of that gospel which he once ridiculed and blasphemed; He can open the eyes of a man's understanding and make him see the kingdom of God; He can open the ears of a man, and make him willing to hear His voice, and to follow Him wheresoever He goeth; He can give power to a man who once walked in the broad way that leadeth unto destruction, to walk in the way of life; He can make hands that were once instruments of sin, serve Him and do His will. The time of miracles is not yet passed. Every conversion is a miracle. Have we ever seen a real instance of conversion? Let us know that we saw in it the hand of Christ. We should have seen nothing really greater if we had seen our Lord making the dumb to speak and the lame to walk, when He was on earth.

Would we know what to do, if we desire to be saved? Do we feel soul-sick and want a cure? We must just go to Christ by faith, and apply to Him for relief. He is not changed: eighteen hundred years have made no difference in Him. He is at the right hand of God, He is still the great Physician. He still 'receiveth sinners' (Luke 15:2). He is still mighty to heal.

July 2

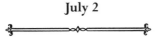

And he came and took her by the hand, and lifted her up; and
immediately the fever left her, and she ministered unto them.
Mark 1:31

W hat a complete and perfect cure the Lord Jesus
makes, when He heals.

He takes the sick woman by the hand, and lifts her up, and
'immediately the fever left her'. But this was not all. A greater miracle
remained behind. At once we are told 'she ministered unto them'. That
weakness and prostration of strength which, as a general rule, a fever
leaves behind it, in her case was entirely removed. The fevered woman
was not only made well in a moment, but in the same moment made
strong and able to work.

We may see in this case a lively emblem of Christ's dealing with sin-
sick souls. That blessed Saviour not only gives mercy and forgiveness;
He gives renewing grace besides. To as many as receive Him as their
Physician, he gives power to become the sons of God. He cleanses them
by His Spirit, when He washes them in His precious blood. Those whom
He justifies, He also sanctifies. When He bestows an absolution, He
also bestows a new heart. When He grants free forgiveness for the past,
He also grants strength to 'minister' to Him for the time to come. The
sin-sick soul is not merely cured, and then left to itself. It is also supplied
with a new heart and a right spirit, and enabled so to live as to please
God.

There is comfort in this thought for all who feel a desire to serve
Christ, but at present are afraid to begin. Let them know that Jesus is
an almighty Saviour, who never forsakes those who once commit
themselves to Him. Once raised by His mighty hand from the death of
sin, and washed in His precious blood, they shall go on 'ministering to
Him' to their life's end. They shall have power to overcome the world,
and crucify the flesh, and resist the devil. Only let them begin, and they
shall go on. Jesus knows nothing of half-cured cases and half-finished
work. Let them trust in Jesus and go forward. The pardoned soul shall
always be enabled to serve Christ.

July 3

And they bring unto him one that was deaf, and had an impediment
in his speech; and they beseech him to put his hand upon him.
Mark 7:32

The mighty miracle which is here recorded.
We read that they brought unto our Lord 'one that was deaf, and had an impediment in his speech', and besought Him that He would 'put his hand upon him'. At once the petition is granted, and the cure is wrought. Speech and hearing are instantaneously given to the man by a word and a touch. '[S]traightway his ears were opened, and the string of his tongue was loosed, and he spake plain.'

We see but half the instruction of this passage, if we only regard it as an example of our Lord's divine power. It is such an example, beyond doubt, but it is something more than that. We must look further, deeper and lower than the surface, and we shall find in the passage precious spiritual truths.

Here we are meant to see our Lord's power to heal the spiritually deaf. He can give the chief of sinners a hearing ear. He can make him delight in listening to the very gospel which he once ridiculed and despised.

Here also we are meant to see our Lord's power to heal the spiritually dumb. He can teach the hardest of transgressors to call upon God. He can put a new song in the mouth of him whose talk was once only of this world. He can make the vilest of men speak of spiritual things, and testify the gospel of the grace of God.

When Jesus pours forth His Spirit, nothing is impossible. We must never despair of others. We must never regard our own hearts as too bad to be changed. He that healed the deaf and dumb still lives. The cases which moral philosophy pronounces hopeless, are not incurable if they are brought to Christ.

July 4

And he took him aside from the multitude, and put his fingers into his
ears, and he spit, and touched his tongue ...
Mark 7:33

The peculiar manner in which our Lord thought good
to work the miracle here recorded.
We are told that when the deaf and dumb person was brought
to Jesus, 'he took him aside from the multitude, and put his fingers into
his ears, and he spit, and touched his tongue; And looking up to heaven,
he sighed' – and then, and not till then, came the words of commanding
power: 'Ephphatha, that is, Be opened'.

There is undoubtedly much that is mysterious in these actions. We
know not why they were used. It would have been as easy to our Lord
to speak the word, and command health to return at once, as to do
what He here did. His reasons for the course He adopted are not
recorded. We only know that the result was the same as on other
occasions: the man was cured.

But there is one simple lesson to be learned from our Lord's conduct
on this occasion. That lesson is, that Christ was not tied to the use of
any one means in doing His works among men. Sometimes He thought
fit to work in one way, sometimes in another. His enemies were never
able to say that unless He employed certain invariable agency He could
not work at all.

We see the same thing going on still in the Church of Christ. We see
continual proof that the Lord is not tied to the use of one means
exclusively in conveying grace to the soul. Sometimes He is pleased to
work by the Word preached publicly, sometimes by the Word read
privately. Sometimes He awakens people by sickness and affliction,
sometimes by the rebukes or counsel of friends. Sometimes He employs
means of grace to turn people out of the way of sin. Sometimes He
arrests their attention by some providence, without any means of grace
at all.

July 5

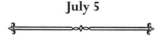

And were beyond measure astonished, saying, He hath done all things
well: he maketh both the deaf to hear, and the dumb to speak.
Mark 7:37

The remarkable testimony which was borne by those
who saw the miracle here recorded.
They said of our Lord, 'He hath done all things well'!

It is more than probable that those who said these words were little
sensible of their full meaning, when applied to Christ. Like Caiaphas,
they 'spake he not of' themselves (John 11:51). But the truth to which
they gave utterance is full of deep and unspeakable comfort, and ought
to be daily remembered by all true Christians.

Let us remember it as we look back over the days past of our lives,
from the hour of our conversion. Our Lord 'hath done all things well'.
In first bringing us out of darkness into marvellous light – in humbling
us and teaching us our weakness, guilt and folly, – in stripping us of our
idols, and choosing all our portions – in placing us where we are, and
giving us what we have – how well everything has been done! How
great the mercy that we have not had our own way!

Let us remember it as we look forward to the days yet to come. We
know not what they may be, bright or dark, many or few. But we know
that we are in the hands of Him who 'doeth all things well'. He will not
err in any of His dealings with us. He will take away and give, He will
afflict and bereave, He will move and He will settle with perfect wisdom,
at the right time, in the right way. The great Shepherd of the sheep
makes no mistakes. He leads every lamb of His flock by the right way to
the city of habitation.

We shall never see the full beauty of these words till the resurrection
morning. We shall then look back over our lives, and know the meaning
of everything that happened from first to last. We shall remember all
the way by which we were led, and confess that all was 'well done'. The
why and the wherefore, the causes and reasons of everything which
now perplexes, will be clear and plain as the sun at noonday. We shall
wonder at our own blindness, and marvel that we could ever have
doubted our Lord's love.

July 6

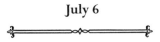

And as he was now going down, his servants met him,
and told him, saying, Thy son liveth.
John 4:51

What benefits affliction can confer on the soul.
We read, that anxiety about a son led the nobleman to Christ,
in order to obtain help in time of need. Once brought into
Christ's company, he learned a lesson of priceless value. In the end, he
'believed, and his whole house'. All this, be it remembered, hinged
upon the son's sickness. If the nobleman's son had never been ill, his
father might have lived and died in his sins.

Affliction is one of God's medicines. By it He often teaches lessons
which would be learned in no other way. By it He often draws souls
away from sin and the world, which would otherwise have perished
everlastingly. Health is a great blessing, but sanctified disease is a greater.
Prosperity and worldly comfort, are what all naturally desire; but losses
and crosses are far better for us, if they lead us to Christ. Thousands at
the last day, will testify with David, and the nobleman before us, 'It is
good for me that I have been afflicted' (Ps. 119:71).

Let us beware of murmuring in the time of trouble. Let us settle it
firmly in our minds, that there is a meaning, a needs-be and a message
from God, in every sorrow that falls upon us. There are no lessons so
useful as those learned in the school of affliction. There is no commentary
that opens up the Bible so much as sickness and sorrow. '[N]o chastening
for the present seemeth to be joyous, but grievous: nevertheless
afterward it yieldeth peaceable fruit' (Heb. 12:11). The resurrection
morning will prove, that many of the losses of God's people were in
reality eternal gains.

July 7

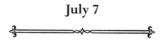

But if I do, though ye believe not me, believe the works: that ye may
know, and believe, that the Father is in me, and I in him.
John 10:38

The importance which our Lord Jesus Christ attaches to His miracles.

He appeals to them as the best evidence of His own divine mission. He bids the Jews look at them, and deny them if they can. 'If I do not the works of my Father, believe me not. But if I do, though ye believe not me, believe the works.'

The mighty miracles which our Lord performed during the three years of His earthly ministry, are probably not considered as much as they ought to be in the present day. These miracles were not few in number. Forty times and more we read in the Gospels of His doing things entirely out of the ordinary course of nature – healing sick people in a moment, raising the dead with a word, casting out devils, calming winds and waves in an instant, walking on the water as on solid ground.

These miracles were not all done in private among friends. Many of them were wrought in the most public manner, under the eyes of unfriendly witnesses. We are so familiar with these things that we are apt to forget the mighty lesson they teach. They teach that He who worked these miracles must be nothing less than very God. They stamp His doctrines and precepts with the mark of divine authority. He only who created all things at the beginning, could suspend the laws of creation at His will. He who could suspend the laws of creation, must be One who ought to be thoroughly believed and implicitly obeyed. To reject One who confirmed His mission by such mighty works, is the height of madness and folly.

Hundreds of unbelieving men, no doubt, in every age, have tried to pour contempt on Christ's miracles, and to deny that they were ever worked at all. But they labour in vain. Proofs upon proofs exist that our Lord's ministry was accompanied by miracles, and that this was acknowledged by those who lived in our Lord's time. Objectors of this sort would do well to take up the one single miracle of our Lord's resurrection from the dead, and disprove it if they can.

July 8

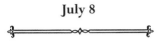

Then Jesus six days before the passover came to Bethany, where Lazarus
was, which had been dead, whom he raised from the dead.
John 12:1

What abounding proofs exist of the truth of our Lord's greatest miracles.

We read of a supper at Bethany, where Lazarus 'sat at the table' among the guests – Lazarus, who had been publicly raised from the dead, after lying four days in the grave. No-one could pretend to say that his resurrection was a mere optical delusion, and that the eyes of the bystanders must have been deceived by a ghost or vision. Here was the very same Lazarus, after several weeks, sitting among his fellow men with a real material body, and eating and drinking real material food. It is hard to understand what stronger evidence of a fact could be supplied. He that is not convinced by such evidence as this may as well say that he is determined to believe nothing at all.

It is a comfortable thought, that the very same proofs which exist about the resurrection of Lazarus, are the proofs which surround that still mightier fact, the resurrection of Christ from the dead. Was Lazarus seen for several weeks by the people of Bethany, going in and coming out among them? So was the Lord Jesus seen by His disciples. Did Lazarus take material food before the eyes of his friends? So did the Lord Jesus eat and drink before His ascension. No-one in his sober senses, who saw Jesus take 'broiled fish, and of an honeycomb', and eat it before several witnesses, would doubt that He had a real body (Luke 24:42).

We shall do well to remember this. In an age of abounding unbelief and scepticism, we shall find that the resurrection of Christ will bear any weight that we can lay upon it. Just as he placed beyond reasonable doubt the rising again of a beloved disciple within two miles of Jerusalem, so in a very few weeks He placed beyond doubt His own victory over the grave. If we believe that Lazarus rose again, we need not doubt that Jesus rose again also.

July 9

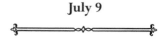

If ye then, being evil, know how to give good gifts unto your children,
how much more shall your Father which is in heaven give good things
to them that ask him?
Matthew 7:11

The duty of prayer, and the rich encouragements there are to pray.

There is a beautiful connection between this lesson and that which goes before it. Would we know when to be 'silent', and when to 'speak' – when to bring forward 'holy things', and produce our 'pearls'? We must pray. This is a subject to which the Lord Jesus evidently attaches great importance: the language that He uses is a plain proof of this. He employs three different words to express the idea of prayer: 'Ask', 'Seek', 'Knock'. He holds out the broadest, fullest promise to those who pray: 'every one that asketh receiveth'. He illustrates God's readiness to hear our prayers by an argument drawn from the well-known practice of parents on earth: 'evil' and selfish as they are by nature, they do not neglect the wants of their children according to the flesh; much more will a God of love and mercy attend to the cries of those who are His children by grace!

Let us take special notice of these words of our Lord about prayer. Few of His sayings, perhaps, are so well-known and so often repeated as this. The poorest and most unlearned can generally tell us, that 'if we do not seek we shall not find'. But what is the good of knowing it, if we do not use it? Knowledge, not improved and well employed, will only increase our condemnation at the last day.

Do we know anything of this 'asking, seeking, and knocking'? Why should we not? There is nothing so simple and plain as praying, if a man really has a will to pray. There is nothing unhappily, which men are so slow to do: they will use many of the forms of religion, attend many ordinances, do many things that are right, before they will do this; and yet without this, no soul can be saved!

July 10

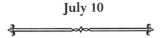

Then Jesus answered and said unto her, O woman, great is thy faith: be it unto thee even as thou wilt. And her daughter was made whole from that very hour.
Matthew 15:28

What encouragement there is to persevere in prayer, both for ourselves and others.

It is hard to conceive a more striking illustration of this truth, than we have in this passage. The prayer of this afflicted mother at first seemed entirely unnoticed: Jesus 'answered her not a word'. Yet she prayed on. The saying which by and by fell from our Lord's lips sounded discouraging: 'I am not sent but unto the lost sheep of the house of Israel'. Yet she prayed on, 'Lord help me'. The second saying of our Lord was even less encouraging than the first: 'It is not meet to take the children's bread, and to cast it to dogs.' Yet 'Hope deferred' did not make her 'heart sick' (Prov. 13:12). Even then she was not silenced: even then she finds a plea for some 'crumbs' of mercy to be granted to her. And her importunity obtained at length a gracious reward: 'O woman, great is thy faith: be it unto thee even as thou wilt'. That promise never yet was broken: 'seek, and ye shall find' (Matt. 7:7).

Let us remember this history, when we pray for ourselves. We are sometimes tempted to think that we get no good by our prayers, and that we may as well give them up altogether. Let us resist the temptation: it comes from the devil. Let us believe, and pray on. Against our besetting sins, against the spirit of the world, against the wiles of the devil, let us pray on, and not faint. For strength to do duty, for grace to bear our trials, for comfort in every trouble, let us 'continue in prayer'. Let us be sure that no time is so well spent in every day as that which we spend upon our knees. Jesus hears us, and in His own good time will give an answer.

Let us remember this history when we intercede for others. Have we children, whose conversion we desire? Have we relations and friends, about whose salvation we are anxious? Let us follow the example of this Canaanitish woman, and lay the state of their souls before Christ.

July 11

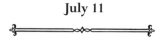

But Simon's wife's mother lay sick of a fever, and anon they tell him of her.
Mark 1:30

To what remedy a Christian ought to resort first, in time of trouble.

He ought to follow the example of the friends of Simon's wife's mother. We read that when she 'lay sick of a fever', they told Jesus 'of her'.

There is no remedy like this. Means are to be used diligently, without question, in any time of need. Doctors are to be sent for in sickness. Lawyers are to be consulted when property or character needs defence. The help of friends is to be sought. But still, after all, the first thing to be done is to cry to the Lord Jesus Christ for help. None can relieve us so effectually as He can. None is so compassionate, and so willing to relieve. When Jacob was in trouble, he turned to his God first: 'Deliver me, I pray thee ... from the hand of Esau' (Gen. 32:11). When Hezekiah was in trouble, he first spread Sennacherib's letter before the Lord: 'I beseech thee, save thou us out of his hand' (2 Kgs. 19:19). When Lazarus fell sick, his sisters sent immediately to Jesus: 'Lord', they said, 'he whom thou lovest is sick' (John 11:3). Now let us do likewise. 'Cast thy burden upon the LORD, and he shall sustain thee....' 'Casting all your care upon him....' '[I]n every thing by prayer and supplication with thanksgiving let your requests be made known unto God' (Ps. 55:22; 1 Pet. 5:7; Phil. 4:6).

Let us not only remember this rule, but practise it too. We live in a world of sin and sorrow. The days of darkness in a man's life are many. It needs no prophet's eye to foresee that we shall all shed many a tear, and feel many a heart-wrench, before we die. Let us be armed with a receipt against despair, before our troubles come. Let us know what to do, when sickness, or bereavement, or cross, or loss, or disappointment breaks in upon us like an armed man. Let us do as they did in Simon's house at Capernaum. Let us at once 'tell him'.

July 12

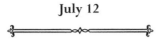

And in the morning, rising up a great while before day, he went out,
and departed into a solitary place, and there prayed.
Mark 1:35

An example of our Lord Jesus Christ's habits about private prayer.
We are told, that 'in the morning, rising up a great while before day, he went out, and departed into a solitary place, and there prayed'. We shall find the same thing often recorded of our Lord in the Gospel history. When He was baptized, we are told that He was 'praying' (Luke 3:21). When He was transfigured, we are told, that 'as he prayed, the fashion of his countenance was altered' (Luke 9:29). Before He chose the twelve apostles, we are told that He 'continued all night in prayer to God' (Luke 6:12). When all men spoke well of Him, and would fain have made Him a King, we are told that 'he went up into a mountain apart to pray' (Matt. 14:23). When tempted in the garden of Gethsemane, he said, 'Sit ye here, while I shall pray' (Mark 14:32). In short, our Lord prayed always, and did not faint. Sinless as He was, He set us an example of diligent communion with His Father. His Godhead did not render Him independent of the use of all means as a man. His very perfection was a perfection kept up through the exercise of prayer. We ought to see in all this the immense importance of private devotion. If He who was 'holy, harmless, undefiled, and separate from sinners', thus prayed continually, how much more ought we who are compassed with infirmity? If He found it needful to offer up supplications with strong crying and tears, how much more needful is it for us, who in many things offend daily?

What shall we say to those who never pray at all, in the face of such a passage as this? There are many such, it may be feared, in the list of baptized people – many who rise up in the morning without prayer, and without prayer lie down at night – many who never speak one word to God. Are they Christians? It is impossible to say so. A praying master, like Jesus, can have no prayerless servants. The Spirit of adoption will always make a man call upon God. To be prayerless is to be Christless, Godless and in the high road to destruction.

July 13

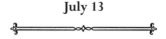

And when he had sent them away, he departed into a mountain to pray.
Mark 6:46

Our Lord Jesus Christ's conduct, when the miracle of feeding the multitude had been performed.

We read, that 'when he had sent them away, he departed into a mountain to pray'.

There is something deeply instructive in this circumstance. Our Lord sought not the praise of man. After one of His greatest miracles we find Him immediately seeking solitude and spending His time in prayer. He practised what He had taught elsewhere, when He said, 'Enter into thy closet, and shut thy door, and pray to thy Father which is in secret'. None ever did such mighty works as He did. None ever spake such words. None ever was so instant in prayer.

Let our Lord's conduct in this respect be our example. We cannot work miracles as He did; in this He stands alone. But we can walk in His steps in the matter of private devotion. If we have the Spirit of adoption, we can pray. Let us resolve to pray more than we have done hitherto. Let us strive to make time, and place, and opportunity for being alone with God. Above all, let us not only pray before we attempt to work for God, but pray also after our work is done.

It would be well for us all if we examined ourselves more frequently as to our habits about private prayer. What time do we give to it in the twenty-four hours of the day? What progress can we mark, one year with another, in the fervency, fullness and earnestness of our prayers? What do we know by experience of 'labouring fervently in prayer'? These are humbling inquiries, but they are useful for our souls. There are few things, it may be feared, in which Christians come so far short of Christ's example as they do in the matter of prayer.

July 14

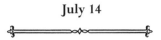

And when it was day, he departed and went into a desert place: and
the people sought him, and came unto him, and stayed him,
that he should not depart from them.
Luke 4:42

Our Lord's practice of occasional retirement from public notice into some solitary place.
We read, that after healing many that were sick and casting out many devils, 'he departed and went into a desert place'. His object in so doing is shown by comparison with other places in the Gospels. He went aside from His work for a season, to hold communion with His Father in heaven, and to pray. Holy and sinless as His human nature was, it was a nature kept sinless in the regular use of means of grace, and not in the neglect of them.

There is an example here which all who desire to grow in grace and walk closely with God would do well to follow. We must make time for private meditation, and for being alone with God. It must not content us to pray daily and read the Scripture, to hear the gospel regularly and to receive the Lord's Supper. All this is well. But something more is needed. We should set apart special seasons for solitary self-examination and meditation on the things of God. How often in a year this practice should be attempted each Christian must judge for himself. But that the practice is most desirable seems clear both from Scripture and experience. We live in hurrying, bustling times. The excitement of daily business and constant engagements keep many men in a perpetual whirl, and entails great peril on souls. The neglect of this habit of withdrawing occasionally from worldly business is the probable cause of many an inconsistency of backsliding which brings scandal on the cause of Christ. The more work we have to do, the more we ought to imitate our Master. If He, in the midst of His abundant labours, found time to retire from the world occasionally, how much more may we? If the Master found the practice necessary, it must surely be a thousand times more necessary for His disciples.

July 15

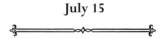

And he withdrew himself into the wilderness, and prayed.
Luke 5:16

Our Lord Jesus Christ's diligence about private prayer. Although 'great multitudes came together to hear, and to be healed by him of their infirmities', He still made time for secret devotion. Holy and undefiled as He was, He would not allow the demands of public business to prevent regular private intercourse with God. We are told that 'he withdrew himself into the wilderness, and prayed'.

There is an example set before us here, which is much overlooked in these latter days. There are few professing Christians, it may be feared, who strive to imitate Christ in this matter of private devotion. There is abundance of hearing, and reading, and talking, and profession, and visiting, and almsgiving, and subscribing to societies, and teaching at schools. But is there, together with all this, a due proportion of private prayer? Are believing men and women sufficiently careful to be frequently alone with God? These are humbling and heart-searching questions. But we shall find it useful to give them an answer.

Why it is that there is so much apparent religious working, and yet so little result in positive conversions to God – so many sermons, and so few souls saved – so much machinery, and so little effect produced – so much running hither and thither, and yet so few brought to Christ? Why is all this? The reply is short and simple. There is not enough private prayer. The cause of Christ does not need less working, but it does need among the workers more praying. Let us each examine ourselves, and amend our ways. The most successful workmen in the Lord's vineyard, are those who are like their Master, often and much upon their knees.

July 16

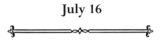

Therefore said he unto them, The harvest truly is great, but the labourers are few: pray ye therefore the Lord of the harvest, that he would send forth labourers into his harvest.
Luke 10:2

The importance of prayer and intercession. This is the leading thought with which our Lord opens His address. Before He tells His ambassadors what to do, He first bids them to pay. '[P]ray ye therefore the Lord of the harvest, that he would send forth labourers into his harvest.'

Prayer is one of the best and most powerful means of helping forward the cause of Christ in the world. It is a means within the reach of all who have the Spirit of adoption. Not all believers have money to give to missions. Very few have great intellectual gifts, or extensive influence among men. But all believers can pray for the success of the gospel, and they ought to pray for it daily. Many and marvellous are the answers to prayer which are recorded for our learning in the Bible. 'The effectual fervent prayer of a righteous man availeth much' (Jas. 5:16).

Prayer is one of the principal weapons which the minister of the gospel ought to use. To be a true successor of the apostles, he must give himself to prayer as well as to the ministry of the Word (Acts. 6:4). He must not only use the sword of the Spirit, but pray always, with all prayer and supplication (Eph. 6:17, 18). This is the way to win a blessing on his own ministry. This, above all, is the way to procure hopers to carry on Christ's work. Colleges may educate men. Bishops may ordain them. Patrons may give them livings. But God alone can raise up and send forth 'labourers' who will do work among souls. For a constant supply of such labourers let us daily pray.

July 17

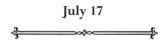

In that hour Jesus rejoiced in spirit, and said, I thank thee, O Father,
Lord of heaven and earth, that thou hast hid these things from the
wise and prudent, and hast revealed them unto babes: even so, Father;
for so it seemed good in thy sight.
Luke 10:21

Τhe one instance on record of our Lord Jesus Christ rejoicing.

We read, that in that hour 'Jesus rejoiced in spirit'. Three times we are told in the Gospels that our Lord Jesus Christ wept. Once only we are told that He rejoiced.

And what was the cause of our Lord's joy? It was the conversion of souls. It was the reception of the gospel by the weak and lowly among the Jews, when the 'wise and prudent' on every side were rejecting it. Our blessed Lord no doubt saw much in this world to grieve Him. He saw the obstinate blindness and unbelief of the vast majority of those among whom He ministered. But when He saw a few poor men and women receiving the glad tidings of salvation, even His heart was refreshed. He saw it and was glad.

Let all Christians mark our Lord's conduct in this matter, and follow His example. They find little in the world to cheer them. They see around them a vast multitude walking in the broad way that leadeth to destruction, careless, hardened and unbelieving. They see a few here and there, and only a few, who believe to the saving of their souls. But let this sight make them thankful. Let them bless God that any at all are converted and that any at all believe. We do not realize the sinfulness of man sufficiently. We do not reflect that the conversion of any soul is a miracle – a miracle as great as the raising of Lazarus from the dead. Let us learn from our blessed Lord to be more thankful. There is always some blue sky as well as black clouds, if we will only look for it. Though only a few are saved, we should find reason for rejoicing. It is only through free grace and undeserved mercy that any are saved at all.

July 18

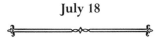

And he said unto them, Which of you shall have a friend, and shall go
unto him at midnight, and say unto him, Friend, lend me three loaves ...
Luke 11:5

The importance of perseverance in prayer.
This lesson is conveyed to us in the simple parable, commonly called the 'Friend at Midnight'. We are there reminded what man can obtain from man by dint of importunity: selfish and indolent as we naturally are, we are capable of being roused to exertion by continued asking. The man who would not give three loaves at midnight for friendship's sake, at length gave them to save himself the trouble of being further entreated. The application of the parable is clear and plain. If importunity succeeds so well between man and man, how much more may we expect it to obtain mercies when used in prayer to God. The lesson is one which we shall do well to remember. It is far more easy to begin a habit of prayer than to keep it up. Myriads of professing Christians are regularly taught to pray when they are young, and then gradually leave off the practice as they grow up. Thousands take up a habit of praying for a little season, after some special mercy or special affliction, and then little by little become cold about it, and at last lay it aside. The secret thought comes stealing over men's minds that 'it is no use to pray'. They see no visible benefit from it; they persuade themselves that they get on just as well without prayer. Laziness and unbelief prevail over their hearts, and at last they altogether 'restrainest prayer before God' (Job 15:4).

Let us resist this feeling whenever we feel it rising within us. Let us resolve by God's grace, that however poor and feeble our prayers may seem to be, we will pray on. It is not for nothing that the Bible tells us so frequently to 'watch in prayer,' to 'pray without ceasing', to 'continue in prayer', to 'pray always and not to faint', to be 'instant in prayer'. These expressions all look one way: they are all meant to remind us of a danger and to quicken us to duty. The time and way in which our prayers shall be answered are matters which we must leave entirely to God; but that every petition which we offer in faith shall certainly be answered, we need not doubt.

July 19

And I say unto you, Ask, and it shall be given you; seek, and ye shall
find; knock, and it shall be opened unto you.
Luke 11:9

How wide and encouraging are the promises which the Lord Jesus holds out to prayer.

The striking words in which they are clothed are familiar to us if any are in the Bible: 'Ask, and it shall be given you; seek, and ye shall find; knock, and it shall be opened unto you'. The solemn declaration which follows appears intended to make assurance doubly sure: 'every one that asketh receiveth; and he that seeketh findeth; and to him that knocketh it shall be opened'. The heart-searching argument which concludes the passage leaves faithlessness and unbelief without excuse: 'If ye then, being evil, know how to give good gifts unto your children: how much more shall your heavenly Father give the Holy Spirit to them that ask him?'

There are few promises in the Bible so broad and unqualified as those contained in this wonderful passage. The last in particular deserves especial notice. The Holy Spirit is beyond doubt the greatest gift which God can bestow upon man: having this gift, we have all things – life, light, hope and heaven. Having this gift, we have God the Father's boundless love, God the Son's atoning blood and full communion with all three Persons of the blessed Trinity. Having this gift, we have grace and peace in the world that now is, glory and honour in the world to come. And yet this mighty gift is held out by our Lord Jesus Christ as a gift to be obtained by prayer! 'Shall your heavenly Father give the Holy Spirit to them that ask him?'

And now let us ask ourselves whether we know anything of real prayer? Do we pray at all? Do we pray in the name of Jesus, and as needy sinners? Do we know what it is to 'ask', and 'seek', and 'knock', and wrestle in prayer, like men who feel that it is a matter of life and death, and that they must have an answer? Or are we content with saying over some old form of words, while our thoughts are wandering and our hearts far away? Truly we have learned a great lesson when we have learned that 'saying prayers' is not praying!

July 20

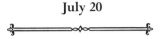

And they lifted up their voices, and said, Jesus, Master, have mercy on us.
Luke 17:13

How earnestly men can cry for help when they feel their need of it.

We read that as our Lord 'entered into a certain village, there met him ten men that were lepers'. It is difficult to conceive any condition more thoroughly miserable than that of men afflicted with leprosy. They were cast out from society: they were cut off from all communion with their fellows. The men described in the passage before us appear to have been truly sensible of their wretchedness. They 'stood afar off'; but they did not stand idly doing nothing. '[T]hey lifted up their voices, and said, Jesus, Master, have mercy on us.' They felt acutely the deplorable state of their bodies. They found words to express their feelings. They cried earnestly for relief when a chance of relief appeared in sight.

The conduct of the ten lepers is very instructive. It throws light on a most important subject in practical Christianity, which we can never understand too well. The subject is prayer.

How is it that many never pray at all? How is it that many others are content to repeat a form of words, but never pray with their hearts? How is it that dying men and women, with souls to be lost or saved, can know so little of real, hearty, business-like prayer? The answer to these questions is short and simple: the bulk of mankind have no sense of sin; they do not feel their spiritual disease; they are not conscious that they are lost, and guilty, and hanging over the brink of hell. When a man finds out his soul's ailment, he soon learns to pray. Like the leper, he finds words to express his want. He cries for help.

How is it, again, that many true believers often pray coldly? What is the reason that their prayers are so feeble, and wandering, and lukewarm, as they frequently are? The answer once more is very plain: their sense of need is not so deep as it ought to be; they are not truly alive to their own weakness and helplessness, and so they do not cry fervently for mercy and grace.

July 21

And fell down on his face at his feet, giving him thanks:
and he was a Samaritan.
Luke 17:16

What a rare thing is thankfulness. We are told that of all the ten lepers whom Christ healed, there was only one who turned back and gave Him thanks. The words that fell from our Lord's lips upon this occasion are very solemn: 'Were there not ten cleansed? but where are the nine?'

The lesson before us is humbling, heart-searching and deeply instructive. The best of us are far too like the nine lepers. We are more ready to pray than to praise, and more disposed to ask God for what we have not than to thank Him for what we have. Murmurings, and complainings, and discontent abound on every side of us. Few indeed are to be found who are not continually hiding their mercies under a bushel, and setting their wants and trials on a hill. These things ought not so to be: but all who know the Church and the world must confess that they are true. The widespread thanklessness of Christians is the disgrace of our day. It is a plain proof of our little humility.

Let us pray daily for a thankful spirit. It is the spirit which God loves and delights to honour: David and St Paul were eminently thankful men. It is the spirit which has marked all the brightest saints in every age of the Church: McCheyne and Bickersteth, and Haldane Stewart, were always full of praise. It is the spirit which is the very atmosphere of heaven: angels and 'just men made perfect' are always blessing God. It is the spirit which is the source of happiness on earth: if we would be careful for nothing, we must make our requests known to God, not only with prayer and supplication, but with thanksgiving (Phil. 4:6).

Above all, let us pray for a deep sense of our own sinfulness, guilt and undeserving. This, after all, is the true secret of a thankful spirit. It is the man who daily feels his debt to grace, and daily remembers that in reality he deserves nothing but hell – this is the man who will be daily blessing and praising God. Thankfulness is a flower which will never bloom well excepting upon a root of deep humility.

July 22

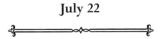

The Pharisee stood and prayed thus with himself, God, I thank thee, that I am not as other men are, extortioners, unjust, adulterers, or even as this publican.
Luke 18:11

The prayer of the Pharisee which our Lord condemns. We read that he said, 'God, I thank thee that I am not as other men are, extortioners, unjust, adulterers, or even as this publican. I fast twice in the week, I give tithes of all that I possess.'

One great defect stands out on the face of this prayer, a defect so glaring that even a child might mark it: it exhibits no sense of sin and need, it contains no confession and no petition, no acknowledgment of guilt and emptiness, no supplication for mercy and grace. It is a mere boasting recital of fancied merits, accompanied by an uncharitable reflection on a brother-sinner. It is a proud, high-minded profession, destitute alike of penitence, humility and charity. In short, it hardly deserves to be called a prayer at all.

No state of soul can be conceived so dangerous as that of the Pharisee. Never are men's bodies in such desperate plight as when mortification and insensibility set in; never are men's hearts in such a hopeless condition as when they are not sensible of their own sins. He that would not make shipwreck on this rock must beware of measuring himself by his neighbours. What does it signify that we are more moral than 'other men'? We are all vile and imperfect in the sight of God. If we 'contend with him', we 'cannot answer him one of a thousand' (Job 9:3). Let us remember this: in all our self-examination let us not try ourselves by comparison with the standard of men: let us look at nothing but the requirements of God. He that acts on this principle will never be a Pharisee.

July 23

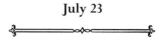

And the publican, standing afar off, would not lift up so much as his
eyes unto heaven, but smote upon his breast, saying,
God be merciful to me a sinner.
Luke 18:13

The prayer of the publican which our Lord commends. That prayer was in every respect the very opposite of that of the Pharisee. We read that he stood afar off, and 'smote upon his breast, saying, God be merciful to me a sinner'. Our Lord Himself stamps this short prayer with the seal of His approbation. He says, 'I tell you, this man went down to his house justified rather than the other'.

The excellence of the publican's prayer consists in five points, each of which deserves attention. For one thing, it was a real petition. A prayer which only contains thanksgiving and profession, and asks nothing, is essentially defective: it may be suitable of an angel, but it is not suitable for a sinner. For another thing, it was a direct personal prayer. The publican did not speak of his neighbours, but himself. Vagueness and generality are the great defects of most men's religion: to get out of 'we', and 'our', and 'us', into 'I', and 'my', and 'me', is a great step toward heaven. For another thing, it was a humble prayer: a prayer which put self in the right place. The publican confessed plainly that he was a sinner. This is the very ABC of saving Christianity: we never begin to be good till we can feel and say that we are bad. For another thing, it was a prayer in which mercy was the chief thing desired, and faith in God's covenant mercy, however weak, displayed. Mercy is the first thing we must ask for in the day we begin to pray: mercy and grace must be the subject of our daily petitions at the throne of grace till the day we die. Finally, the publican's prayer was one which came from his heart. He was deeply moved in uttering it: he smote upon his breast, like one who felt more than he could express. Such prayers are the prayers which are God's delight. A broken and a contrite heart He will not despise (Ps. 51:17).

July 24

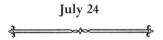

But I have prayed for thee, that thy faith fail not:
and when thou art converted, strengthen thy brethren.
Luke 22:32

One great secret of a believer's perseverance in the faith.

We read that our Lord said to Peter, 'I have prayed for thee, that thy faith fail not'. It was owing to Christ's intercession that Peter did not entirely fall away.

The continued existence of grace in a believer's heart is a great standing miracle. His enemies are so mighty, and his strength is so small, the world is so full of snares, and his heart is so weak, that it seems at first sight impossible for him to reach heaven. The passage before us explains his safety: he has a mighty Friend at the right hand of God, who ever lives to make intercession for him; there is a watchful Advocate, who is daily pleading for him, seeing all his daily necessities, and obtaining daily supplies of mercy and grace for his soul. His grace never altogether dies, because Christ always lives to intercede (Heb. 7:25).

If we are true Christians we shall find it essential to our comfort in religion to have clear views of Christ's priestly office and intercession. Christ lives, and therefore our faith shall not fail. Let us beware of regarding Jesus only as one who died for us: let us never forget that He is alive for evermore. St Paul bids us specially remember that He is risen again, and is at the right hand of God, and also maketh intercession for us (Rom. 8:34). The work that He does for His people is not yet over; He is still appearing in the presence of God for them, and doing for their souls what He did for Peter. His present life for them is just as important as His death on the cross eighteen hundred years ago. Christ lives, and therefore true Christians 'shall live also'.

July 25

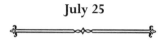

And he was withdrawn from them about a stone's cast,
and kneeled down, and prayed ...
Luke 22:41

An example of what believers ought to do in time of trouble.

The great Head of the Church Himself supplies the pattern. We are told that when He came to the Mount of Olives, the night before He was crucified, He 'kneeled down and prayed'.

It is a striking fact that both the Old and New Testaments give one and the same receipt for bearing trouble. What says the book of Psalms? '[C]all upon Me in the day of trouble: I will deliver thee' (Ps. 50:15). What says the Apostle James? Is any afflicted? '[L]et him pray' (Jas. 5:13). Prayer is the receipt which Jacob used, when he feared his brother Esau; prayer is the receipt which Job used when property and children were suddenly taken from him; prayer is the receipt which Hezekiah used when Sennacherib's threatening letter arrived; and prayer is the receipt which the Son of God Himself was not ashamed to use in the days of His flesh. In the hour of His mysterious agony He 'prayed'.

Let us take care that we use our Master's remedy, if we want comfort in affliction. Whatever other means of relief we use, let us pray. The first Friend we should turn to ought to be God; the first message we should send ought to be to the throne of grace. No depression of spirits must prevent us; no crushing weight of sorrow must make us dumb. It is a prime device of Satan to supply the afflicted man with false reasons for keeping silence before God. Let us beware of the temptation to brood sullenly over our wounds. If we can say nothing else, we can say, 'I am oppressed; undertake for me' (Isa. 38:14).

Like Jesus, he should tell his desires openly to his heavenly Father, and spread his wishes unreservedly before Him; but like Jesus, he should do it all with an entire submission of will to the will of God. He should never forget that there may be wise and good reasons for his affliction.

July 26

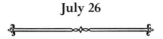

Then said Jesus, Father, forgive them; for they know not what they do.
And they parted his raiment, and cast lots.
Luke 23:34

Our Lord's words of gracious intercession.
We read that when He was crucified, His first words were, 'Father, forgive them; for they know not what they do.' His own racking agony of body did not make Him forget others: the first of His seven sayings on the cross was a prayer for the souls of His murderers. His prophetical office He had just exhibited by a remarkable prediction; His kingly office He was about to exhibit soon by opening the door of paradise to the penitent thief; His priestly office He now exhibited by interceding for those who crucified Him: 'Father,' He said, 'forgive them'.

The fruits of this wonderful prayer will never be fully seen until the day when the books are opened, and the secrets of all hearts are revealed. We have probably not the least idea how many of the conversions to God at Jerusalem which took place during the first six months after the crucifixion, were the direct reply to this marvellous prayer. Perhaps this prayer was the first step towards the penitent thief's repentance; perhaps it was one means of affecting the centurion, who declared our Lord 'a righteous man'; perhaps the three thousand converted on the day of Pentecost, foremost, it may be at one time among our Lord's murderers, owed their conversion to this very prayer. The day will declare it: there is nothing secret that shall not be revealed. This only we know, that the Father heareth the Son always (John 11:42). We may be sure that this wondrous prayer was heard.

Let us see in our Lord's intercession for those who crucified Him, one more proof of Christ's infinite love to sinners. The Lord Jesus is indeed most pitiful, most compassionate, most gracious. None are too wicked for Him to care for: none are too far gone in sin for His almighty heart to take interest in their souls.

July 27

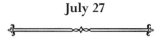

Therefore his sisters sent unto him, saying,
Lord, behold, he whom thou lovest is sick.
John 11:3

Jesus Christ is the Christian's best Friend in the time of need.

We read that when Lazarus was sick, his sisters at once sent to Jesus, and laid the matter before Him. Beautiful, touching, and simple was the message they sent. They did not ask Him to come at once, or to work a miracle, and command the disease to depart. They only said, 'Lord, behold, he whom thou lovest is sick', and left the matter there, in the full belief that He would do what was best. Here was the true faith and humility of saints! Here was gracious submission of will!

The servants of Christ, in every age and climate, will do well to follow this excellent example. No doubt when those whom we love are sick, we are to use diligently every reasonable means for their recovery. We must spare no pains to obtain the best medical advice. We must assist nature in every possible manner to fight a good fight against its enemy. But in all our doing, we must never forget that the best and ablest and wisest Helper is in heaven, at God's right hand. Like afflicted Job, our first action must be to fall on our knees and worship. Like Hezekiah, we must spread our matters before the Lord. Like the holy sisters at Bethany, we must send up a prayer to Christ. Let us not forget, in the hurry and excitement of our feelings, that none can help like Him, and that He is merciful, loving and gracious.

Let us turn from the passage with a settled determination to trust Christ entirely with all the concerns of this world, both public and private. Let us believe that He by whom all things were made at first is He who is managing all with perfect wisdom. The affairs of kingdoms, families and private individuals, are all alike overruled by Him. He chooses all the portions of His people. When we are sick, it is because He knows it to be for our good: when He delays coming to help us, it is for some wise reason.

July 28

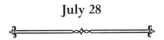

Then they took away the stone from the place where the dead was laid.
And Jesus lifted up his eyes, and said,
Father, I thank thee that thou hast heard me.
John 11:41

The words which our Lord addressed to God the Father, when the stone was taken from the grave.

We read that he said, 'Father, I thank thee that thou hast heard me. And I knew that thou hearest me always: but because of the people which stand by I said it, that they may believe that thou hast sent me'. This wonderful language is totally unlike anything said by prophets or apostles, when they worked miracles. In fact, it is not prayer, but praise. It evidently implies a constant mysterious communion going on between Jesus and His Father in heaven, which it is past the power of man either to explain or conceive. We need not doubt that here, as elsewhere in St John, our Lord meant to teach the Jews the entire and complete unity there was between Him and His Father, in all that He did, as well as in all that He taught. Once more He would remind them that He did not come among them as a mere Prophet, but as the Messiah, who was sent by the Father. Once more He would have them know that as the words which He spake were the very words which the Father gave Him to speak, so the works which He wrought were the very works which the Father gave Him to do. In short, He was the promised Messiah, whom the Father always hears, because He and the Father are One.

Deep and high as this truth is, it is for the peace of our souls to believe it thoroughly, and to grasp it tightly. Let it be a settled principle of our religion that the Saviour in whom we trust is nothing less than eternal God, One whom the Father hears always, One who in very deed is God's Fellow. A clear view of the dignity of our Mediator's Person, is one secret of inward comfort. Happy is he who can say, 'I know whom I have believed, and am persuaded that he is able to keep that which I have committed unto him' (2 Tim. 1:12).

July 29

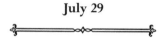

Hitherto have ye asked nothing in my name: ask, and ye shall receive, that your joy may be full.
John 16:24

While Christ is absent believers must ask much in prayer.

It is written, 'Hitherto have ye asked nothing in my name: ask, and ye shall receive, that your joy may be full.'

We may well believe that up to this time the disciples had never realized their Master's full dignity. They had certainly never understood that He was the one Mediator between God and man, in whose name and for whose sake they were to put up their prayers. Here they are distinctly told that henceforward they are to 'ask in His name'. Nor can we doubt that our Lord would have all His people, in every age, understand that the secret of comfort during His absence is to be instant in prayer. He would have us know that if we cannot see Him with our bodily eyes any longer, we can talk with Him, and through Him have special access to God. '[A]sk, and ye shall receive', He proclaims to all His people in every age; 'and your joy shall be full.'

Let the lesson sink down deeply into our hearts. Of all the list of Christian duties there is none to which there is such abounding encouragement as prayer. It is a duty which concerns all. High and low, rich and poor, learned and unlearned – all must pray. It is a duty for which all are accountable. All cannot read, or hear, or sing; but all who have the Spirit of adoption can pray. Above all, it is a duty in which everything depends on the heart and motive within. Our words may be feeble and ill-chosen, and our language broken and ungrammatical, and unworthy to be written down. But if the heart be right, it matters not. He that sits in heaven can spell out the meaning of every petition sent up in the name of Jesus, and can make him that asks know and feel that he receives.

'If we know these things, happy are we if we do them.' Let prayer in the name of Jesus be a daily habit with us every morning and evening of our lives.

July 30

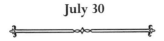

I pray for them: I pray not for the world, but for them which thou hast given me; for they are thine.
John 17:9

The Lord Jesus does things for His believing people which He does not do for the wicked and unbelieving. He helps their souls by special intercession. He says, 'I pray for them: I pray not for the world, but for them which thou hast given me'.

The doctrine before us is one which is specially hated by the world. Nothing gives such offence, and stirs up such bitter feeling among the wicked, as the idea of God making any distinction between man and man, and loving one person more than another. Yet the world's objections to the doctrine are, as usual, weak and unreasonable. Surely a little reflection might show us that a God who regarded good and bad, holy and unholy, righteous and unrighteous, with equal complacency and favour, would be a very strange kind of God! The special intercession of Christ for His saints is agreeable to reason and to common sense.

Of course, like every other gospel truth, the doctrine before us needs careful statement and scriptural guarding. On the one hand, we must not narrow the love of Christ to sinners, and on the other we must not make it too broad. It is true that Christ loves all sinners, and invites all to be saved; but it is also true that He specially loves the 'blessed company of all faithful people', whom He sanctifies and glorifies. It is true that He has wrought out a redemption sufficient for all mankind, and offers it freely to all; but it is also true that His redemption is effectual only to them that believe. Just so it is true that He is the Mediator between God and man; but it is also true that He intercedes actively for none but those that come unto God by Him. Hence it is written, 'I pray for them: I pray not for the world'.

The special intercession of the Lord Jesus is one grand secret of the believer's safety. He is daily watched, and thought for, and provided for with unfailing care, by One whose eye never slumbers and never sleeps. Jesus is able 'to save them to the uttermost that come unto God by him, seeing he ever liveth to make intercession for them' (Heb. 7:25).

July 31

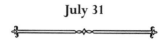

Sanctify them through thy truth: thy word is truth.
John 17:17

How Jesus prays that His people may be sanctified.
'Sanctify them', He says, 'through thy truth: thy word is truth.'
We need not doubt that, in this place at any rate, the word 'sanctify' means 'make holy'. It is a prayer that the Father would make His people more holy, more spiritual, more pure, more saintly in thought and word and deed, in life and character. Grace had done something for the disciples already – called, converted, renewed and changed them. The great Head of the Church prays that the work of grace may be carried higher and further, and that His people may be more thoroughly sanctified and made holy in body, soul and spirit – in fact more like Himself.

Surely we need not say much to show the matchless wisdom of this prayer. More holiness is the very thing to be desired for all servants of Christ. Holy living is the great proof of the reality of Christianity. Men may refuse to see the truth of our arguments, but they cannot evade the evidence of a godly life. Such a life adorns religion and makes it beautiful, and sometimes wins those who are not won by the Word (1 Pet. 3:1). Holy living trains Christians for heaven. The nearer we live to God while we live, the more ready shall we be to dwell for ever in His presence when we die. Our entrance into heaven will be entirely by grace, and not of works; but heaven itself would be no heaven to us if we entered it with an unsanctified character. Our hearts must be in tune for heaven if we are to enjoy it. There must be a moral meetness for 'the inheritance of the saints in light', as well as a title (Col. 1:12). Christ's blood alone can give us a title to enter the inheritance. Sanctification must give us a capacity to enjoy it.

Who, in the face of such facts as these, need wonder that increased sanctification should be the first thing that Jesus asks for His people? Who that is really taught of God can fail to know that holiness is happiness, and that those who walk with God most closely, are always those who walk with Him most comfortably?

AUGUST

August 1

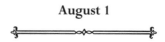

*Father, I will that they also, whom thou hast given me, be with me
where I am; that they may behold my glory, which thou hast given me:
for thou lovedst me before the foundation of the world.*
John 17:24

How Jesus prays that His people may at last be with him and behold His glory.

'I will', He says, that those 'whom thou hast given me, be with me where I am: that they may behold my glory.'

This is a singularly beautiful and touching conclusion to our Lord's remarkable prayer. We may well believe that it was meant to cheer and comfort those who heard it, and to strengthen them for the parting scene which was fast drawing near. But for all who read it even now, this part of His prayer is full of sweet and unspeakable comfort.

We do not see Christ now. We read of Him, hear of Him, believe in Him and rest our souls in His finished work. But even the best of us, at our best, walk by faith and not by sight, and our poor halting faith often makes us walk very feebly in the way to heaven. There shall be an end of all this state of things one day. We shall at length see Christ as He is, and know as we have been known. We shall behold Him face to face, and not through a glass darkly. We shall actually be in His presence and company, and go out no more. If faith has been pleasant, much more will certainty be. No wonder that when St Paul has written, we shall 'ever be with the Lord', he adds, 'comfort one another with these words' (1 Thess. 4:17, 18).

We know little of heaven now. Our thoughts are all confounded, when we try to form an idea of a future state in which pardoned sinners shall by perfectly happy. '[I]t doth not yet appear what we shall be' (1 John 3:2). But we may rest ourselves on the blessed thought, that after death we shall be 'with Christ'. Whether before the resurrection in paradise, or after the resurrection in final glory, the prospect is still the same. True Christians shall be 'with Christ'. We need no more information.

August 2

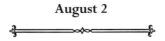

I came not to call the righteous, but sinners to repentance.
Luke 5:32

O ne of the chief objects of Christ's coming into the world.
We have it in the well-known words, 'I came not to call the righteous, but sinners to repentance.'

This is that great lesson of the gospel which, in one form or another, we find continually taught in the New Testament. It is one which we can never have too strongly impressed upon our minds. Such is our natural ignorance and self-righteousness in religion, that we are constantly losing sight of it. We need to be frequently reminded, that Jesus did not come merely as a teacher, but as the Saviour of that which was utterly lost, and that those only can receive benefit from Him who will confess that they are ruined, bankrupt, hopeless, miserable sinners.

Let us use this mighty truth, if we never used it before. Are we sensible of our own wickedness and sinfulness? Do we feel that we are unworthy of anything but wrath and condemnation? Then let us understand that we are the very persons for whose sake Jesus came into the world. If we feel ourselves righteous, Christ has nothing to say to us. But if we feel ourselves sinners, Christ calls us to repentance. Let not the call be made in vain.

Let us go on using this mighty truth, if we have used it in time past. Do we find our own hearts weak and deceitful? Do we often feel that 'when I would do good, evil is present with me'? (Rom. 7:21). It may be all true, but it must not prevent our resting on Christ. He came into the world to save sinners, and if we feel ourselves such, we have warrant for applying to, and trusting in Him to our life's end. One thing only let us never forget: Christ came to call us to repentance, and not to sanction our continuing in sin.

August 3

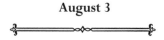

I tell you, Nay: but, except ye repent, ye shall all likewise perish.
Luke 13:3

How strongly our Lord lays down the universal necessity of repentance.

Twice He declares emphatically, 'except ye repent, ye shall all likewise perish'.

The truth here asserted is one of the foundations of Christianity. All of us are born in sin. We are fond of sin, and are naturally unfit for friendship with God. Two things are absolutely necessary to the salvation of every one of us: we must repent, and we must believe the gospel. Without repentance towards God, and faith towards our Lord Jesus Christ, no man can be saved.

The nature of true repentance is clearly and unmistakably laid down in holy Scripture. It begins with knowledge of sin. It goes on to work sorrow for sin. It leads to confession of sin before God. It shows itself before man by a thorough breaking off from sin. It results in producing a habit of deep hatred for all sin. Above all, it is inseparably connected with lively faith in the Lord Jesus Christ. Repentance like this is the characteristic of all true Christians.

The necessity of repentance to salvation will be evident to all who search the Scriptures, and consider the nature of the subject. Without it there is no forgiveness of sins. There never was a pardoned man who was not also a penitent. There never was one washed in the blood of Christ who did not feel, and mourn, and confess, and hate his own sins. Without it there can be no meetness for heaven. We could not be happy if we reached the kingdom of glory with a heart loving sin. The company of saints and angels would give us no pleasure. Our minds would not be in tune for an eternity of holiness. Let these things sink down into our hearts. We must repent as well as believe, if we hope to be saved.

August 4

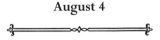

*Likewise, I say unto you, there is joy in the presence of the angels of
God over one sinner that repenteth.*
Luke 15:10

The wide encouragement which our Lord holds out to
repentance.

We read these striking words: 'joy shall be in heaven over one
sinner that repenteth'. We read the same thought again after a few verses:
'there is joy in the presence of the angels of God over one sinner that
repenteth'. The thing is doubled, to make doubt impossible. The idea is
repeated, in order to meet man's unbelief.

There are deep things in these sayings, beyond doubt. Our poor
weak minds are little able to understand how the perfect joy of heaven
can admit the increase. But one thing, at any rate, stands out clearly on
the face of these expressions – there is an infinite willingness on God's
part to receive sinners. However wicked a man may have been, in the
day that he really turns from his wickedness and comes to God by Christ,
God is well pleased. God has no pleasure in the death of him that dieth,
and God has pleasure in true repentance.

Let the man who is afraid to repent consider well the verses we are
now looking at, and be afraid no more. There is nothing on God's part
to justify his fears. An open door is set before him: a free pardon awaits
him. 'If we confess our sins, he is faithful and just to forgive us our sins,
and to cleanse us from all unrighteousness' (1 John 1:9).

Let the man who is ashamed to repent consider these verses and
cast shame aside. What though the world mocks and jests at his
repentance? While man is mocking, angels are rejoicing. The very change
which sinners call foolishness is a change which fills heaven with joy.

Have we repented ourselves? This, after all, is the principal question
which concerns us. What shall it profit us to know Christ's love if we do
not use it? 'If ye know these things, happy are ye if ye do them' (John
13:17).

August 5

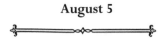

I will arise and go to my father, and will say unto him,
Father, I have sinned against heaven, and before thee ...
Luke 15:18

Man awaking to a sense of his natural state, and resolving to repent.

Our Lord tells us that the younger son 'came to himself, he said, How many hired servants of my father's have bread enough and to spare, and I perish with hunger! I will arise and go to my father, and will say unto him, Father, I have sinned'.

The thoughts of thousands are vividly painted in these words. Thousands have reasoned in this way, and are saying such things to themselves every day. And we must be thankful when we see such thoughts arise. Thinking is not change of heart, but it may be the beginning of it: conviction is not conversion, but it is one step, at any rate, in a right direction. The ruin of many people's souls is simply this — that they never think at all.

One caution, however, must always be given: men must beware that they do not stop short in 'thinking'. Good thoughts are all very well, but they are not saving Christianity. If the younger son had never got beyond thinking, he might have kept from home to the day of his death.

The man in whose heart a true work of the Holy Ghost has begun will never be content with thinking and resolving. He will break off from sin: he will come out from its fellowship. He will cease to do evil: he will learn to do well. He will turn to God in humble prayer. He will confess his iniquities: he will not attempt to excuse his sins. He will say with David, 'I acknowledge my transgressions'. He will say with the publican, 'God be merciful to me a sinner' (Ps. 51:3; Luke 18:13).

Let us beware of any repentance, falsely so-called, which is not of this character. Action is the very life of 'repentance unto salvation'. Feelings, and tears, and remorse, and wishes, and resolutions, are all useless, until they are accompanied by action and a change of life.

August 6

*And the Lord turned, and looked upon Peter. And Peter remembered the
word of the Lord, how he had said unto him,
Before the cock crow, thou shalt deny me thrice.*
Luke 22:61

How bitter sin is to believers, when they have fallen
into it and discovered their fall.

This is a lesson which stands out plainly on the face of the
verses before us. We are told that when Peter remembered the warning
he had received, and saw how far he had fallen, he 'went out and wept
bitterly'. He found out by experience the truth of Jeremiah's words: 'it
is an evil thing and bitter, that thou hast forsaken the LORD' (Jer. 2:19).
He felt keenly the truth of Solomon's saying: 'The backslider in heart
shall be filled with his own ways' (Prov. 14:14). No doubt he could
have said with Job, 'I abhor myself, and repent in dust and ashes' (Job
42:6).

Sorrow like this, let us always remember, is an inseparable companion
of true repentance. Here lies the grand distinction between 'repentance
unto salvation', and unavailing remorse. Remorse can make a man
miserable, like Judas Iscariot, but it can do no more: it does not lead
him to God. Repentance makes a man's heart soft and his conscience
tender, and shows itself in real turning to a Father in heaven. The falls of
a graceless professor are falls from which there is no rising again; but
the fall of a true saint always ends in deep contrition, self-abasement
and amendment of life.

Let us take heed, ere we leave this passage, that we always make a
right use of Peter's fall. Let us never make it an excuse for sin: let us
learn from his sad experience, to watch and pray, lest we fall into
temptation. If we do fall, let us believe that there is hope for us as there
was for him. But above all, let us remember, that if we fall as Peter fell,
we must repent as Peter repented, or else we shall never be saved.

August 7

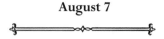

And he said unto Jesus,
Lord, remember me when thou comest into thy kingdom.
Luke 23:42

The unvarying character of repentance unto salvation. This is a point in the penitent thief's story which is fearfully overlooked. Thousands look at the broad fact that he was saved in the hour of death, and look no further; they do not look at the distinct and well-defined evidences of repentance which fell from his lips before he died. Those evidences deserve our closest attention.

The first notable step in the thief's repentance was his concern about his companion's wickedness in reviling Christ: 'Dost not thou fear God', he said, 'seeing thou art in the same condemnation?' The second step was a full acknowledgment of his own sin: 'we indeed are justly in condemnation; we receive the due reward of our deeds'. The third step was an open confession of Christ's innocence: 'this man hath done nothing amiss'. The fourth step was faith in Jesus Christ's power and will to save him: he returned to a crucified sufferer, and called Him 'Lord', and declared his belief that He had a kingdom. The fifth step was prayer: he cried to Jesus when he was hanging on the cross, and asked Him even then to think upon his soul. The sixth and last step was humility: he begged to be 'remembered' by our Lord. He mentions no great thing: enough for him if he is remembered by Christ. These six points should always be remembered in connection with the penitent thief. His time was very short for giving proof of his conversion; but it was time well used. Few dying people have ever left behind them such good evidences as were left by this man.

Let us beware of a repentance without evidences. Thousands, it may be feared, are every year going out of the world with a lie in their right hand. They fancy they will be saved because the thief was saved in the hour of death; they forget that if they would be saved as he was, they must repent as he repented. The shorter a man's time is, the better must be the use he makes of it; the nearer he is to death, when he first begins to think, the clearer must be the evidence he leaves behind.

August 8

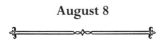

And, behold, there was a great earthquake: for the angel of the Lord descended from heaven, and came and rolled back the stone from the door, and sat upon it.
Matthew 28:2

The glory and majesty with which Christ rose from the dead.

We are told that 'there was a great earthquake'. We are told that 'the angel of the Lord descended from heaven, and came and rolled back the stone from the door [of the sepulchre], and sat upon it'. We need not suppose that our blessed Lord needed the help of any angel, when He came forth from the grave; we need not for a moment doubt that He rose again by His own power: but it pleased God, that His resurrection should be accompanied and followed by signs and wonders. It seemed good that the earth should shake, and a glorious angel appear, when the Son of God arose from the dead as a conqueror.

Let us not fail to see in the manner of our Lord's resurrection, a type and pledge of the resurrection of His believing people. The grave could not hold Him beyond the appointed time, and it shall not be able to hold them; a glorious angel was a witness of His rising, and glorious angels shall be the messengers who shall gather believers when they rise again: He rose with a renewed body, and yet a body, real, true and material, and so also shall His people have a glorious body, and be like their Head. When we see Him 'we shall be like him' (1 John 3:2).

Let us take comfort in this thought. Trial, sorrow and persecution are often the portion of God's people; sickness, weakness and pain often hurt and wear their poor earthly tabernacle: but their good time is yet to come. Let them wait patiently, and they shall have a glorious resurrection. When we die, and where we are buried, and what kind of a funeral we have, matters little: the great question to be asked is this, 'How shall we rise again?'

August 9

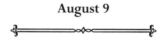

Now when Jesus was risen early the first day of the week, he appeared first to Mary Magdalene, out of whom he had cast seven devils.
Mark 16:9

What abundant proof we have that our Lord Jesus Christ really rose again from the dead.

In this one passage St Mark records no less than three distinct occasions on which He was seen after His resurrection. First, he tells us, our Lord appeared to one witness – Mary Magdalene; then to two witnesses – two disciples walking into the country; and, lastly, to eleven witnesses – the eleven apostles all assembled together. Let us remember, in addition to this, that other appearances of our Lord are described by other writers in the New Testament, beside those mentioned by St Mark. And then let us not hesitate to believe, that of all the facts of our Lord's history, there is none more thoroughly established than the fact that He rose from the dead.

There is great mercy in this. The resurrection of Christ is one of the foundation-stones of Christianity. It was the seal of the great work that He came on earth to do. It was the crowning proof that the ransom He paid for sinners was accepted, the atonement for sin accomplished, the head of him who had the power of death bruised, and the victory won. It is well to remark how often the resurrection of Christ is referred to by the apostles. He 'was delivered for our offences,' says Paul, 'and was raised again for our justification' (Rom. 4:25). He 'hath begotten us again unto a lively hope', says Peter, 'by the resurrection of Jesus Christ from the dead' (1 Pet. 1:3).

We ought to thank God that the fact of the resurrection is so clearly established. The Jew, the Gentile, the priests, the Roman guard, the women who went to the tomb, the disciples who were so backward to believe, are all witnesses whose testimony cannot be gainsaid. Christ has not only died for us, but has also risen again. To deny it shows far greater credulity than to believe it. To deny it a man must put credit in monstrous and ridiculous improbabilities. To believe it a man has only to appeal to simple undeniable facts.

August 10

_The men of Nineveh shall rise up in the judgment with this
generation, and shall condemn it: for they repented at the preaching of
Jonas; and, behold, a greater than Jonas is here._
Luke 11:32

How our Lord Jesus Christ testifies to the truth of a
resurrection and a life to come.

He speaks of the Queen of the South, whose name and
dwelling-place are now alike unknown to us. He says she 'shall rise up
in the judgment'. He speaks of the men of Nineveh, a people who have
passed away from the face of the earth. He says of them also, they 'shall
rise up'.

There is something very solemn and instructive in the language which
our Lord here uses. It reminds us that this world is not all, and that the
life which a man lives in the body on earth is not the only life of which
we ought to think. The Kings and Queens of olden time are all to live
again one day, and to stand before the bar of God. The vast multitudes
who once swarmed round palaces of Nineveh are all to come forth
from their graves, and to give an account of their works. To our eyes
they seem to have passed away for ever. We read with wonder of their
empty halls, and talk of them as a people who have completely perished.
Their dwelling-places are a desolation: their very bones are dust. But to
the eye of God they all live still. The Queen of the South and the men of
Nineveh will all rise again. We shall yet see them face to face.

Let the truth of the resurrection be often before our minds. Let the
life to come be frequently before our thoughts. All is not over when the
grave receives its tenant, and man goes to his long home. Other people
may dwell in our houses, and spend our money. Our very names may
soon be forgotten. But still all is not over! Yet a little time and we all
shall live again. '[T]he earth shall cast out the dead' (Isa. 26:19). Many,
like Felix, may well tremble when they think of such things. But men
who live by faith in the Son of God, like St Paul, should lift up their
heads and rejoice.

August 11

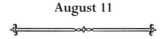

And thou shalt be blessed; for they cannot recompense thee:
for thou shalt be recompensed at the resurrection of the just.
Luke 14:14

The great importance of looking forward to the resurrection of the dead.

This lesson stands out in a striking manner in the language used by our Lord on the subject of showing charity to the poor. He says to the Pharisee who entertained Him, the poor 'cannot recompense thee: for thou shalt be recompensed at the resurrection of the just'.

There is a resurrection after death. Let this never be forgotten. The life that we live here in the flesh is not all: the visible world around us is not the only world with which we have to do; all is not over when the last breath is drawn, and men and women are carried to their long home in the grave. 'The trumpet shall' one day 'sound, and the dead shall be raised incorruptible.' 'All that are in the graves shall hear Christ's voice, and come forth; they that have done good, to the resurrection of life; and they that have done evil, to the resurrection of damnation.' This is one of the great foundation truths of the Christian religion. Let us cling to it firmly, and never let it go.

Let us strive to live like men who believe in a resurrection and a life to come, and desire to be always ready for another world. So living, we shall look forward to death with calmness: we shall feel that there remains some better portion for us beyond the grave. So living, we shall take patiently all that we have to bear in this world: trials, losses, disappointments, ingratitude, will affect us little. We shall not look for our reward here: we shall feel that all will be rectified one day, and that the Judge of all the earth will do right (Gen. 18:25).

But how can we bear the thought of the resurrection? What shall enable us to look forward to a world to come without alarm? Nothing can do it, but faith in Christ. Believing on Him we have nothing to fear: our sins will not appear against us; the demands of God's law will be found completely satisfied. We shall stand firm in the great day, and none shall lay anything to our charge (Rom. 8:33).

August 12

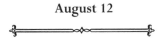

Now upon the first day of the week, very early in the morning, they
came unto the sepulchre, bringing the spices which they had prepared,
and certain others with them.
Luke 24:1

The reality of Christ's resurrection.

We read, that 'upon the first day of the week', certain women came to the sepulchre in which the body of Jesus had been laid, in order to anoint Him. But when they came to the place, 'they found the stone rolled away ... And they entered in, and found not the body of the Lord Jesus.'

This simple fact is the starting point in the history of the resurrection of Christ. On Friday morning His body was safe in the tomb: on Sunday morning His body was gone: by whose hands had it been taken away? Who had removed it? Not surely the priests and scribes and other enemies of Christ! If they had Christ's body to show in disproof of His resurrection, they would gladly have shown it. Not the apostles and other disciples of our Lord! They were far too much frightened and dispirited to attempt such an action, and the more so when they had nothing to gain by it. One explanation, and one only, can meet the circumstance of the case. That explanation is the one supplied by the angels in the verse before us: Christ 'had risen' from the grave. To seek Him in the sepulchre was seeking 'the living among the dead'. He had risen again, and was soon seen alive and conversing in the body by many credible witnesses.

Let us cling firmly to the resurrection of Christ, as one of the pillars of the gospel. It ought to produce in our minds a settled conviction of the truth of Christianity: our faith does not depend merely on a set of texts and doctrines; it is founded on a mighty fact which the sceptic has never been able to overturn. It ought to assure us of the certainty of the resurrection of our bodies after death. If our Master has risen from the grave, we need not doubt that His disciples shall rise again at the last day. Above all, it ought to fill our hearts with a joyful sense of the fullness of gospel salvation.

August 13

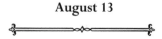

And their words seemed to them as idle tales, and they believed them not.
Luke 24:11

How slow of belief the first disciples were on the subject of Christ's resurrection.

We read that when the women returned from the sepulchre and told the things they had heard from the angels to the eleven apostles, 'their words seemed to them as idle tales, and they believed them not'. In spite of the plainest declarations from their Master's own lips that He would rise again the third day – in spite of the distinct testimony of five or six credible witnesses that the sepulchre was empty, and that angels had told them He was risen – in spite of the manifest impossibility of accounting for the empty tomb on any other supposition than that of a miraculous resurrection – in spite of all this, these eleven faithless ones would not believe!

Perhaps we marvel at their unbelief. No doubt it seems at first sight most senseless, most unreasonable, most provoking, most unaccountable. But shall we not do well to look at home? Do we not see around us, in the Christian Churches, a mass of unbelief far more unreasonable and far more blameworthy than that of the apostles? Do we not see, after eighteen centuries of additional proofs that Christ has risen from the dead, a general want of faith, which is truly deplorable? Do we not see myriads of professing Christians who seem not to believe that Jesus died and rose again, and is coming to judge the world? These are painful questions. Strong faith is indeed a rare thing: no wonder that our Lord said, 'when the Son of man cometh, shall he find faith on the earth?' (Luke 18:8).

The unbelief of the apostles is one of the strongest indirect evidences that Jesus rose from the dead. If the disciples were at first so backward to believe our Lord's resurrection, and were at last so thoroughly persuaded of its truth that they preached it everywhere, Christ must have risen indeed.

August 14

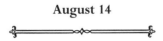

Verily, verily, I say unto you, The hour is coming, and now is, when the dead
shall hear the voice of the Son of God: and they that hear shall live.
John 5:25

A most solemn prophecy of the final resurrection of all the dead.

Our Lord tells us that 'the hour is coming, in the which all that are in the graves shall hear his voice, And shall come forth; they that have done good, unto the resurrection of life; and they that have done evil, unto the resurrection of damnation'.

The passage is one of those that ought to sink down very deeply into our hearts, and never be forgotten. All is not over when men die. Whether they like it or not, they will have to come forth from their graves at the last day, and to stand at Christ's bar. None can escape His summons. When His voice calls them before Him, all must obey. When men rise again, they will not all rise in the same condition. There will be two classes – two parties – two bodies. Not all will go to heaven. Not all will be saved. Some will rise again to inherit eternal life, but some will rise again only to be condemned. These are terrible things! But the words of Christ are plain and unmistakable. Thus it is written, and thus it must be.

Let us make sure that we hear Christ's quickening voice now, and are numbered among His true disciples. Let us know the privileges of true believers, while we have life and health. Then, when His voice shakes heaven and earth, and is calling the dead from their graves, we shall feel confidence, and not be 'ashamed before him at his coming' (1 John 2:28).

August 15

At that time Jesus went on the sabbath day through the corn;
and his disciples were an hungred,
and began to pluck the ears of corn and to eat.
Matthew 12:1

O**ur Lord Jesus Christ does not do away with the observance of a weekly Sabbath day.**
He neither does so here nor elsewhere in the four Gospels. We often find His opinion expressed about Jewish errors on the subject of the Sabbath; but we do not find a word to teach us that His disciples were not to keep the Sabbath at all.

It is of much importance to observe this. The mistakes that have arisen from a superficial consideration of our Lord's sayings on the Sabbath question, are neither few nor small; thousands have rushed to the hasty conclusion that Christians have nothing to do with the fourth commandment, and that it is no more binding on us than the Mosaic law about sacrifices: there is nothing in the New Testament to justify any such conclusion.

The plain truth is that our Lord did not abolish the law of the weekly Sabbath: He only freed it from incorrect interpretations, and purified it from man-made additions. He did not tear out of the decalogue the fourth commandment: He only stripped off the miserable traditions with which the Pharisees had incrusted the day, and by which they had made it, not a blessing, but a burden. He left the fourth commandment where He found it – a part of the eternal law of God, of which no jot or tittle was ever to pass away. May we never forget this!

Saving Christianity is closely bound up with Sabbath observance. May we never forget that our great aim should be to 'keep the Sabbath holy!' Works of necessity may be done: 'it is lawful to do well', and show mercy; but to give the Sabbath to idleness, pleasure-seeking or the world, is utterly unlawful. It is contrary to the example of Christ, and a sin against a plain commandment of God.

August 16

And he said unto them, The sabbath was made for man,
and not man for the sabbath ...
Mark 2:27

The true principle by which all questions about the observance of the Sabbath ought to be decided.

'The Sabbath', says our Lord, 'was made for man, and not man for the Sabbath ...'

There is a mine of deep wisdom in those words. They deserve close attention, and the more so because they are not recorded in any Gospel but that of St Mark. Let us see what they contain.

'The Sabbath was made for man ...' God made it for Adam in paradise, and renewed it to Israel on Mount Sinai. It was made for all mankind: not for the Jew only, but for the whole family of Adam. It was made for man's benefit and happiness. It was for the good of his body, the good of his mind and the good of his soul. It was given to him as a boon and a blessing, and not as a burden. This was the original institution.

But 'man was not made for the Sabbath'. The observance of the day of God was never meant to be so enforced as to be an injury to his health, or to interfere with his necessary wants. The original command to 'keep holy the Sabbath Day', was not intended to be so interpreted as to do harm to his body, or prevent acts of mercy to his fellow-creatures. This was the point that the Pharisees had forgotten, or buried under their traditions. There is nothing in all this to warrant the rash assertion of some, that our Lord has done away with the fourth commandment. On the contrary, He manifestly speaks of the Sabbath day as a privilege and a gift, and only regulates the extent to which its observance should be enforced. He shows that works of necessity and mercy may be done on the Sabbath day; but He says not a word to justify the notion that Christians need not 'remember the day to keep it holy'.

Let us be jealous over our own conduct in the matter of observing the Sabbath. Let us contend earnestly for its preservation among us all in its integrity. We may rest assured that national prosperity and personal growth in grace are intimately bound up in the maintenance of a holy Sabbath.

August 17

And they returned, and prepared spices and ointments;
and rested the sabbath day according to the commandment.
Luke 23:56

The respect paid by Christ's disciples to the fourth
commandment.

We are told that the women who had prepared spices and
ointment to anoint our Lord's body, 'rested the sabbath day according
to the commandment'.

This little fact is a strong indirect argument in reply to those who
tell us that Christ abolished the fourth commandment. Neither here
nor elsewhere do we find anything to warrant any such conclusion. We
see our Lord frequently denouncing the man-made traditions of the
Jews about Sabbath observance: we see Him purifying the blessed day
from superstitious and unscriptural opinions; we see Him maintaining
firmly that works of necessity and works of mercy were not breaches
of the fourth commandment: but nowhere do we find Him teaching
that the Sabbath was not to be kept at all; and here, in the verse before
us, we find His disciples as scrupulous as any about the duty of keeping
holy a Sabbath day. Surely they could never have been taught by their
Master that the fourth commandment was not intended to be binding
on Christians.

Let us cling firmly to the old doctrine that the Sabbath is not a mere
Jewish institution, but a day which was meant for man from the
beginning, and which was intended to be honoured by Christians quite
as much as by Jews. Let us not doubt that the apostles were taught by
our Lord to change the day from the last day of the week to the first,
although mercifully checked from publicly proclaiming the change in
order to avoid giving offence to Israel. Above all, let us regard the Sabbath
as an institution of primary importance to man's soul, and contend
earnestly for its preservation amongst us in all its integrity. It is good
for body, mind and soul: it is good for the Nation which observes it,
and for the Church which gives it honour. It is but a few steps from 'no
Sabbath' to 'no God'.

August 18

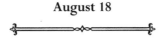

Again, the kingdom of heaven is like unto treasure hid in a field; the
which when a man hath found, he hideth, and for joy thereof goeth
and selleth all that he hath, and buyeth that field.
Matthew 13:44

Men really convinced of the importance of salvation will give up everything to win Christ and eternal life.

What was the conduct of the two men our Lord describes? The one was persuaded that there was a 'treasure hid in a field', which would amply repay him, if he bought the field, however great the price that he might give. The other was persuaded that the 'pearl' he had found was so immensely valuable, that it would answer to him to purchase it at any cost. Both were convinced that they had found a thing of great value: both were satisfied that it was worth a great present sacrifice to make this thing their own. Others might wonder at them; others might think them foolish for paying such a sum of money for the 'field' and 'pearl': but they knew what they were about. They were sure that they were making a good bargain.

We see, in this simple picture, the conduct of a true Christian explained. He is what he is, and does what he does in his religion, because he is thoroughly persuaded that it is worthwhile. He comes out from the world; he puts off the old man; he forsakes the vain companion of his past life. Like Matthew, he gives up everything, and, like Paul, he 'counts all things loss' for Christ's sake. And why? Because he is convinced that Christ will make amends to him for all he gives up. He sees in Christ an endless 'treasure'; he sees in Christ a precious 'pearl'; to win Christ he will make any sacrifice. This is true faith: this is the stamp of a genuine work of the Holy Ghost.

We see in these two parables the real clue to the conduct of many unconverted people. They are what they are in religion, because they are not fully persuaded that it is worthwhile to be different. They flinch from decision, they shrink from taking up the cross; they halt between two opinions; they will not commit themselves: they will not commit themselves: they have not faith.

August 19

And, behold, one came and said unto him,
Good Master, what good thing shall I do, that I may have eternal life?
Matthew 19:16

A person may have desires after salvation, and yet not be saved.

Here is one who in a day of abounding unbelief comes of his own accord to Christ. He comes not to have a sickness healed; he comes not to plead about a child: he comes about his own soul. He opens the conference with the frank question, 'Good Master, what good thing shall I do, that I may have eternal life?' Surely we might have thought, 'This is a promising case: this is no prejudiced ruler or Pharisee: this is a hopeful inquirer.' Yet by and by this very young man goes 'away sorrowful'; and we never read a word to show that he was converted! We must never forget that good feelings alone in religion are not the grace of God. We may know the truth intellectually; we may often feel pricked in conscience; we may have religious affections awakened within us, have many anxieties about our souls and shed many tears: but all this is not conversion. It is not the genuine saving work of the Holy Ghost.

Unhappily this is not all that must be said on this point. Not only are good feelings alone not grace, but they are even positively dangerous, if we content ourselves with them, and do not act as well as feel. It is a profound remark of that mighty master on moral questions, Bishop Butler, that passive impressions, often repeated, gradually lose all their power; actions, often repeated, produce a habit in man's mind; feelings often indulged in, without leading to corresponding actions, will finally exercise no influence at all.

Let us apply this lesson to our own state. Perhaps we know what it is to feel religious fears, wishes and desires. Let us beware that we do not rest in them. Let us never be satisfied till we have the witness of the Spirit in our hearts, that we are actually born again and new creatures; let us never rest till we know that we have really repented, and laid hold on the hope set before us in the gospel.

August 20

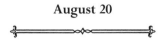

*And Levi made him a great feast in his own house: and there was a
great company of publicans and of others that sat down with them.*
Luke 5:29

C onversion is a cause of joy to a true believer.
We read, that when Levi was converted he made 'a great feast
in his own house'. A feast is made for laughter and merriment
(Eccles. 10:19). Levi regarded the change in himself as an occasion of
rejoicing, and wished others to rejoice with him.

We can easily imagine that Levi's conversion was a cause of grief to
his worldly friends. They saw him giving up a profitable calling, to follow
a new teacher from Nazareth! They doubtless regarded his conduct as a
grievous piece of folly, and an occasion for sorrow rather than joy. They
only looked at his temporal losses by becoming a Christian. Of his
spiritual gains they knew nothing. And there are many like them. There
are always thousands of people who, if they hear of a relation being
converted, consider it rather a misfortune. Instead of rejoicing, they
only shake their heads and mourn.

Let us, however, settle it in our minds that Levi did right to rejoice,
and if we are converted, let us rejoice likewise. Nothing can happen to
a man which ought to be such an occasion of joy, as his conversion. It is
a far more important event than being married, or coming of age, or
being made a nobleman, or receiving a great fortune. It is the birth of
an immortal soul! It is the rescue of a sinner from hell! It is a passage
from death to life! It is being made a king and priest for evermore! It is
being provided for, both in time and eternity! It is adoption into the
noblest and richest of all families, the family of God! Let us not heed
the opinion of the world in this matter. They speak evil of things which
they know not. Let us, with Levi, consider every fresh conversion as a
cause for great rejoicing. Never ought there to be such joy, gladness and
congratulation, as when our sons, or daughters, or brethren, or sisters,
or friends are born again and brought to Christ.

August 21

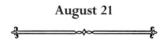

And Levi made him a great feast in his own house: and there was a
great company of publicans and of others that sat down with them.
Luke 5:29

Converted souls desire to promote the conversion of others.

We are told that when Levi was converted, and had made a feast on the occasion, he invited 'a great company of publicans' to share it. Most probably these men were his old friends and companions. He knew well what their souls needed, for he had been one of them. He desired to make them acquainted with that Saviour who had been merciful to himself. Having found mercy, he wanted them also to find it. Having been graciously delivered from the bondage of sin, he wished others also to be set free.

This feeling of Levi will always be the feeling of a true Christian. It may be safely asserted that there is no grace in the man who cares nothing about the salvation of his fellow men. The heart which is really taught by the Holy Ghost, will always be full of love, charity and compassion. The soul which has been truly called of God, will earnestly desire that others may experience the same calling. A converted man will not wish to go to heaven alone.

How is it with ourselves in this matter? Do we know anything of Levi's spirit after his conversion? Do we strive in every way to make our friends and relatives acquainted with Christ? Do we say to others, as Moses to Hobab, 'come thou with us, and we will do thee good'? (Num. 10:29)? Do we say, as the Samaritan woman, 'Come, see a man that told me all that ever I did'? Do we cry to our brethren, as Andrew did to Simon, 'We have found the Christ'? These are very serious questions. They supply a most searching test of the real condition of our souls. Let us not shrink from applying it. There is not enough of a missionary spirit amongst Christians. It should not satisfy us to be safe ourselves. We ought to also try to do good to others. All cannot go to the heathen, but every believer should strive to be a missionary to his fellow men. Having received mercy, we should not hold our peace.

August 22

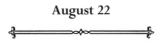

Then they went out to see what was done; and came to Jesus, and
found the man, out of whom the devils were departed, sitting at the
feet of Jesus, clothed, and in his right mind: and they were afraid.
Luke 8:35

The wonderful change which Christ can work in Satan's
slaves.

We are told that the Gadarenes found the man 'out of whom the devils were departed, sitting at the feet of Jesus, clothed, and in his right mind'. That sight must indeed have been strange and astonishing! The man's past history and condition, no doubt, were well-known. He had probably been a nuisance and a terror to all the neighbourhood. Yet here, in one moment, a complete change had come over him. Old things had passed away, and all things had become new. The power by which such a cure was wrought must indeed have been almighty. When Christ is the Physician nothing is impossible.

One thing, however, must never be forgotten. Striking and miraculous as this cure was, it is not really more wonderful than every case of decided conversion to God. Marvellous as the change was which appeared in this demoniac's condition when healed, it is not one whit more marvellous than the change which passes over everyone who is born again, and turned from the power of Satan to God. Never is a man in his right mind till he is converted, or in his right place till he sits by faith at the feet of Jesus, or rightly clothed till he has put on the Lord Jesus Christ. Have we ever considered what real conversion to God is? It is nothing else but the miraculous release of a captive, the miraculous restoration of a man to his right mind, the miraculous deliverance of a soul from the devil.

What are we ourselves? This, after all, is the grand question which concerns us. Are we bondsmen of Satan or servants of God? Has Christ made us free, or does the devil yet reign in our hearts? Do we sit at the feet of Jesus daily? Are we in our right minds? May the Lord help us to answer these questions aright!

August 23

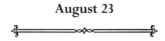

And, behold, a certain lawyer stood up, and tempted him, saying,
Master, what shall I do to inherit eternal life?
Luke 10:25

The solemn question which was addressed to our Lord Jesus Christ.

We are told that a certain lawyer asked Him, 'what shall I do to inherit eternal life?' The motive of this man was evidently not right. He only asked this question to 'tempt' our Lord, and to provoke Him to say something on which His enemies might lay hold. Yet the question he propounded was undoubtedly one of the deepest importance.

It is a question which deserves the principal attention of every man, woman, and child on earth. We are all sinners – dying sinners, and sinners going to be judged after death. 'How shall our sins be pardoned? Wherewith shall we come before God? How shall we escape the damnation of hell? Whither shall we flee from the wrath to come? What must we do to be saved?' These are inquiries which people of every rank ought to put to themselves, and never to rest till they find an answer.

It is a question which unhappily few care to consider. Thousands are constantly inquiring, 'What shall we eat? What shall we drink? Wherewithal shall we be clothed? How can we get money? How can we enjoy ourselves? How can we prosper in the world?' Few, very few, will ever give a moment's thought to the salvation of their souls. They hate the subject. It makes them uncomfortable. They turn from it and put it away. Faithful and true is that saying of our Lord's, 'wide is the gate, and broad is the way, that leadeth to destruction, and many there be which go in thereat' (Matt. 7:13).

Let us not be ashamed of putting the lawyer's question to our souls. Let us rather ponder it, think about it and never be content till it fills the first place in our minds. Let us seek to have the witness of the Spirit within us, that we repent us truly of sin, that we have a lively faith in God's mercy through Christ, and that we are really walking with God. This is the character of the heirs of eternal life. These are they who shall one day receive the kingdom prepared for the children of God.

August 24

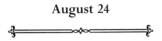

When thou goest with thine adversary to the magistrate, as thou art in the way, give diligence that thou mayest be delivered from him; lest he hale thee to the judge, and the judge deliver thee to the officer, and the officer cast thee into prison.
Luke 12:58

The immense importance of seeking reconciliation with God before it be too late.

This is a lesson which our Lord illustrates by a parable or comparison. He compares us to a man on his way to a magistrate with an adversary, in consequence of a difference of dispute, and describes the course which such a man ought to take. Like him, we are upon our way to the presence of a Judge: we shall all stand at the bar of God. Like him, we have an adversary: the holy law of God is against us, and contrary to us, and its demands must be satisfied. Like him, we ought to give diligence to get our case settled, before it comes before the Judge: we ought to seek pardon and forgiveness before we die. Like him, if we let our opportunity slip, the judgment will go against us, and we shall be cast into the prison of hell. Such appears to be the meaning of the parable in the passage before us. It is a vivid picture of the care which men ought to take in the great matter of reconciliation with God.

Peace with God is by far the first thing in religion. We are born in sin and children of wrath. We have no natural love towards God: the carnal mind is enmity against God. It is impossible that God can take pleasure in us: 'the wicked ... his soul hateth' (Ps. 11:5). The chief and foremost desire of everyone who professes to have any religion, should be to obtain reconciliation. Till this is done nothing is done: we have got nothing worth having in Christianity, until we have peace with God. The law brings us in guilty: the judgment is sure to go against us. Without reconciliation, the end of our life's journey will be hell.

August 25

There shall be weeping and gnashing of teeth,
when ye shall see Abraham, and Isaac, and Jacob, and all the prophets,
in the kingdom of God, and you yourselves thrust out.
Luke 13:28

A **remarkable question asked.**
We are told that a certain man said to our Lord, 'are there few that be saved?'

We do not know who this inquirer was. He may have been a self-righteous Jew, trained to believe that there was no hope for the uncircumcised, and no salvation for any but the children of Abraham. He may have been an idle trifler with religion, who was ever wasting his time on curious and speculative questions. In any case, we must all feel that he asked a question of deep and momentous importance.

He that desires to know the number of the saved, in the present dispensation, need only turn to the Bible, and his curiosity will be satisfied. He will read in the Sermon on the Mount these solemn words: 'strait is the gate, and narrow is the way, which leadeth unto life, and few there be that find it' (Matt. 7:14). He has only to look around him, and compare the ways of the many with the Word of God, and he will soon come to the conclusion, if he is an honest man, that the saved are few. It is an awful conclusion: our souls naturally turn away from it; but Scripture and facts alike combine to shut us up to it. Salvation to the uttermost is offered to men. All things are ready on God's part: Christ is willing to receive sinners; but sinners are not willing to come to Christ. And hence few are saved.

August 26

And he arose, and came to his father. But when he was yet a great way off, his father saw him, and had compassion, and ran, and fell on his neck, and kissed him.
Luke 15:20

The penitent man received readily, pardoned freely and completely accepted with God.

Our Lord shows us this, in this part of the younger son's history, in the most touching manner. We read that 'when he was yet a great way off, his father saw him, and had compassion, and ran, and fell on his neck, and kissed him. And the son said unto him, Father, I have sinned against heaven, and in thy sight, and am no more worthy to be called thy son. But the father said to his servants, Bring forth the best robe, and put it on him; and put a ring on his hand, and shoes on his feet: And bring hither the fatted calf, and kill it; and let us eat, and be merry: For this my son was dead, and is alive again; he was lost, and is found. And they began to be merry.'

More deeply affecting words than these, perhaps, were never written. To comment on them seems almost needless: it is like gilding refined gold, and painting the lily. They show us in great broad letters the infinite love of the Lord Jesus Christ towards sinners. They teach how infinitely willing He is to receive all who come to Him, and how complete, and full, and immediate is the pardon which He is ready to bestow. '[B]y him all that believe are justified from all things.' He is 'plenteous in mercy' (Acts 13:39; Ps. 86:5).

Let this boundless mercy of our Lord Jesus Christ be graven deeply in our memories, and sink into our minds. Let us never forget that He is One 'that receiveth sinners'. With Him and His mercy sinners ought to begin, when they first begin to desire salvation. On Him and His mercy saints must live, when they have been taught to repent and believe. '[T]he life which I now live in the flesh', says St Paul, 'I live by the faith of the Son of God, who loved me, and gave himself for me' (Gal. 2:20).

August 27

It was meet that we should make merry, and be glad: for this thy
brother was dead, and is alive again; and was lost, and is found.
Luke 15:32

The conversion of any soul ought to be an occasion of joy to all who see it.

Our Lord shows us this by putting the following words into the mouth of the prodigal's father: 'It was meet that we should make merry, and be glad: for this thy brother was dead, and is alive again; and was lost, and is found.'

The lesson of these words was primarily meant for the scribes and Pharisees. If their hearts had been in a right state, they would never have murmured at our Lord for receiving sinners. They would have remembered that the worst of publicans and sinners were their own brethren, and that if they themselves were different, it was grace alone that had made the difference. They would have been glad to see such helpless wanderers returning to the fold. They would have been thankful to see them plucked as brands from the burning, and not cast away for ever. Of all these feelings, unhappily, they knew nothing. Wrapped in their own self-righteousness they murmured and found fault, when in reality they ought to have thanked God and rejoiced.

The lesson is one which we shall all do well to lay to heart. Nothing ought to give us such true pleasure as the conversion of souls. It makes angels rejoice in heaven: it ought to make Christians rejoice on earth. What if those who are converted were lately the vilest of the vile? What if they have served sin and Satan for many long years, and wasted their substance in riotous living? It matters nothing. 'Has grace come into their hearts? Are they truly penitent? Have they come back to their father's house? Are they new creatures in Christ Jesus? Are the dead made alive and the lost found?' These are the only questions we have any right to ask.

August 28

───◈◇◈───

And, behold, there was a man named Zacchaeus, which was the chief
among the publicans, and he was rich.
Luke 19:2

No-one is too bad to be saved, or beyond the power of Christ's grace.

We are told of a wealthy publican becoming a disciple of Christ: a more unlikely event we cannot well imagine! We see the 'camel passing through the eye of a needle', and the 'rich man entering the kingdom of God': we behold a plain proof that 'all things are possible with God'. We see a covetous tax gatherer transformed into a liberal Christian!

The door of hope which the gospel reveals to sinners, is very wide open. Let us leave it open, as we find it: let us not attempt, in narrow-minded ignorance, to shut it. We should never be afraid to maintain that Christ is 'able to save to the uttermost', and that the vilest of sinners may be freely forgiven if they will only come to Him. We should offer the gospel boldly to the worst and wickedest, and say, 'There is hope. Only repent and believe.' '[T]hough your sins be as scarlet, they shall be as white as snow; though they be red like crimson, they shall be as wool' (Isa. 1:18). Such doctrine may seem to worldly people foolishness and licentiousness, but such doctrine is the gospel of Him who saved Zacchaeus at Jericho. Hospitals discharge many cases as incurable; but there are no incurable cases under the gospel: any sinner may be healed, if he will only come to Christ.

The ways by which the Holy Ghost leads men and women to Christ are wonderful and mysterious: He is often beginning in a heart a work which shall stand to eternity, when a looker-on observes nothing remarkable. In every work there must be a beginning, and in spiritual work that beginning is often very small. Do we see a careless brother beginning to use means of grace, which in time past he neglected? Do we see him coming to church and listening to the gospel after a long course of Sabbath-breaking? When we see such things let us remember Zacchaeus, and be hopeful.

August 29

Jesus answered and said unto him, Verily, verily, I say unto thee,
Except a man be born again, he cannot see the kingdom of God.
John 3:3

What a mighty change our Lord declares to be needful to salvation, and what a remarkable expression He uses in describing it. He speaks of a new birth. He says to Nicodemus, 'Except a man be born again, he cannot see the kingdom of God'. He announces the same truth in other words, in order to make it more plain to his hearer's mind: 'Except a man be born of water and of the Spirit, he cannot enter into the kingdom of God'. By this expression He meant Nicodemus to understand that 'no-one could become His disciple, unless his inward man was as thoroughly cleansed and renewed by the Spirit, as the outward man is cleansed by water'. To possess the privileges of Judaism a man only needed to be born of the seed of Abraham after the flesh. To possess the privileges of Christ's kingdom, a man must be born again of the Holy Ghost.

The change which our Lord here declares needful to salvation is evidently no slight or superficial one. It is not merely reformation, or amendment, or moral change, or outward alteration of life. It is a thorough change of heart, will and character. It is a resurrection. It is a new creation. It is a passing from death to life. It is the implanting in our dead hearts of a new principle from above. It is the calling into existence of a new being, with a new nature, new habits of life, new tastes, new desires, new appetites, new judgments, new opinions, new hopes and new fears. All this, and nothing less than this is implied, when our Lord declares that we all need a 'new birth'.

This mighty change, it must never be forgotten, we cannot give to ourselves. The very name which our Lord gives to it is a convincing proof of this. He calls it 'a birth'. No man is the author of his own existence, and no man can quicken his own soul. We might as well expect a dead man to give himself life, as expect a natural man to make himself spiritual. To give life is the peculiar prerogative of God. Well may our Lord declare that we need to be 'born again'!

August 30

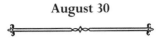

Verily, verily, I say unto you, He that believeth on me hath everlasting life.
John 6:47

The salvation of a believer is a present thing.
Our Lord Jesus Christ says, 'Verily, verily, I say unto you, He that believeth on me hath everlasting life.' Life, we should observe, is a present possession. It is not said that he shall have it at last, in the judgment day. It is now, even now, in this world, his property. He hath it the very day that he believes.

The subject is one which it much concerns our peace to understand, and one about which errors abound. How many seem to think that forgiveness and acceptance with God are things which we cannot attain in this life – that they are things which are to be earned by a long course of repentance and faith and holiness – things which we may receive at the bar of God at last, but must never pretend to touch while we are in this world! It is a complete mistake to think so. The very moment a sinner believes on Christ he is justified and accepted. There is no condemnation for him. He has peace with God, and that immediately and without delay. His name is in the book of life, however little he may be aware of it. He has a title to heaven, which death and hell and Satan cannot overthrow. Happy are they that know this truth! It is an essential part of the good news of the gospel.

After all, the great point we have to consider is whether we believe. What shall it profit us that Christ has died for sinners, if we do not believe on Him? 'He that believeth on the Son hath everlasting life: and he that believeth not the Son shall not see life; but the wrath of God abideth on him' (John 3:36).

August 31

*The thief cometh not, but for to steal, and to kill, and to destroy: I am come
that they might have life, and that they might have it more abundantly.*
John 10:10

The great object for which Christ came into the world.
He says, I am come that men 'might have life, and that they
might have it more abundantly'.

The truth contained in these words is of vast importance. They supply
an antidote to many crude and unsound notions which are abroad in
the world. Christ did not come to be only a teacher of new morality, or
an example of holiness and self-denial, or a founder of new ceremonies,
as some have vainly asserted. He left heaven, and dwelt for thirty-three
years on earth for far higher ends than these. He came to procure eternal
life for man, by the price of His own vicarious death. He came to be a
mighty fountain of spiritual life for all mankind, to which sinners coming
by faith might drink; and, drinking, might live for evermore. By Moses
came laws, rules, ordinances, ceremonies. By Christ came grace, truth
and eternal life.

Important as this doctrine is, it requires to be fenced with one word
of caution. We must not overstrain the meaning of our Lord Jesus Christ's
words. We must not suppose that eternal life was a thing entirely
unknown until Christ came, or that the Old Testament saints were in
utter darkness about the world to come. The way of life by faith in a
Saviour was a way well-known to Abraham and Moses and David. A
Redeemer and a Sacrifice was the hope of all God's children from Abel
down to John the Baptist: but their vision of these things was necessarily
imperfect. They saw them afar off, and not distinctly. They saw them in
outline only, and not completely. It was the coming of Christ which
made all things plain, and caused the shadows to pass away. Life and
immortality were brought into full light by the gospel. In short, to use
our Lord's own words, even those who had life had it 'more abundantly',
when Christ came into the world.

SEPTEMBER

September 1

My sheep hear my voice, and I know them, and they follow me ...
John 10:27

Ｔhe vast privileges which the Lord Jesus Christ bestows on true Christians.

He uses words about them of singular richness and strength. 'I know them ... I give unto them eternal life ... they shall never perish, neither shall any man pluck them out of my hand.' This sentence is like the cluster of grapes which came from Eschol. A stronger form of speech perhaps can hardly be found in the whole range of the Bible.

Christ 'knows' His people with a special knowledge of approbation, interest, and affection. By the world around them they are comparatively unknown, uncared for or despised. But they are never forgotten or overlooked by Christ.

Christ 'gives' His people 'eternal life'. He bestows on them freely a right and title to heaven, pardoning their many sins, and clothing them with a perfect righteousness. Money, and health, and worldly prosperity He often wisely withholds from them. But He never fails to give them grace, peace and glory.

Christ declares that His people 'shall never perish'. Weak as they are, they shall all be saved. Not one of them shall be lost and cast away: not one of them shall miss heaven. If they err, they shall be brought back: if they fall, they shall be raised. The enemies of their souls may be strong and mighty, but their Saviour is mightier, and none shall pluck them out of their Saviour's hands.

A promise like this deserves the closest attention. If words mean anything, it contains that great doctrine, the perseverance or continuance in grace, of true believers. That doctrine is literally hated by worldly people. No doubt, like every other truth of Scripture, it is liable to be abused. But the words of Christ are too plain to be evaded. He has said it, and He will make it good: my sheep 'shall never perish'.

Whatever men may please to say against this doctrine it is one which God's children ought to hold fast, and defend with all their might.

September 2

Believest thou not that I am in the Father, and the Father in me? the
words that I speak unto you I speak not of myself: but the Father that
dwelleth in me, he doeth the works.
John 14:10

How expressly the Lord Jesus shuts out all ways of salvation but Himself.
'[N]o man', He declares, 'no man cometh unto the Father but by me.'

It avails nothing that a man is clever, learned, highly gifted, amiable, charitable, kind-hearted and zealous about some sort of religion. All this will not save his soul, if he does not draw near to God by Christ's atonement, and make use of God's own son as his Mediator and Saviour. God is so holy that all men are guilty and debtors in His sight. Sin is so sinful that no mortal man can make satisfaction for it. There must be a mediator, a ransom-payer, a redeemer, between ourselves and God, or else we can never be saved. There is only one door, one bridge, one ladder, between earth and heaven, the crucified Son of God. Whosoever will enter in by that door may be saved, but to him who refuses to use that door the Bible holds out no hope at all. '[W]ithout shedding of blood is no remission' (Heb. 9:22).

Let us beware, if we love life, of supposing that mere earnestness will take a man to heaven, though he know nothing of Christ. The idea is a deadly and ruinous error. Sincerity will never wipe away our sins. It is not true that every man will be saved by his own religion, no matter what he believes, provided he is diligent and sincere. We must not pretend to be wiser than God. Christ has said, and Christ will stand to it, 'no man cometh unto the Father, but by me'.

September 3

Yet a little while, and the world seeth me no more; but ye see me:
because I live, ye shall live also.
John 14:19

Christ's life secures the life of His believing people. He says, 'Because I live, ye shall live also'.

There is a mysterious and indissoluble union between Christ and every true Christian. The man that is once joined to Him by faith, is as closely united as a member of the body is united to the head. So long as Christ, his Head, lives, so long he will live: he cannot die unless Christ can be plucked from heaven, and Christ's life destroyed; but this, since Christ is very God, is totally impossible! 'Christ being raised from the dead dieth no more; death hath no more dominion over him' (Rom. 6:9). That which is divine, in the very nature of things, cannot die.

Christ's life secures the continuance of spiritual life to His people. They shall not fall away: they shall persevere unto the end. The divine nature of which they are partakers, shall not perish. The incorruptible seed within them shall not be destroyed by the devil and the world. Weak as they are in themselves, they are closely knit to an immortal Head, and not one member of His mystical body shall ever perish.

Christ's life secures the resurrection life of His people. Just as He rose again from the grave, because death could not hold Him one moment beyond the appointed time, so shall all His believing members rise again, in the day when He calls them from the tomb. The victory that Jesus won when He rolled the stone away and came forth from the tomb, was a victory not only for Himself but for His people. If the Head rose, much more shall the members.

Truths like these ought to be often pondered by true Christians. The careless world knows little of a believer's privileges. It sees little but the outside of him. It does not understand the secret of his present strength, and of his strong hope of good things to come. And what is that secret? Invisible union with an invisible Saviour in heaven! Each child of God is invisibly linked to the throne of the Rock of Ages.

September 4

But he turned, and said unto Peter, Get thee behind me, Satan: thou
art an offence unto me: for thou savourest not the things that be of
God, but those that be of men.
Matthew 16:23

There is no doctrine of Scripture so deeply important as the doctrine of Christ's atoning death.

We cannot have clearer proof of this than the language used by our Lord in rebuking Peter. He addresses him by the awful name of 'Satan', as if he was an adversary, and doing the devil's work, in trying to prevent His death. He says to him, whom He had so lately called 'blessed', 'Get thee behind me … thou art an offence unto me'. He tells the man whose noble confession He had just commended so highly, 'thou savourest not the things that be of God, but those that be of men'. Stronger words than these never fell from our Lord's lips. The error that drew from such a loving Saviour such a stern rebuke to such a true disciple, must have been a mighty error indeed.

The truth is that our Lord would have us regard the crucifixion as the central truth of Christianity. Right views of His vicarious death, and the benefits resulting from it, lie at the very foundation of Bible-religion. Never let us forget this. On matters of Church-government, and the form of worship, men may differ from us, and yet reach heaven in safety. On the matter of Christ's atoning death, as the way of peace, truth is only one. If we are wrong here, we are ruined for ever. Error on many points is only a skin disease; error about Christ's death is a disease at the heart. Here let us take our stand: let nothing move us from this ground. The sum of all our hopes must be, that Christ has 'died for us' (1 Thess. 5:10). Give up that doctrine, and we have no solid hope at all.

September 5

As it is written in the prophets, Behold, I send my messenger before thy
face, which shall prepare thy way before thee.
Mark 1:2

How the beginning of the Gospel was a fulfilment of
Scripture.
John the Baptist began his ministry, 'As it is written in the
prophets'.

There was nothing unforeseen and suddenly contrived in the coming
of Jesus Christ into the world. In the very beginning of Genesis we find
it predicted that 'the seed of the woman shall bruise the serpent's head'
(Gen. 3:15). All through the Old Testament we find the same event
foretold with constantly increasing clearness. It was a promise often
renewed to patriarchs, and repeated by prophets, that a Deliverer and
Redeemer should one day come. His birth, His character, His life, His
death, His resurrection, His forerunner, were all prophesied of long
before He came. Redemption was worked out and accomplished in
every step, just as it was written.

We should always read the Old Testament with a desire to find
something in it about Jesus Christ. We study this portion of the Bible
with little profit, if we can see in it nothing but Moses, and David, and
Samuel, and the Prophets. Let us search the books of the Old Testament
more closely. It was said by Him whose words can never pass away,
these 'are they which testify of Me' (John 5:39).

September 6

And he said unto them, Have ye never read what David did, when he
had need, and was an hungred, he, and they that were with him?
Mark 2:25

The value of a knowledge of Holy Scripture.
Our Lord replies to the accusation of the Pharisees by a reference
to Holy Scripture. He reminds His enemies of the conduct of
David, when 'he had need, and was an hungred'. 'Have ye never read
what David did ....'

They could not deny that the writer of the book of Psalms, and the
man after God's own heart, was not likely to set a bad example. They
knew in fact that he had not turned aside from God's commandment,
all the days of his life, 'save only in the matter of Uriah the Hittite' (1
Kings 15:5). Yet what had David done? He had gone into the house of
God, when pressed by hunger, and eaten the 'shewbread, which is not
lawful to eat but for the priests'. He had thus shown that some
requirements of God's laws might be relaxed in case of necessity. To
this Scripture example our Lord refers His adversaries. They found
nothing to reply to it. The sword of the Spirit was a weapon which they
could not resist. They were silenced, and put to shame.

Now the conduct of our Lord on this occasion ought to be a pattern
to all His people. Our grand reason for our faith and practice, should
always be, 'Thus it is written in the Bible.' 'What saith the Scripture?'
We should endeavour to have the Word of God on our side in all
debatable questions. We should seek to be able to give a scriptural answer
for our behaviour in all matters of dispute. We should refer our enemies
to the Bible as our rule of conduct. We shall always find a plain text of
the most powerful argument we can use. In a world like this we must
expect our opinions to be attacked, if we serve Christ, and we may be
sure that nothing silences adversaries so soon as a quotation from
Scripture.

September 7

And he came to Nazareth, where he had been brought up: and, as his custom was, he went into the synagogue on the sabbath day, and stood up for to read.
Luke 4:16

What marked honour our Lord Jesus Christ gave to public means of grace.

We are told that 'he went into the synagogue [of Nazareth] on the sabbath day, and stood up for to read' the Scriptures. In the days when our Lord was on earth, the scribes and Pharisees were the chief teachers of the Jews. We can hardly suppose that a Jewish synagogue enjoyed much of the Spirit's presence and blessing under such teaching. Yet even then we find our Lord visiting a synagogue, and reading and preaching in it. It was the place where His Father's day and Word were publicly recognised, and as such He thought it good to do it honour.

We need not doubt that there is a practical lesson for us in this part of our Lord's conduct. He would have us know that we are not lightly to forsake any assembly of worshippers, which presses to respect the name, the day and the Book of God. There may be many things in such an assembly which might be done better. There may be want of fullness, clearness and distinctness in the doctrine preached. There may be a lack of unction and devoutness in the manner in which the worship is conducted. But so long as no positive error is taught, and there is no choice between worshipping with such an assembly, and having no public worship at all, it becomes a Christian to think much before he stays away. If there be but two or three in the congregation who meet in the name of Jesus, there is a special blessing promised. But there is no like blessing promised to him who tarries at home.

We are told that He chose a passage from the book of Isaiah, in which the prophet foretold the nature of the work Messiah was to do when He came into the world. And when our Lord had read this prophecy, He told the listening crowd around Him, that He Himself was the Messiah of whom these words were written, and that in Him and in His gospel the marvellous figures of the passage were about to be fulfilled.

September 8

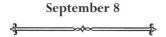

He said unto him, What is written in the law? how readest thou?
Luke 10:26

The high honour which our Lord Jesus Christ places on the Bible.

He refers the lawyer at once to the Scriptures, as the only rule of faith and practice. He does not say in reply to his question, 'What does the Jewish Church say about eternal life? What do the scribes, and Pharisees, and priests think? What is taught on the subject in the traditions of the elders?' He takes a far simpler and more direct course. He sends His questioner at once to the writings of the Old Testament: 'What is written in the law? how readest thou?'

Let the principle contained in these words be one of the foundation principles of our Christianity. Let the Bible, the whole Bible and nothing but the Bible, be the rule of our faith and practice. Holding this principle we travel upon the King's highway. The road may sometimes seem narrow, and our faith may be sorely tried, but we shall not be allowed greatly to err. Departing from this principle we enter on a pathless wilderness. There is no telling what we may be led to believe or do. For ever let us bear this in mind. Here let us cast anchor. Here let us abide. It matters nothing who says a thing in religion, whether an ancient Father, or a modern Bishop, or a learned divine. Is it in the Bible? Can it be proved by the Bible? If not, it is not to be believed. It matters nothing how beautiful and clever sermons or religious books may appear. Are they in the smallest degree contrary to Scripture? If they are, they are rubbish and poison, and guides of no value. What saith the Scripture? This is the only rule, measure, and gauge of religious truth. '[T]o the law and to the testimony', says Isaiah: 'if they speak not according to this word, it is because there is no light in them' (Isa. 8:20).

September 9

And he said unto him, If they hear not Moses and the prophets,
neither will they be persuaded, though one rose from the dead.
Luke 16:31

The greatest miracles would have no effect on men's hearts if they will not believe God's Word.

The rich man thought that 'if one went ... [to his brethren] from the dead they' would repent. He argued that the sight of one who came from another world must surely make them feel, though the old familiar words of Moses and the prophets had been heard in vain. The reply of Abraham is solemn and instructive: 'If they hear not Moses and the prophets, neither will they be persuaded, though one rose from the dead'.

The principle laid down in these words is of deep importance. The Scriptures contain all that we need to know in order to be saved, and a messenger from the world beyond the grave could add nothing to them. It is not more evidence that is wanted in order to make men repent, but more heart and will to make use of what they already know. The dead could tell us nothing more than the Bible contains, if they rose from their graves to instruct us. After the first novelty of their testimony was worn away, we should care no more for their words than the words of any other. This wretched waiting for something which we have not, and neglect of what we have, is the ruin of thousands of souls. Faith, simple faith in the Scriptures which we already possess, is the first thing needful to salvation. The man who has the Bible, and can read it, and yet awaits for more evidence before he becomes a decided Christian, is deceiving himself. Except he awakens from this delusion he will die in his sins.

September 10

*And beginning at Moses and all the prophets, he expounded unto them
in all the scriptures the things concerning himself.*
Luke 24:27

How full the Old Testament is of Christ.
We are told that our Lord began 'at Moses and all the prophets
... expounded ... in all the Scriptures the things concerning
himself'.

How shall we explain these words? In what way did our Lord show
'things concerning himself', in every part of the Old Testament field?
The answer to this question is short and simple: Christ was the substance
of every Old Testament sacrifice ordained in the law of Moses; Christ
was the true Deliverer and King, of whom all the judges and deliverers
in Jewish history were types; Christ was the coming Prophet greater
than Moses, whose glorious advent filled the pages of prophets; Christ
was the true seed of the woman who was to bruise the serpent's head,
the true seed in whom all nations were to be blessed, the true scape-
goat, the true brazen serpent, the true lamb to which every daily offering
pointed, the true High Priest of whom every descendant of Aaron was
a figure. These things, or something like them, we need not doubt,
were some of the things which our Lord expounded in the way to
Emmaus.

Let it be a settled principle in our minds, in reading the Bible, that
Christ is the central sum of the whole Book: so long as we keep Him in
view, we shall never greatly err in our search for spiritual knowledge,
once losing sight of Christ, we shall find the whole Bible dark and full
of difficulty. The key of Bible knowledge is Jesus Christ.

September 11

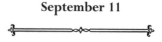

Then opened he their understanding,
that they might understand the scriptures ...
Luke 24:45

The gift which our Lord bestowed on His disciples immediately before He left the world.

We read that He opened 'their understanding, that they might understand the scriptures.'

We must not misapprehend these words. We are not to suppose that the disciples knew nothing about the Old Testament up to this time, and that the Bible is a book which no ordinary person can expect to comprehend; we are simply to understand that Jesus showed His disciples the full meaning of many passages, which had hitherto been hid from their eyes: above all, He showed the true interpretation of many prophetical passages concerning the Messiah.

We all need a like enlightenment of our understanding. '[T]he natural man receiveth not the things of the Spirit of God: for they are foolishness unto him: neither can he know them, because they are spiritually discerned' (1 Cor. 2:14). Pride, and prejudice, and love of the world blind our intellects, and throw a veil over the eyes of our minds in the reading of the Scriptures. We see the words, but do not thoroughly understand them until we are taught from above.

He that desires to read his Bible with profit, must first ask the Lord Jesus to open the eyes of his understanding by the Holy Ghost. Human commentaries are useful in their way: the help of good and learned men is not to be despised; but there is no commentary to be compared with the teaching of Christ. A humble and prayerful spirit will find a thousand things in the Bible, which the proud, self-conceited student will utterly fail to discern.

September 12

Philip findeth Nathanael, and saith unto him, We have found him, of
whom Moses in the law, and the prophets, did write,
Jesus of Nazareth, the son of Joseph.
John 1:45

How much of Christ there is in the Old Testament Scriptures.

We read that when Philip described Christ to Nathanael, he says, 'We have found him, of whom Moses in the law, and the prophets, did write'.

Christ is the sum and substance of the Old Testament. To Him the earliest promises pointed in the days of Adam, and Enoch, and Noah, and Abraham, and Isaac, and Jacob. To Him every sacrifice pointed in the ceremonial worship appointed at Mount Sinai. Of Him every high priest was a type, and every part of the tabernacle was a shadow, and every judge and deliverer of Israel was a figure. He was the Prophet like unto Moses, whom the Lord God promised to send, and the King of the house of David, who came to be David's Lord as well as son. He was the Son of the virgin, and the Lamb foretold by Isaiah – the righteous Branch mentioned by Jeremiah – the true Shepherd foreseen by Ezekiel – the Messenger of the covenant promised by Malachi – and the Messiah, who, according to Daniel, was to be cut off, thought not for Himself. The further we read in the volume of the Old Testament, the clearer do we find the testimony about Christ. The light which the inspired writers enjoyed in ancient days was, at best, but dim, compared to that of the gospel. But the coming Person they all saw afar off, and on whom they all fixed their eyes, was one and the same. The Spirit, which was in them, testified of Christ (1 Pet. 1:11).

Do we stumble at this saying? Do we find it hard to see Christ in the Old Testament, because we do not see His name? Let us be sure that the fault is all our own. It is our spiritual vision which is to blame, and not the Book. The eyes of our understanding need to be enlightened. The veil has yet to be taken away. Let us pray for a more humble, childlike and teachable spirit, and let us take up 'Moses and the prophets' again. Christ is there, though our eyes may not yet have seen Him.

September 13

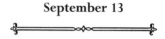

For had ye believed Moses, ye would have believed me: for he wrote of me.
John 5:46

The manner in which Christ speaks of Moses.
He says to the Jews, 'had ye believed Moses, ye would have believed me: for he wrote of me'.

These words demand our special attention in these latter days. That there really was such a person as Moses, that he really was the author of the writings commonly ascribed to him, on both these points our Lord's testimony is distinct. '[H]e wrote of me.' Can we suppose for a moment that our Lord was only accommodating Himself to the prejudices and traditions of His hearers, and that He spoke of Moses as a writer, though He knew in His heart that Moses never wrote at all? Such an idea is profane. It would make out our Lord to have been dishonest. Can we suppose for a moment that our Lord was ignorant about Moses, and did not know the wonderful discoveries which learned men, falsely so-called, have made in the nineteenth century? Such an idea is ridiculous blasphemy. To imagine the Lord Jesus speaking ignorantly in such a chapter as the one before us, is to strike at the root of all Christianity. There is but one conclusion about the matter. There was such a person as Moses. The writings commonly ascribed to him were written by him. The facts recorded in them are worthy of all credit. Our Lord's testimony is an unanswerable argument. The sceptical writers against Moses and the Pentateuch have greatly erred.

Let us beware of handling the Old Testament irreverently, and allowing our minds to doubt the truth of any part of it, because of alleged difficulties. The simple fact that the writers of the New Testament continually refer to the Old Testament, and speak even of the most miraculous events recorded in it as undoubtedly true, should silence our doubts. Is it at all likely, probable or credible, that we of the nineteenth century are better informed about Moses than Jesus and His apostles? God forbid that we should think so! Then let us stand fast, and not doubt that every word in the Old Testament, as well as in the New, was given inspiration by God.

September 14

If he called them gods, unto whom the word of God came,
and the scripture cannot be broken ...
John 10:35

The high honour that Jesus Christ puts on the holy Scriptures.

We find Him using a text out of the Psalms as an argument against His enemies, in which the whole point lies in the single word 'gods'. And then having quoted the text, He lays down the great principle, 'the scripture cannot be broken'. It is as though He said, 'Wherever the Scripture speaks plainly on any subject, there can be no more question about it. The case is settled and decided. Every jot and tittle of Scripture is true, and must be received as conclusive.'

The principle here laid down by our Lord is one of vast importance. Let us grasp it firmly, and never let it go. Let us maintain boldly the complete inspiration of every word of the original Hebrew and Greek Scriptures. Let us believe that not only every book of the Bible, but every chapter, and not only every chapter, but every verse, and not only every verse, but every word, was originally given by inspiration of God. Inspiration, we must never shrink from asserting, extends not only to the thoughts and ideas of Scripture, but to the least words.

The principle before us, no doubt, is rudely assaulted in the present day. Let no Christian's heart fail because of these assaults. Let us stand our ground manfully, and defend the principle of plenary inspiration as we would the apple of our eye. There are difficulties in Scripture, we need not shrink from conceding: things hard to explain, hard to reconcile and hard to understand. But in almost all these difficulties, the fault, we may justly suspect, is not so much in Scripture as in our own weak minds. In all cases we may well be content to wait for more light, and to believe that all shall be made clear at last. One thing we may rest assured is very certain – if the difficulties of plenary inspiration are to be numbered by thousands. The wisest course is to walk in the old path – the path of faith and humility; and say, 'I cannot give up a single word of my Bible. All Scripture is given by inspiration of God. The Scripture cannot be broken.'

September 15

These things understood not his disciples at the first: but when Jesus
was glorified, then remembered they that these things were written of
him, and that they had done these things unto him.
John 12:16

How minutely the prophecies concerning Christ's first coming were fulfilled.

The riding into Jerusalem on an ass, which is here recorded, might seem at first sight a simple action and in no way remarkable. But when we turn to the Old Testament, we find that this very thing had been predicted by the Prophet Zechariah five hundred years before (Zech. 9:9). We find that the coming of a Redeemer some day, was not the only thing which the Holy Ghost had revealed to the Fathers, but that even the least particulars of His earthly career were predicted and written down with precise accuracy.

Such fulfilments of prophecy as this deserve the special attention of all who love the Bible and read it with reverence. They show us that every word of holy Scripture was given by inspiration of God. They teach us to beware of the mischievous practice of spiritualizing and explaining away the language of Scripture. We must settle it in our minds that the plain, literal meaning of the Bible is generally the true and correct meaning. Here is a prediction of Zechariah literally and exactly fulfilled. Our Lord was not merely a very humble person, as some spiritualizing interpreters would have explained Zechariah's words to mean, but He literally rode into Jerusalem on an ass. Above all, such fulfilments teach us what we may expect in looking forward to the second advent of Jesus Christ. They show us that we must look for a literal accomplishment of the prophecies concerning that second coming, and not for a figurative and spiritual one. For ever let us hold fast this great principle. Happy is that Bible-reader who believes the words of the Bible to mean exactly what they seem to mean. Such a man has got the true key of knowledge in looking forward to things to come. To know that predictions about the second advent of Christ will be fulfilled literally, just as predictions about the first advent of Christ were fulfilled literally, is the first step towards a right understanding of unfulfilled prophecy.

September 16

And was transfigured before them: and his face did shine as the sun,
and his raiment was white as the light.
Matthew 17:2

A striking pattern of the glory in which Christ and His people will appear when He comes the second time. There can be little question that this was one main object of this wonderful vision. It was meant to encourage the disciples, by giving them a glimpse of good things yet to come. That 'face shining as the sun', and that 'raiment white as the light', were intended to give the disciples some idea of the majesty in which Jesus will appear to the world, when He comes the second time, and all His saints with Him. The corner of the veil was lifted up, to show them their Master's true dignity. They were taught that if He did not yet appear to the world in the guise of a King, it was only because the time for putting on His royal apparel was not yet come. It is impossible to draw any other conclusion from St Peter's language, when writing on the subject. He says with distinct reference to the transfiguration, 'We were eye witnesses of His majesty' (2 Pet. 1:16).

It is good for us to have the coming glory of Christ and His people deeply impressed in our minds. We are sadly apt to forget it. There are few visible indications of it in the world: 'we see not yet all things put under' our Lord's feet (Heb. 2:8). Sin, unbelief and superstitions abound. Thousands are practically saying, 'We will not have this man to reign over us.' It doth not yet appear what His people shall be: their crosses, their tribulations, their weaknesses, their conflicts, are all manifest enough; but there are few signs of their future reward. Let us beware of giving way to doubts in this matter: let us silence such doubts by reading over the history of transfiguration. There is laid up for Jesus, and all that believe on Him, such glory as the heart of man never conceived.

September 17

And after six days Jesus taketh with him Peter, and James, and John,
and leadeth them up into an high mountain apart by themselves:
and he was transfigured before them.
Mark 9:2

The marvellous vision they contain of the glory which Christ and His people shall have at His second coming. There can be no doubt that this was one of the principal purposes of the transfiguration. It was meant to teach the disciples, that though their Lord was lowly and poor in appearance now, He would one day appear in such royal majesty as became the Son of God. It was meant to teach them, that when their Master came the second time, His saints, like Moses and Elias, would appear with Him. It was meant to remind them, that though reviled and persecuted now, because they belonged to Christ, they would one day be clothed with honour, and be partakers of their Master's glory.

We have reason to thank God for this vision. We are often tempted to give up Christ's service, because of the cross and affliction which it entails. We see few with us, and many against us. We find our names cast out as evil, and all manner of evil said of us, because we believe and love the gospel. Year after year we see our companions in Christ's service removed by death, and we feel as if we knew little about them, except that they are gone to an unknown world, and that we are left alone. All these things are trying to flesh and blood. No wonder that the faith of believers sometimes languishes, and their eyes fail while they look for their hope.

Let us see in the story of the transfiguration, a remedy for such doubting thoughts as these. The vision of the holy mount is a gracious pledge that glorious things are in store for the people of God. Their crucified Saviour shall come again in power and great glory. His saints shall all come with Him, and are in safekeeping until that happy day. We may wait patiently. 'When Christ, who is our life, shall appear, then shall ye also appear with him in glory' (Col. 3:4).

September 18

And then shall they see the Son of man coming in the clouds with
great power and glory.
Mark 13:26

What solemn majesty will attend our Lord Jesus Christ's second coming to this world.

The language that is used about the sun, moon and stars, conveys this idea of some universal convulsion of the universe at the close of the present dispensation. It reminds us of the Apostle Peter's words: 'the heavens shall pass away with a great noise, and the elements shall melt with fervent heat' (2 Pet. 3:10). At such time as this, amidst terror and confusion, exceeding all that even earthquakes or hurricanes are known to produce, men 'shall see the Son of man coming in the clouds with great power and glory'.

The second coming of Christ shall be utterly unlike the first. He came the first time in weakness, a tender infant, born of a poor woman in the manger at Bethlehem, unnoticed, unhonoured and scarcely known. He shall come the second time in royal dignity, with the armies of heaven around Him, to be known, recognised and feared, by all the tribes of the earth. He came the first time to suffer, to bear our sins, to be reckoned a curse, to be despised, rejected, unjustly condemned and slain. He shall come the second time to reign, to put down every enemy beneath His feet, to take the kingdoms of this world for His inheritance, to rule them with righteousness, to judge all men and to live for evermore.

Here are comfortable thoughts for Christ's friends. Their own King will soon be here. They shall reap according as they have sown. They shall receive a rich reward for all that they have endured for Christ's sake. They shall exchange their cross for a crown. Here are confounding thoughts for Christ's foes. That same Jesus of Nazareth, whom they have so long despised and rejected, shall at length have pre-eminence. That very Christ whose gospel they have refused to believe shall appear as their Judge, and helpless, hopeless and speechless, they will have to stand before His bar.

September 19

Take ye heed, watch and pray: for ye know not when the time is.
Mark 13:33

W
hat are the practical duties of all true believers in the prospect of the second coming of Jesus Christ. Our Lord mentions three things, to which His people should attend. He tells them plainly that He is coming again one day, in power and great glory. He tells them at the same time, that the precise hour and date of that coming are not known. What then are His people to do? In what position of mind are they to live? They are to watch. They are to pray. They are to work.

We are to watch. We are to live always on our guard. We are to keep our souls in a wakeful, lively state, prepared at any time to meet our Master. We are to beware of anything like spiritual lethargy, dullness, deadness and torpor. The company, the employment of time, the society which induces us to forget Christ and His second advent, should be marked, noted and avoided. '[L]et us not sleep, as do others;' says the apostle, 'but let us watch and be sober' (1 Thess. 5:6).

We are to pray. We are to keep up habits of regular communion and intercourse with God. We are to allow no strangeness to come in between us and our Father in heaven, but to speak with Him daily; that so we may be ready at any moment to see Him face to face. Moreover, we are to make special prayer about the Lord's coming, that we may be 'found of him in peace, without spot, and blameless', with the cares of this life, and so the day comes upon us unawares (2 Pet. 3:14; Luke 21: 34).

Finally, we are to work. We are to realize that we are all servants of a great Master, who has given to every man his work, and expects that work to be done. We are to labour to glorify God, each in our particular sphere and relation. There is always something for everyone to do. We are to strive each of us to shine as a light – to be salt of our own times – to be faithful witnesses for our Master, and to honour Him by conscientiousness and consistency in our daily conversation.

September 20

For as the lightning, that lighteneth out of the one part under heaven,
shineth unto the other part under heaven;
so shall also the Son of man be in his day.
Luke 17:24

The second coming of Jesus Christ will be a very sudden event.

Our Lord describes this by a striking figure. He says, 'as the lightning, that lighteneth out of the one part under heaven, shineth unto the other part under heaven; so shall also the Son of man be in his day.'

The second personal advent of Christ is the real fulfilment of these words. Of the precise day and hour of that advent we know nothing; but whenever it may take place, one thing at least is clear – it will come on the Church and the world suddenly, instantaneously and without previous notice. The whole tenor of Scripture points this way. It shall be 'in such an hour as ye think not'. It shall come 'as a thief in the night' (Matt. 24:44; 1 Thess. 5:2).

This suddenness of Christ's second advent is a solemn thought. It ought to make us study a continual preparedness of mind. Our heart's desire and endeavour should be to be always ready to meet our Lord; our life's aim should be to do nothing, and say nothing, which could make us ashamed if Christ were suddenly to appear. 'Blessed', says the Apostle John, 'is he that watcheth, and keepeth his garments' (Rev. 16:15).

Those who denounce the doctrine of the second advent as speculative, fanciful and unpractical, would do well to reconsider the subject. The doctrine was not so regarded in the days of the apostles. In their eyes patience, hope, diligence, moderation, personal holiness, were inseparably connected with an expectation of the Lord's return. Happy is the Christian who has learned to think with them! To be ever looking for the Lord's appearing is one of the best helps to a close walk with God.

September 21

And when these things begin to come to pass, then look up,
and lift up your heads; for your redemption draweth nigh.
Luke 21:28

How complete will be the security of true Christians at the second advent of Christ.

We read that our Lord said to His disciples, 'when these things begin to come to pass, then look up, and lift up your heads; for your redemption draweth nigh'.

However terrible the signs of Christ's second coming may be to the impenitent, they need not strike terror into the heart of the true believer: they ought rather to fill him with joy. They ought to remind him that his complete deliverance from sin, the world and the devil, is close at hand, and that he shall soon bid an eternal farewell to sickness, sorrow, death and temptation. The very day when the unconverted man shall lose everything, shall be the day when the believer shall enter on his eternal reward; the very hour when the worldly man's hopes shall perish, shall be the hour when the believer's hope shall be exchanged for joyful certainty and full possession.

The servant of God should often look forward to Christ's second advent. He will find the thought of that day a cordial to sustain him under all the trials and persecutions of this present life. Yet a little time, let him remember, 'and he that shall come will come, and will not tarry'. The words of Isaiah shall be fulfilled: 'the Lord God will wipe away tears from off all faces; and the rebuke of his people shall he take away from off all the earth'. One sure receipt for a patient spirit is to expect little from this world, and to be ever 'waiting for the coming of our Lord Jesus Christ' (Heb. 10:37; Is. 25:8; 1 Cor. 1:7).

September 22

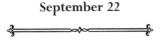

Then answered all the people, and said, His blood be on us, and on our children.
Matthew 27:25

The desperate wickedness of human nature.

The behaviour of Pilate afforded the chief priests and elders an occasion of reconsidering what they were about. The difficulties he raised about condemning our Lord, gave time for second thoughts: but there were no second thoughts in the minds of our Lord's enemies. They pressed on their wicked deed; they rejected the compromise that Pilate offered: they actually preferred having a wretched felon, named Barabbas, set at liberty rather than Jesus. They clamoured loudly for our Lord's crucifixion; and they wound up all by recklessly taking on themselves all the guilt of our Lord's death, in words of portentous meaning: 'His blood be on us, and on our children'.

And what had our Lord done, that the Jews should hate Him so? He was no robber, or murderer: He was no blasphemer of their God, or reviler of their prophets. He was one whose life was love: He was one who 'went about doing good, and healing all that were oppressed of the devil' (Acts 10:38). He was innocent of any transgression against the law of God or man, and yet the Jews hated Him, and never rested till He was slain! They hated Him, because He testified of their works that they were evil: they hated the light, because it made their own darkness visible. In a word, they hated Christ, because He was righteous and they were wicked, because He was holy and they were unholy, because He testified against sin, and they were determined to keep their sins and not let them go.

Let us never be surprised at the wickedness there is in the world. Let us mourn over it, and labour to make it less, but let us never be surprised at its extent. There is nothing which the heart of man is not capable of conceiving, or the hand of man of doing. As long as we live, let us mistrust our own hearts: even renewed by the Spirit, they are still 'deceitful above all things, and desperately wicked' (Jer. 17:9).

SIN

September 23

And there came a leper to him, beseeching him, and kneeling down to him, and saying unto him, If thou wilt, thou canst make me clean.
Mark 1:40

The dreadful nature of the disease which Jesus cured. Leprosy is a complaint of which we know little or nothing in our northern climate. In Bible lands it is far more common. It is a disease which is utterly incurable. It is no mere skin infection, as some ignorantly suppose. It is a radical disease of the whole man. It attacks, not merely the skin, but the blood, the flesh and the bones, until the unhappy patient begins to lose his extremities, and to rot by inches – let us remember beside this, that amongst the Jews the leper was reckoned unclean, and was cut off from the congregation of Israel and the ordinances of religion. He was obliged to dwell in a separate house. None might touch him or minister to him. Let us remember all this, and then we may have some idea of the remarkable wretchedness of a leprous person. To use the words of Aaron, when he interceded for Miriam, he was, 'as one dead, of whom the flesh is half consumed' (Num. 12:12).

But is there nothing like leprosy among ourselves? Yes: indeed there is! There is a foul soul-disease which is engrained into our very nature, and cleaves to our bones and marrow with deadly force. That disease is the plague of sin. Like leprosy, it is a deep-seated disease, infecting every part of our nature, heart, will, conscience, understanding, memory and affections. Like leprosy, it makes us loathsome and abominable, unfit for the company of God, and unmeet for the glory of heaven. Like leprosy, it is incurable by any earthly physician, and is slowly but surely dragging us down to the second death. And worst of all, far worse than leprosy, it is a disease from which no mortal man is exempt. '[W]e are all', in God's sight, 'as an unclean thing' (Isa. 64:6).

September 24

And saith unto them, My soul is exceeding sorrowful unto death:
tarry ye here, and watch.
Mark 14:34

How keenly our Lord felt the burden of a world's sin.
It is written that He 'began to be sore amazed, and to be very
heavy; And saith unto them, My soul is exceeding sorrowful
unto death', and that He 'fell on the ground, and prayed that, if it were
possible, the hour might pass from him'. There is only one reasonable
explanation of these expressions. It was no mere fear of the physical
suffering of death, which drew them from our Lord's lips. It was a
sense of the enormous load of human guilt, which began at that time to
press upon Him in a peculiar way. It was a sense of the unutterable
weight of our sins and transgressions which were then specially laid
upon Him. He was being 'made a curse for us'. He was bearing our
griefs and carrying our sorrows, according to the covenant He came on
earth to fulfil. He was being 'made sin for us who Himself knew no
sin'. His holy nature felt acutely the hideous burden laid upon Him.
These were the reasons of His extraordinary sorrow. We ought to see in
our Lord's agony in Gethsemane the exceeding sinfulness of sin. It is a
subject on which the thoughts of professing Christians are far below
what they should be. The careless, light way in which such sins as
swearing, Sabbath-breaking, lying and the like are often spoken of, is a
painful evidence of the low condition of men's moral feelings. Let the
recollection of Gethsemane have a sanctifying effect upon us. Whatever
others do, let us never 'make a mock at sin'.

September 25

When Simon Peter saw it, he fell down at Jesus' knees, saying,
Depart from me; for I am a sinful man, O Lord.
Luke 5:8

H<small>OW</small> **much a sense of God's presence abases man and makes him feel his sinfulness.**

We see this strikingly illustrated by Peter's words, when the miraculous draught convinced him that One greater than man was in his boat. We read that 'he fell down at Jesus' knees saying, Depart from me; for I am a sinful man, O Lord'.

In measuring these words of Peter, we must of course remember the time at which they were spoken. He was, at best, but a babe in grace, weak in faith, weak in experience and weak in knowledge. At a later period in his life, he would, doubtless, have said, 'Abide with me', and not, 'Depart'. But still, after every deduction of this kind, the words of Peter exactly express the first feelings of man when he is brought into anything like close contact with God. The sight of divine greatness and holiness makes him feel strongly his own littleness and sinfulness. Like Adam after the fall, his first thought is to hide himself. Like Israel under Sinai, the language of his heart is, 'Let not God speak with us, lest we die' (Exod. 20:19).

Let us strive to know more and more, every year we live, our need of a mediator between ourselves and God. Let us seek more and more to realize that without a mediator our thoughts of God can never be comfortable, and the more clearly we see God the more uncomfortable we must feel. Above all, let us be thankful that we have in Jesus the very Mediator whose help our souls require, and that through Him we may draw near to God with boldness, and cast fear away. Out of Christ God is a consuming fire. In Christ He is a reconciled Father. Without Christ the strictest moralist may well tremble, as he looks forward to his end. Through Christ the chief of sinners may approach God with confidence, and feel perfect peace.

September 26

And why call ye me, Lord, Lord, and do not the things which I say?
Luke 6:46

W hat an old and common sin is profession without
practice.

It is written, that our Lord said, 'why call ye me Lord, Lord, and do not the things which I say?' The Son of God Himself had many followers, who pretended to honour Him by calling Him Lord, but yielded no obedience to His commandments.

The evil which our Lord exposes here, has always existed in the Church of God. It was found six hundred years before our Lord's time, in the days of Ezekiel: 'they come unto thee', we read, 'as the people cometh, and they sit before thee as my people, and they hear thy words, but they will not do them: for with their mouth they shew much love, but their heart goeth after their covetousness' (Ezek. 33:31). It was found in the primitive Church of Christ in the days of St James: 'be ye doers of the word,' he says, 'and not hearers only, deceiving your own selves' (Jas. 1:22). It is a disease which has never ceased to prevail all over Christendom. It is a soul-ruining plague, which is continually sweeping away crowds of gospel-hearers down the broad way to destruction. Open sin, and avowed unbelief, no doubt slay their thousands. But profession without practice slays its tens of thousands.

Let us settle it in our minds, that no sin is so foolish and unreasonable as the sin which Jesus here denounces. Common sense alone might tell us, that the name and form of Christianity can profit us nothing, so long as we cleave to sin in our hearts, and live unchristian lives. Let it be a fixed principle in our religion, that obedience is the only sound evidence of saving faith, and that the talk of the lips is worse than useless, if it is not accompanied by sanctification of the life. The man in whose heart the Holy Ghost really dwells, will never be content to sit still, and do nothing to show his love to Christ.

September 27

Now when he came nigh to the gate of the city, behold, there was a
dead man carried out, the only son of his mother, and she was a
widow: and much people of the city was with her.
Luke 7:12

What sorrow sin has brought into the world. We are told of a funeral at Nain. All funerals are mournful things, but it is difficult to imagine a funeral more mournful than the one here described. It was the funeral of a young man, and that young man the only son of his mother, and that mother a widow. There is not an item in the whole story which is not full of misery. And all this misery, be it remembered, was brought into the world by sin. God did not create it at the beginning, when He made all things 'very good'. Sin is the cause of it all. '[S]in entered into the world' when Adam fell, 'and death by sin' (Rom. 5:12).

Let us never forget this great truth. The world around us is full of sorrow. Sickness, and pain, and infirmity, and poverty, and labour, and trouble, abound on every side. From one end of the world to the other, the history of families is full of lamentation, and weeping, and mourning, and woe. And whence does it all come? Sin is the fountain and root to which all must be traced. There would neither have been tears, nor cares, nor illness, nor deaths, nor funerals in the earth, if there had been no sin. We must bear this state of things patiently. We cannot alter it. We may thank God that there is a remedy in the gospel, and that this life is not all. But in the meantime let us lay the blame at the right door. Let us lay the blame on sin.

How much ought we to hate sin! Instead of loving it, cleaving to it, dallying with it, excusing it, playing with it, we ought to hate it with a deadly hatred. Sin is the great murderer, and thief, and pestilence, and nuisance of this world. Let us make no peace with it. Let us wage a ceaseless warfare against it. It is 'the abominable thing which God hateth'. Happy is he who is of one mind with God, and can say, I 'Abhor that which is evil' (Rom. 12:9).

September 28

*And a woman having an issue of blood twelve years, which had spent
all her living upon physicians, neither could be healed of any …*
Luke 8:43

A **striking picture of the condition of many souls.**
We are told that she had been afflicted with a wearing disease
for 'twelve years', and that she 'had spent all her living upon
physicians', and that she could not be 'healed of any'. The state of many
a sinner's heart is placed before us in this description, as in a glass.
Perhaps it describes ourselves.

There are men and women in most congregations who have felt
their sins deeply, and been sore afflicted by the thought that they are
not forgiven and not fit to die. They have desired relief and peace of
conscience, but have not known where to find them. They have tried
many false remedies, and found themselves 'nothing bettered, but rather
worse'. They have gone the round of all the forms of religion, and
wearied themselves with every imaginable man-made device for
obtaining spiritual health. But all has been in vain. Peace of conscience
seems as far off as ever. The wound within appears a fretting, intractable
sore, which nothing can heal. They are still wretched, still unhappy, still
thoroughly discontented with their own state. In short, like the woman
of whom we read today, they are ready to say, 'There is no hope for me.
I shall never be saved'.

Let all such take comfort in the miracle which we are now
considering. Let them know that 'there is balm in Gilead', which can
cure them, if they will only seek it. There is one door at which they
have never knocked in all their efforts to obtain relief. There is one
Physician to whom they have not applied, who never fails to heal. Let
them consider the conduct of the woman before us in her necessity.
When all other means had failed she went to Jesus for help. Let them
go and do likewise.

September 29

But I say unto you, that it shall be more tolerable in that day for Sodom, than for that city.
Luke 10:12

The great sinfulness of those who reject the offer of Christ's gospel.

Our Lord declares that it shall be 'more tolerable' at the last day 'for Sodom', than for those who receive not the message of His disciples. And He proceeds to say that the guilt of Chorazin and Bethsaida, cities in Galilee, where he had often preached and worked miracles, but where the people had nevertheless not repented, was greater than the guilt of Tyre and Sidon.

Declarations like these are peculiarly awful. They throw light on some truths which men are very apt to forget. They teach us that all will be judged according to their spiritual light, and that from those who have enjoyed most religious privileges, most will be required. They teach us the exceeding hardness and unbelief of the human heart. It was possible to hear Christ preach, and to see Christ's miracles, and yet to remain unconverted. They teach us, not least, that man is responsible for the state of his own soul. Those who reject the gospel, and remain impenitent and unbelieving, are not merely objects of pity and compassion, but deeply guilty and blameworthy in God's sight. God called, but they refused. God spoke to them, but they would not regard. The condemnation of the unbelieving will be strictly just. Their blood will be upon their own heads. The Judge of all the earth will do right.

Let us lay these things to heart, and beware of unbelief. It is not open sin and flagrant profligacy alone which ruin souls. We have only to sit still and do nothing, when the gospel is pressed on our acceptance, and we shall find ourselves one day in the pit.

We have only to remain cold, careless, indifferent, unmoved and unaffected, and our end will be in hell. This was the ruin of Chorazin and Bethsaida. And this, it may be feared, will be the ruin of thousands, as long as the world stands. No sin makes less noise, but none so surely damns the soul, as unbelief.

September 30

*And he said, Woe unto you also, ye lawyers! for ye lade men with
burdens grievous to be borne, and ye yourselves touch not the burdens
with one of your fingers.*
Luke 11:46

How great is the sin of professing to teach others what we do not practise ourselves.

He says to the lawyers, 'ye lade men with burdens grievous to be borne, while ye yourselves touch not the burdens with one of your fingers'. They required others to observe wearisome ceremonies in religion which they themselves neglected. They had the impudence to lay yokes upon the consciences of other men, and yet to grant exemptions from these yokes for themselves. In a word, they had one set of measures and weights for their hearers, and another set for their own souls.

The stern reproof which our Lord here administers should come home with special power to certain classes in the Church. It is a word in season to all teachers of young people. It is a word to all masters of families and heads of households. It is a word to all fathers and mothers. Above all, it is a word to all clergymen and ministers of religion. Let all such mark well our Lord's language in this passage. Let them beware of telling others to aim at a standard which they do not aim at themselves. Such conduct, to say the least, is gross inconsistency.

Perfection, no doubt, is unattainable in this world. If nobody is to lay down rules, or teach, or preach, until he is faultless himself, the whole fabric of society would be thrown into confusion. But we have a right to expect some agreement between a man's words and a man's works, between his teaching and his doing, between his preaching and his practice. One thing at all events is very certain: no lessons produce such effects on men as those which the teacher illustrates by his own daily life. Happy is he who can say with Paul, 'Those things, which ye have ... heard, and seen in me, do' (Phil. 4:9).

OCTOBER

October 1

*And when he had spent all, there arose a mighty famine in that land;
and he began to be in want.*
Luke 15:14

Man finding out that the ways of sin are hard, by bitter experience.

Our Lord shows us the younger son spending all his property and reduced to want, obliged to take service and 'feed swine' so hungry that he is ready to eat swine's food, and cared for by none.

These words describe a common case. Sin is a hard master, and the servants of sin always find it out, sooner or later, to their cost. Unconverted people are never really happy: under a profession of high spirits and cheerfulness, they are often ill at ease within. Thousands of them are sick at heart, dissatisfied with themselves, weary of their own ways, and thoroughly uncomfortable. 'There be many that say, Who will shew us any good?' 'There is no peace, saith my God, to the wicked' (Ps. 4:6; Isa. 57:21).

Let this truth sink down into our hearts. It is a truth, however loudly unconverted people may deny it. '[T]he way of transgressors is hard' (Prov. 13:15). The secret wretchedness of natural men is exceedingly great: there is a famine within, however much they may try to conceal it. They are 'in want'. He that 'soweth to his flesh shall of the flesh reap corruption'. No wonder that St Paul said, 'What fruit had ye then in those things whereof ye are now ashamed?' (Gal. 6:8; Rom. 6:21).

October 2

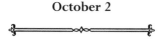

Now when Jesus heard these things, he said unto him, Yet lackest thou
one thing: sell all that thou hast, and distribute unto the poor, and
thou shalt have treasure in heaven: and come, follow me.
Luke 18:22

What harm one master-sin may do to a soul.
The desires which the rich ruler expressed were right and
good: he wanted 'eternal life'. There seemed at first sight
no reason why he should not be taught the way of God, and become a
disciple. But there was one thing unhappily, which he loved better than
'eternal life': that thing was his money. When invited by Christ to give
up all that he had on earth and seek treasure in heaven, he had not faith
to accept the invitation. The love of money was his master-sin.

Shipwrecks like this are sadly common in the Church of Christ.
Few are the ministers who could not put their finger on many cases like
that of the man before us. Many are ready to give up everything for
Christ's sake, excepting one darling sin, and for the sake of that sin are
lost for evermore. When Herod heard John the Baptist, 'he did many
things, and heard him gladly'; but there was one thing he could not do:
he could not part with Herodias. That one thing cost Herod his soul
(Mark 6:20).

There must be no reserve in our hearts, if we would receive anything
at Christ's hands. We must be willing to part with anything, however
dear it may be, if it stands between us and our salvation; we must be
ready to cut off the right hand and pluck out the right eye, to make any
sacrifice, and to break any idol. Life, we must remember, eternal life is
at stake! One leak neglected, is enough to sink a mighty ship; one
besetting sin, obstinately clung to, is enough to shut a soul out of heaven.
The love of money, secretly nourished in the heart, is enough to bring
a man, in other respects moral and irreproachable, down to the pit of
hell.

October 3

And shall lay thee even with the ground, and thy children within thee;
and they shall not leave in thee one stone upon another;
because thou knewest not the time of thy visitation.
Luke 19:44

There is a religious ignorance which is sinful and blameworthy.

We read that our Lord denounced judgments on Jerusalem, because she knew not the time of her visitation. She might have known that the times of Messiah had fully come, and that Jesus of Nazareth was the Messiah: but she would not know. Her rulers were wilfully ignorant: they would not calmly examine evidences, and impartially consider great plain facts, her people would not see 'the signs of the times'. Therefore judgment was soon to come upon Jerusalem to the uttermost. Her wilful ignorance left her without excuse.

The principle laid down by our Lord in this place is deeply important. It contradicts an opinion which is very common in the world. It teaches distinctly that all ignorance is not excusable, and that when men might know truth but refuse to know it, their guilt is very great in the sight of God. There is a degree of knowledge for which all are responsible, and if from indolence or prejudice we do not attain that knowledge, the want of it will ruin our souls.

Let us impress this great principle deeply on our own hearts, let us urge it diligently on others, when we speak to them about religion, let us not flatter ourselves that ignorance will excuse everyone who dies in ignorance, and that he will be pardoned because he knew no better! Did he live up to the light he had? Did he use every means for attaining knowledge? Did he honestly employ every help within his reach, and search industriously after wisdom? These are grave questions. If a man cannot answer them, he will certainly be condemned in the judgment day. A wilful ignorance will never be allowed as a plea in a man's favour; on the contrary, it will rather add to his guilt.

October 4

*And being in an agony he prayed more earnestly: and his sweat was as
it were great drops of blood falling down to the ground.*
Luke 22:44

An example of the exceeding guilt and sinfulness of sin.
We are meant to learn this in Christ's agony and blood sweat,
and all the mysterious distress of body and mind, which the
passage describes. The lesson at first sight may not be clear to a careless
reader of the Bible; but the lesson is there.

How can we account for the deep agony which our Lord underwent
in the garden? What reason can we assign for the intense suffering, both
mental and bodily, which He manifestly endured? There is only one
satisfactory answer: it was caused by the burden of a world's imputed
sin, which then began to press upon Him in a peculiar manner. He had
undertaken to be 'sin for us', to be 'made a curse for us', and to allow
our iniquities to be laid on Himself (2 Cor. 5:21; Gal. 3:13; Isa. 53:6).
It was the enormous weight of these iniquities which made Him suffer
agony; it was the sense of a world's guilt pressing Him down which
made even the eternal Son of God sweat great drops of blood, and
called from Him 'strong crying and tears'. The cause of Christ's agony
was man's sin (Heb. 5:7).

We must beware jealously of the modern notion that our blessed
Lord's life and death were nothing more than a great example of self-
sacrifice. Such a notion throws darkness and confusion over the whole
gospel: it dishonours the Lord Jesus, and represents Him as less resigned
in the day of death than many a modern martyr. We must cling firmly
to the old doctrine that Christ was 'bearing our sins', both in the garden
and on the cross. No other doctrine can ever explain the passage before
us, or satisfy the conscience of guilty man.

October 5

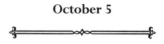

He came unto his own, and his own received him not.
John 1:11

The desperate wickedness of man's natural heart.
We have it in the words, Christ 'was in the world, and the world was made by him, and the world knew him not. He came unto his own, and his own received him not.'

Christ was in the world invisibly, long before he was born of the Virgin Mary. He was there from the very beginning, ruling, ordering, and governing the whole creation. By Him all things consisted (Col. 1:17). He gave to all life and breath, rain from heaven, and fruitful seasons. By Him kings reigned, and nations were increased or diminished. Yet men knew Him not, and honoured Him not. They 'worshipped and served the creature more than the Creator' (Rom. 1:25). Well may the natural heart be called 'wicked'!

But Christ came visibly into the world when He was born at Bethlehem, and fared no better. He came to the very people whom He had brought out from Egypt, and purchased for His own. He came to the Jews, whom He had separated from other nations, and to whom He had revealed Himself by the prophets. He came to those very Jews who had read of Him in the Old Testament Scriptures, seen Him under types and figures in their temple services, and professed to be waiting for His coming. And yet, when He came, those very Jews received Him not. They even rejected Him, despised Him and slew Him. Well may the natural heart be called 'desperately wicked'!

October 6

The woman answered and said, I have no husband. Jesus said unto her,
Thou hast well said, I have no husband ...
John 4:17

The absolute necessity of conviction of sin before a soul can be converted to God.

The Samaritan woman seems to have been comparatively unmoved until our Lord exposed her breach of the seventh commandment. Those heart-searching words, 'Go, call thy husband', appear to have pierced her conscience like an arrow. From that moment, however ignorant, she speaks like an earnest, sincere inquirer after truth. And the reason is evident. She felt that her spiritual disease was discovered. For the first time in her life she saw herself.

To bring thoughtless people to this state of mind should be the principal aim of all teachers and ministers of the gospel. They should carefully copy their Master's example in this place. Till men and women are brought to feel their sinfulness and need, no real good is ever done to their souls. Till a sinner sees himself as God sees him, he will continue careless, trifling and unmoved. By all means we must labour to convince the unconverted man of sin, to prick his conscience, to open his eyes, to show him himself. To this end we must expound the length and breadth of God's holy law. To this end we must denounce every practice contrary to that law, however fashionable and customary. This is the only way to do good. Never does a soul value the gospel medicine until it feels its disease. Never does a man see any beauty in Christ as a Saviour, until he discovers that he is himself a lost and ruined sinner. Ignorance of sin is invariably attended by neglect of Christ.

October 7

The world cannot hate you; but me it hateth, because I testify of it,
that the works thereof are evil.
John 7:7

One principal reason why many hate Christ.
We are told that our Lord said to His unbelieving brethren,
'The world cannot hate you; but me it hateth, because I testify
of it, that the works thereof are evil.'

These words reveal one of those secret principles which influence
men in their treatment of religion. They help to explain that deadly
enmity with which many during our Lord's earthly ministry regarded
Him and His gospel. It was not so much the high doctrines which He
preached, as the high standard of practice which He proclaimed, which
gave offence. It was not even His claim to be received of the Messiah
which men disliked so much, as His witness against the wickedness of
their lives. In short, they could have tolerated His opinions if He would
only have spared their sins.

The principle, we may be sure, is one of universal application. It is
at work now just as much as it was eighteen hundred years ago. The real
cause of many people's dislike to the gospel, is the holiness of living
which it demands. Teach abstract doctrines only, and few will find any
fault. Denounce the fashionable sins of the day, and call on men to repent
and walk consistently with God, and thousands at once will be offended.
The true reason why many profess to be infidels and abuse Christianity,
is the witness that Christianity bears against their own bad lives. Like
Ahab, they hate it, because it does 'not prophesy good concerning them,
but evil' (1 Kgs. 22:8).

October 8

*And Peter followed him afar off, even into the palace of the high
priest: and he sat with the servants, and warmed himself at the fire.*
Mark 14:54

How foolishly Christians sometimes thrust themselves
into temptation.

We are told that when our Lord was led away prisoner, 'Peter
followed him afar off, even into the palace of the high priest: and he sat
with the servants, and warmed himself at the fire'. There was no wisdom
in this act. Having once forsaken his Master and fled, he ought to have
remembered his own weakness, and not to have ventured into danger
again. It was an act of rashness and presumption. It brought on him
fresh trials of faith, for which he was utterly unprepared. It threw him
into bad company, where he was not likely to get good but harm. It
paved the way for his last and greatest transgression, his thrice-repeated
denial of his Master.

But it is an experimental truth that ought never to be overlooked,
that when a believer has once begun to backslide and leave his first
faith, he seldom stops short at his first mistake. He seldom makes only
one stumble. He seldom commits only one fault. A blindness seems to
come over the eyes of his understanding. He appears to cast overboard
his common sense and discretion. Like a stone rolling downhill, the
further he goes on in sinning, the faster and more decided is his course.
Like David, he may begin with idleness, and end with committing every
possible crime. Like Peter, he may begin with cowardice, go on to foolish
trifling with temptation and then end with denying Christ.

If we know anything of true, saving religion, let us ever beware of
the beginnings of backsliding. It is like the letting out of water – first a
drop, then a torrent. Once out of the way of holiness, there is no saying
to what we may come. Once giving way to petty inconsistencies, we
may find ourselves one day committing every sort of wickedness. Let
us keep far from the brink of evil. Let us not play with fire. No petition
in the Lord's Prayer is more important than the last but one: 'lead us
not into temptation'.

October 9

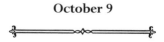

*Being forty days tempted of the devil. And in those days he did eat
nothing: and when they were ended, he afterward hungered.*
Luke 4:2

The power and unwearied malice of the devil.
That old serpent who tempted Adam to sin in paradise was not
afraid to assault the Second Adam, the Son of God. Whether he
understood that Jesus was 'God manifest in the flesh' may perhaps be
doubted. But that he saw in Jesus One who had come into the world to
overthrow his kingdom, is clear and plain. He had seen what happened
at our Lord's baptism. He had heard the marvellous words from heaven.
He felt that the great Friend of man was come, and that his own dominion
was in peril. The Redeemer had come. The prison door was about to be
thrown open. The lawful captives were about to be set free. All this, we
need not doubt, Satan saw, and resolved to fight for his own. The prince
of this world would not give way to the Prince of peace without a mighty
struggle. He had overcome the first Adam in the garden of Eden; why
should he not overcome the Second Adam in the wilderness? He had
spoiled man once of paradise; why should he not spoil him of the
kingdom of God.

Let it never surprise us if we are tempted by the devil. Let us rather
expect it, as a matter of course, if we are living members of Christ. The
Master's lot will be the lot of His disciples. That mighty spirit who did
not fear to attack Jesus himself, is still going about as a roaring lion,
seeking whom he may devour. That murderer and liar who vexed Job,
and overthrew David and Peter, still lives, and is not yet bound. If he
cannot rob us of heaven, he will at any rate make our journey thither
painful. If he cannot destroy our souls, he will at least bruise our heels
(Gen. 3:15). Let us beware of despising him, or thinking lightly of his
power. Let us rather put on the whole armour of God, and cry to the
strong for strength. 'Resist the devil, and he will flee from you' (Jas.
4:7).

October 10

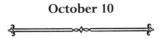

And the devil said unto him, If thou be the Son of God,
command this stone that it be made bread.
Luke 4:3

Our Lord Jesus Christ's ability to sympathize with those that are tempted.
This is a truth that stands out prominently in this passage. Jesus has been really and literally tempted Himself.

It was meet that He who came 'to destroy the works of the devil', should begin His own work by a special conflict with Satan. It was meet that the great Shepherd and Bishop of souls should be fitted for His earthly ministry by strong temptation, as well as by the Word of God and prayer. But, above all, it was meet that the great High Priest and advocate of sinners should be one who had personal experience of conflict, and has known what it is to be in the fire. And this was the case with Jesus. It is written that he 'suffered being tempted' (Heb. 2:18). How much He suffered, we cannot tell. But that His pure and spotless nature did suffer intensely, we may be sure.

Let all true Christians take comfort in the thought that they have a Friend in heaven who can be touched with the feeling of their infirmities (Heb. 4:15). When they pour out their hearts before the throne of grace, and groan under the burden that daily harasses them, there is One making intercession, who knows their sorrows. Let us take courage. The Lord Jesus is not an 'austere man'. He knows what we mean when we complain of temptation, and is both able and willing to give us help.

October 11

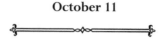

And the devil said unto him, If thou be the Son of God,
command this stone that it be made bread.
Luke 4:3

The exceeding subtlety of our great spiritual enemy, the devil.

Three times we see him assaulting our Lord, and trying to draw Him into sin. Each assault showed the hand of a master in the art of temptation. Each assault was the work of one acquainted by long experience with every weak point in human nature. Each deserves an attentive study.

Satan's first device was to persuade our Lord to distrust His Father's providential care. He comes to Him, when weak and exhausted with forty days hunger, and suggests to Him to work a miracle, in order to gratify a carnal appetite. Why should He wait any longer? Why should the Son of God sit still and starve? Why not 'command this stone that it be made bread'?

Satan's first device was to persuade our Lord to grasp at worldly power by unlawful means. He takes Him to the top of a mountain and shows Him 'all the kingdoms of the world in a moment of time'. All these he promises to give Him, if He will but 'fall down and worship him'. The concession was small. The promise was large. Why not by a little momentary act, obtain an enormous gain?

Satan's last device was to persuade our Lord to an act of presumption. He takes Him to a pinnacle of the temple and suggests to Him to cast Himself down. By so doing He would give public proof that He was one sent by God. In so doing He might even depend on being kept from harm. Was there not a text of Scripture which specially applied to the Son of God, in such a position? Was it not written that angels should bear Him up?

October 12

And Jesus answered him, saying, It is written,
That man shall not live by bread alone, but by every word of God.
Luke 4:4

The manner in which our Lord resisted Satan's temptations.

Three times we see Him foiling and baffling the great enemy who assaulted Him. He does not yield a hair's breadth to him. He does not give him a moment's advantage. Three times we see Him using the same weapon, in reply to his temptations: 'the sword of the Spirit, which is the word of God' (Eph. 6:17). He who was 'full of the Holy Ghost', was yet not ashamed to make the holy Scripture His weapon of defence and His rule of action.

Let us learn from this single fact, if we learn nothing else from this wondrous history, the high authority of the Bible, and the immense value of a knowledge of its contents. Let us read it, search it, pray over it diligently, perseveringly, unweariedly. Let us strive to be so thoroughly acquainted with its pages that its texts may abide in our memories, and stand ready at our right hand in the day of need. Let us be able to appeal from every perversion and false interpretation of its meaning, to those thousand plain passages which are written as it were with a sunbeam. The Bible is indeed a sword, but we must take heed that we know it well, if we would use it with effect.

October 13

Verily I say unto you, It shall be more tolerable for the land of Sodom
and Gomorrah in the day of judgment, than for that city.
Matthew 10:15

It is a most dangerous thing to neglect the offers of the
gospel.
It shall prove 'more tolerable for the land of Sodom and Gomorrah',
in the judgment day, than for those who have heard Christ's truth, and
not received it.

This is a doctrine fearfully overlooked, and one that deserves serious
consideration. Men are apt to forget that it does not require great open
sins to be sinned in order to ruin a soul for ever. They have only to go
on hearing without believing, listening without repenting, going to
church without going to Christ, and by and by they will find themselves
in hell! We shall all be judged according to our light; we shall have to
give account of our use of religious privileges: to hear of the 'great
salvation', and yet neglect it, is one of the worst sins man can commit
(John 16:9; Heb. 2:3).

What are we doing ourselves with the gospel? This is the question
which everyone who reads this passage should put to his conscience.
Let us assume that we are decent and respectable in our lives, correct
and moral in all the relations of life, regular in our formal attendance
on the means of grace: it is all well, so far as it goes; but is this all that
can be said of us? Are we really receiving the love of the truth? Is Christ
dwelling in our hearts by faith? If not, we are in fearful danger: we are
far more guilty than the men of Sodom, who never heard the gospel at
all; we may awake to find, that in spite of our regularity, and morality,
and correctness, we have lost our souls to all eternity. It will not save us
to have lived in the full sunshine of Christian privileges, and to have
heard the gospel faithfully preached every week: there must be
experimental acquaintance with Christ; there must be personal
reception of His truth; there must be vital union with Him: we must
become His servants and disciples.

October 14

*He that is not with me is against me; and he that gathereth not with
me scattereth abroad.*
Matthew 12:30

The impossibility of neutrality in religion.
He that is not with Christ is against Him, and he that gathereth
not with Him, scattereth abroad.

There are many persons in every age of the Church, who need to
have this lesson pressed upon them. They endeavour to steer a middle
course in religion: they are not so bad as many sinners, but still they are
not saints. They feel the truth of Christ's gospel, when it is brought
before them; but they are afraid to confess what they feel. Because they
have these feelings, they flatter themselves they are not so bad as others;
and yet they shrink from the standard of faith and practice which the
Lord Jesus sets up. They are not boldly fighting on Christ's side, and yet
they are not openly against Him. Our Lord warns all such that they are
in a dangerous position. There are only two parties in religious matters:
there are only two camps: there are only two sides. Are we with Christ,
and working in His cause? If not, we are against Him. Are we doing
good in the world? If not, we are doing harm.

The principle here laid down is one which it concerns us all to
remember. Let us settle it in our minds that we shall never have peace
and do good to others unless we are thorough going and decided in our
Christianity. The way of Gamaliel never yet brought happiness and
usefulness to any one, and never will.

October 15

Then certain of the scribes and of the Pharisees answered, saying,
Master, we would see a sign from thee.
Matthew 12:38

T he amazing power of unbelief.
We should mark how the scribes and Pharisees call upon our
Lord to show them more miracles. 'Master, we would see a sign
from thee.' They pretended that they only wanted more evidence in
order to be convinced and become disciples: they shut their eyes to the
many wonderful works which Jesus had already done. It was not enough
for them that He had healed the sick, and cleansed the lepers, raised
the dead, and cast out devils: they were not yet persuaded; they yet
demanded more proof. They would not see what our Lord plainly
pointed at in His reply, that they had no real will to believe. There was
evidence enough to convince them, but they had no wish to be
convinced.

There are many in the Church of Christ who are exactly in the state
of these scribes and Pharisees: they flatter themselves that they only
require a little more proof to become decided Christians; they fancy
that if their reason and intellect could only be met with some additional
arguments, they would at once give up all for Christ's sake, take up the
cross and follow Him. But in the meantime they wait. Alas, for their
blindness! They will not see that there is abundance of evidence on
every side of them. The truth is that they do not want to be convinced.

May we all be on our guard against the spirit of unbelief: it is a
growing evil in these latter days. Want of simple childlike faith is an
increasing feature of the times, in every rank of society. The true
explanation of a hundred strange things that startle us in the conduct of
leading men in churches and states, is downright want of faith. Men
who do not believe all that God says in the Bible, must necessarily take
a vacillating and undecided line on moral and religious questions. 'If ye
will not believe, surely ye shall not be established' (Isa. 7:9).

October 16

Is not this the carpenter's son? is not his mother called Mary?
and his brethren, James, and Joses, and Simon, and Judas?
Matthew 13:55

The strange treatment which our Lord received in His own country.

He came to the town of Nazareth, where He had been brought up, and taught in their synagogue. His teaching, no doubt, was the same as it always was: 'Never man spake like this man.' But it had no effect on the people of Nazareth. They were 'astonished', but their hearts were unmoved. They said, 'Is not this the carpenter's son? is not his mother called Mary?' They despised Him, because they were so familiar with Him. '[T]hey were offended in Him.' And they drew from our Lord the solemn remark, 'A prophet is not without honour, save in his own country, and in his own house.'

Let us see, in this history, a melancholy page of human nature unfolded to our view. We are all apt to despise mercies, if we are accustomed to them, and have them cheap. The Bibles and religious books, which are so plentiful in England, the means of grace, of which we have so abundant a supply, the preaching of the gospel, which we hear every week – all, all are liable to be undervalued. It is mournfully true, that in religion, more than anything else, 'familiarity breeds contempt'. Men forget that truth is truth, however old and hackneyed it may sound, and despise it because it is old. Alas, by doing so, they provoke God to take it away!

Do we wonder that the relatives, servants and neighbours of godly people are not always converted? Do we wonder that the parishioners of eminent ministers of the gospel are often their hardest and most impenitent hearers? Let us wonder no more. Let us mark the experience of our Lord at Nazareth, and learn wisdom.

October 17

*And he sighed deeply in his spirit, and saith, Why doth this generation
seek after a sign? verily I say unto you,
There shall no sign be given unto this generation.*
Mark 8:12

How much sorrow unbelief occasions to our Lord Jesus Christ.

We are told that when 'the Pharisees ... began to question with him, seeking of him a sign from heaven, tempting him ... he sighed deeply in his spirit'. There was a deep meaning in that sigh! It came from a heart which mourned over the ruin which these wicked men were bringing on their own souls. Enemies as they were, Jesus could not behold them hardening themselves in unbelief without sorrow.

The feeling which our Lord Jesus Christ here expressed, will always be the feeling of all true Christians. Grief over the sins of others is one leading evidence of true grace. The man who is really converted, will always regard the unconverted with pity and concern. This was the mind of David: 'I beheld the transgressors, and was grieved' (Ps. 119:158). This was the mind of the godly in the days of Ezekiel: 'they sighed and cried for the abominations done in the land' (Ezek. 9:4). This was the mind of Lot: he 'vexed his righteous soul ... with' the 'unlawful deeds' of those around him (2 Pet. 2:8). This was the mind of Paul: 'I have great heaviness and continual sorrow in my heart ... for my brethren' (Rom. 9:2). In all these cases we see something of the mind of Christ. As the great Head feels, so feel the members. They all grieve when they see sin.

Let us leave the passage with solemn self-inquiry. Do we know anything of likeness to Christ, and fellow-feeling with Him? Do we feel hurt, and pained, and sorrowful, when we see men continuing in sin and unbelief? Do we feel grieved and concerned about the state of the unconverted? These are heart-searching questions, and demand serious consideration. There are few surer marks of an unconverted heart than carelessness and indifference about the souls of others.

October 18

And when he was gone forth into the way, there came one running,
and kneeled to him, and asked him,
Good Master, what shall I do that I may inherit eternal life?
Mark 10:17

The self-ignorance of man.

We are told of one who 'came running' to our Lord, 'and kneeled to him, and asked' the solemn question, 'what shall I do that I may inherit eternal life?' At first sight there was much that was promising in this man's case. He showed anxiety about spiritual things, while most around him were careless and indifferent. He showed a disposition to reverence our Lord, by kneeling to Him, while scribes and Pharisees despised Him. Yet all this time this man was profoundly ignorant of his own heart. He hears our Lord recite those commandments which make up our duty to our neighbour, and at once declares, 'All these have I observed from my youth'. The searching nature of the moral law, its application to our thoughts, and words, as well as actions, are matters with which he is utterly unacquainted.

The spiritual blindness here exhibited is unhappily most common. Myriads of professing Christians at the present day have not an idea of their own sinfulness and guilt in the sight of God. They flatter themselves that they have never done anything very wicked: they have never murdered, or stolen, or committed adultery, or borne false witness; they cannot surely be in much danger of missing heaven. They forget the holy nature of that God with whom they have to do. They forget how often they break His law in temper, or imagination, even when their outward conduct is correct. They never study such portions of Scripture as the fifth chapter of St Matthew, or at any rate they study it with a thick veil over their hearts, and do not apply it to themselves. The result is, that they are wrapped up in self-righteousness. Like the Church of Laodicea, they are 'rich, and increased with goods, and have need of nothing' (Rev. 3:17). Self-satisfied they live, and self-satisfied too often they die.

October 19

And Zacharias said unto the angel, Whereby shall I know this?
for I am an old man, and my wife well stricken in years.
Luke 1:18

The power of unbelief in a good man.

Righteous and holy as Zacharias was, the announcement of the angel appears to him incredible. He cannot think it possible that an old man like himself should have a son. 'Whereby shall I know this?' he says, 'for I am an old man, and my wife well stricken in years'.

A well-instructed Jew, like Zacharias, ought not to have raised such a question. No doubt he was well acquainted with the Old Testament Scriptures. He ought to have remembered the wonderful births of Isaac, and Samson, and Samuel, in old times. He ought to have remembered that what God has done once, He can do again, and that with Him nothing is impossible. But he forgot all this. He thought of nothing but the arguments of mere human reason and sense; and it often happens in religious matters, that where reason begins, faith ends.

Let us learn wisdom from the fault of Zacharias. It is a fault to which God's people in every age have been sadly liable. The histories of Abraham, and Isaac, and Moses, and Hezekiah, and Jehoshaphat, will all show us that a true believer may sometimes be overtaken by unbelief. It is one of the first corruptions which came into man's heart in the day of the fall, when Eve believed the devil rather than God. It is one of the most deep-rooted sins by which a saint is plagued, and from which he is never entirely freed till he dies. Let us pray daily, 'Lord, increase my faith.' Let us not doubt then when God says a thing, that thing shall be fulfilled.

October 20

And whosoever will not receive you, when ye go out of that city,
shake off the very dust from your feet for a testimony against them.
Luke 9:5

Our Lord prepares His disciples to meet with unbelief and impenitence in those to whom they preached. He speaks of those who will not receive them as a class which they must expect to see. He tells them how to behave, when not received, as if it was a state of things to which they must make up their mind.

All ministers of the gospel would do well to read carefully this portion of our Lord's instructions. All missionaries, and district visitors, and Sunday-school teachers, would do well to lay it to heart. Let them not be cast down if their work seems in vain, and their labour without profit. Let them remember that the very first preachers and teachers whom Jesus employed were sent forth with a distinct warning, that not all would believe. Let them work on patiently, and sow the good seed without fainting. Duties are their's. Events are God's. Apostles may plant and water. The Holy Ghost alone can give spiritual life. The Lord Jesus knows what is in the heart of man. He does not despise His labourers because little of the seed they sow bears fruit. The harvest may be small. But every labourer shall be rewarded according to his work.

October 21

And that servant, which knew his lord's will, and prepared not himself,
neither did according to his will, shall be beaten with many stripes.
Luke 12:47

The greater a man's religious light is, the greater is his guilt if he is not converted.

The servant which knew his Lord's will, but did it not, shall be beaten with many stripes. '[U]nto whomsoever much is given, of him shall be much required ...'

The lesson of these words is one of wide application. It demands the attention of many classes. It should come home to the conscience of every British Christian: his judgment shall be far more strict than that of the heathen who never saw the Bible. It should come home to every Protestant who has the liberty to read the Scriptures: his responsibility is far greater than that of the priest-ridden Romanist, who is debarred from the use of God's Word. It should come home to every hearer of the gospel: if he remains unconverted he is far more guilty than the inhabitant of some dark parish, who never hears any teaching but a sort of semi-heathen morality. It should come home to every child and servant in religious families. All such are far more blameworthy, in God's sight, than those who live in houses where there is no honour paid to the Word of God and prayer. Let these things never be forgotten. Our judgment at the last day will be according to our light and opportunities.

What are we doing ourselves with our religious knowledge? Are we using it wisely, and turning it to good account? Or are we content with the barren saying, 'We know it: we know it!' and secretly flattering ourselves that the knowledge of our Lord's will makes us better than others, while that will is not done? Let us beware of mistakes. The day will come when knowledge unimproved will be found the most perilous of possessions. Thousands will awake to find that they are in a lower place than the most ignorant and idolatrous heathen. Their knowledge not used, and their light not followed, will only add to their condemnation.

October 22

And they all with one consent began to make excuse.
The first said unto him, I have bought a piece of ground,
and I must needs go and see it: I pray thee have me excused.
Luke 14:18

Many who receive gospel invitations refuse to accept them.

We read that when the servants announced that all things were ready, those who were invited 'all with one consent began to make excuse'. One had one trivial excuse, and another had another. In one point only all were agreed: they would not come.

We have in this part of the parable a vivid picture of the reception which the gospel is continually meeting with wherever it is proclaimed. Thousands are continually doing what the parable describes. They are invited to come to Christ, and they will not come. It is not ignorance of religion that ruins most men's souls. It is want of will to use knowledge, or love of this present world. It is not open profligacy that fills hell. It is excessive attention to things which in themselves are lawful. It is not avowed dislike to the gospel which is so much to be feared. It is that procrastinating, excuse-making spirit, which is always ready with a reason why Christ cannot be served today. Let the words of our Lord on this subject sink down into our hearts. Infidelity and immorality, no doubt slay their thousands, but decent, plausible, smooth-spoken excuses slay their tens of thousands. No excuse can justify a man in refusing God's invitation, and not coming to Christ.

October 23

Then came to him certain of the Sadducees,
which deny that there is any resurrection; and they asked him ...
Luke 20:27

What an old thing unbelief is.

We are told that there came to our Lord 'certain of the Sadducees, which deny that there is any resurrection'. Even in the Jewish Church, the Church of Abraham, and Isaac, and Jacob, the Church of Moses, and Samuel, and David, and the Prophets, we find that there were bold, avowed, unblushing sceptics. If infidelity like this existed among God's peculiar people, the Jews, what must the state of heathenism have been? If these things existed in a green tree, what must have been the condition of the dry?

We must never be surprised when we hear of infidels, deists, heretics and free-thinkers rising up in the Church, and drawing away disciples after them. We must not count it a rare and a strange thing, it is only one among many proofs that man is a fallen and corrupt being. Since the day when the devil said to Eve, 'Ye shall not surely die', and Eve believed him, there never has been wanting a constant succession of forms of unbelief. There is nothing new about any of the modern theories of infidelity; there is not one of them that is not an old disease under a new name: they are all mushrooms which spring up spontaneously in the hot bed of human nature. It is not in reality a wonderful thing that there should rise up so many who call in question the truths of the Bible: the marvel is rather, that in a fallen world the sect of the Sadducees should be so small.

Let us take comfort in the thought that in the long run of years the truth will always prevail. Its advocates may often be feeble, and their arguments very weak; but there is an inherent strength in the cause itself which keeps it alive. The great evidences of Christianity remain, like the pyramids, unshaken and unmoved. The 'gates of hell' shall never prevail against Christ's truth (Matt. 16:18).

October 24

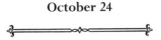

And ye will not come to me, that ye might have life.
John 5:40

The reason why many souls are lost.
The Lord Jesus says to the unbelieving Jews, 'ye will not come to me, that ye might have life'.

These words are a golden sentence, which ought to be engraven in our memories, and treasured up in our minds. It is want of will to come to Christ for salvation that will be found, at last, to have shut the many out of heaven. It is not men's sins: all manner of sin may be forgiven. It is not any decree of God. We are not told in the Bible of any whom God has only created to be destroyed. It is not any limit in Christ's word of redemption: He has paid a price sufficient for all mankind. It is something far more than this: it is man's own innate unwillingness to come to Christ, repent and believe. Either from pride, or laziness, or love of sin, or love of the world, the many have no mind, or wish, or heart, or desire to seek life in Christ. 'God hath given to us eternal life, and this life is in his Son' (1 John 5:11). But men stand still, and will not stir hand or foot to get life. And this is the whole reason why many of the lost are not saved.

This is a painful and solemn truth, but one that we can never know too well. It contains a first principle in Christian theology. Thousands, in every age, are constantly labouring to shift the blame of their condition from off themselves. They talk of their inability to change. They tell you, complacently, that they cannot help being what they are! They know, forsooth, that they are wrong, but they cannot be different! It will not do. Such talk will not stand the test of the Word of Christ before us. The unconverted are what they are because they have no will to be better. '[L]ight is come into the world, and men loved darkness rather than light' (John 3:19). The words of the Lord Jesus will silence many: 'I would have gathered you, and you would not be gathered' (Matt. 23:37).

October 25

How can ye believe, which receive honour one of another ,
and seek not the honour that cometh from God only?
John 5:44

One principal cause of unbelief.

The Lord Jesus says to the Jews, 'How can ye believe, which receive honour one of another, and seek not the honour that cometh from God only?' He meant by that saying, that they were not honest in their religion. With all their apparent desire to hear and learn, they cared more in reality for pleasing man than God. In this state of mind they were never likely to believe.

A deep principle is contained in this saying of our Lord's and one that deserves special attention. True faith does not depend merely on the state of man's head and understanding, but on the state of his heart. His mind may be convinced: his conscience may be pricked: but so long as there is anything the man is secretly loving more than God, there will be no true faith. The man himself may be puzzled, and wonder why he does not believe. He does not see that he is like a child sitting on the lid of his box, and wishing to open it, but not considering that his own weight keeps it shut. Let a man make sure that he honestly and really desires first the praise of God. It is the want of an honest heart which makes many stick fast in their religion all their days, and die at length without peace. Those who complain that they hear, and approve, and assent, but make no progress, and cannot get any hold on Christ, should ask themselves this simple question, 'Am I honest? Am I sincere? Do I really desire first the praise of God?'

October 26

Then said they unto him,
What shall we do, that we might work the works of God?
John 6:28

The spiritual ignorance and unbelief of the natural man.** Twice over we see this brought out and exemplified. When our Lord bade His hearers labour for the 'meat which endureth unto everlasting life', they immediately began to think of works to be done, and a goodness of their own to be established. 'What shall we do, that we might work the works of God?' Doing, doing, doing, was their only idea of the way to heaven. Again, when our Lord spoke of Himself as one sent of God, and the need of believing on Him at once, they turn round with the question, 'What sign showest thou? what dost thou work?' Fresh from the mighty miracle of the loaves and fishes, one might have thought they had had a sign sufficient to convince them. Taught by our Lord Jesus Christ Himself, one might have expected a greater readiness to believe. But alas! there are no limits to man's dullness, prejudice and unbelief in spiritual matters. It is a striking fact that the only thing which our Lord is said to have 'marvelled' at during His earthly ministry, was man's unbelief (Mark 6:6).

We shall do well to remember this, if we ever try to do good to others in the matter of religion. We must not be cast down because our words are not believed, and our efforts seem thrown away. We must not complain of it as a strange thing, and suppose that the people we have to deal with are peculiarly stubborn and hard. We must recollect that this is the very cup of which our Lord had to drink, and like Him we must patiently work on. If ever He, so perfect and so plain a Teacher, was not believed, what right have we to wonder if men do not believe us?

October 27

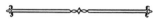

From that time many of his disciples went back,
and walked no more with him.
John 6:66

What an old sin backsliding is.
We read that when our Lord had explained what He meant by eating and drinking his flesh and blood, 'From that time many of his disciples went back, and walked no more with him.'

The true grace of God no doubt is an everlasting possession. From this men never fall away entirely, when they have once received it. '[T]he foundation of God standeth sure ...' 'My sheep [shall never perish]' (2 Tim. 2:19; John 10:28). But there is counterfeit grace and unreal religion in the Church, wherever there is true; and from counterfeit grace thousands may and do fall away. Like the stony-ground hearers, in the parable of the sower, many 'have no root' in themselves, and so 'in time of temptation fall away'. All is not gold that glitters. All blossoms do not come to fruit. All are not Israel which are called Israel. Men may have feelings, desires, convictions, resolutions, hopes, joys, sorrows in religion, and yet never have the grace of God. They may run well for a season, and bid fair to reach heaven, and yet break down entirely after a time, go back to the world, and end like Demas, Judas Iscariot and Lot's wife.

It must never surprise us to see and hear of such cases in our own days. If it happened in our Lord's time, and under our Lord's teaching, much more may we expect it to happen now. Above all, it must never shake our faith and discourage us in our course. On the contrary, we must make up our minds that there will be backsliders in the Church as long as the world stands. The sneering infidel, who defends his unbelief by pointing at them, must find some better argument than their example. He forgets that there will always be counterfeit coins where there is true money.

October 28

After these things Jesus walked in Galilee:
for he would not walk in Jewry, because the Jews sought to kill him.
John 7:1

The desperate hardness and unbelief of human nature. We are told that even our Lord's 'brethren did not believe in Him'.

Holy and harmless as He was in life, some of his nearest relatives, according to the flesh, did not receive Him as the Messiah. It was bad enough that His own people, 'the Jews sought to kill Him'. But it was even worse that 'His brethren did not believe'.

That great scriptural doctrine, man's need of preventing and converting, grace, stands out here, as if written with a sunbeam. It becomes all who question that doctrine to look at this passage and consider. Let them observe that seeing Christ's miracles, hearing Christ's teaching, living in Christ's own company, were not enough to make men believers. The mere possession of spiritual privileges never yet made anyone a Christian. All is useless without the effectual and applying work of God the Holy Ghost. No wonder that our Lord said in another place, 'No man can come to me, except the Father which hath sent me draw him' (John 6:44).

The true servants of Christ in every age will do well to remember this. They are often surprised and troubled to find that in religion they stand alone. They are apt to fancy that it must be their own fault that all around them are not converted like themselves. They are ready to blame themselves because their families remain worldly and unbelieving. But let them look at the verse before us. In our Lord Jesus Christ there was no fault either in temper, word or deed. Yet even Christ's own brethren did not believe in Him.

Our blessed Master has truly learned by experience how to sympathize with all His people who stand alone. He has drunk this bitter cup. He has passed through this fire. Let all who are fainting and cast down, because brothers and sisters despise their religion, turn to Christ for comfort, and pour out their hearts before Him.

October 29

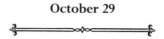

*What manner of saying is this that he said, Ye shall seek me, and shall
not find me: and where I am, thither ye cannot come?*
John 7:36

The miserable end to which unbelievers may one day
come.

We find our Lord saying to His enemies, 'ye shall seek me, and
shall not find me: and where I am, thither ye cannot come'.

We can hardly doubt that these words were meant to have prophetical
sense. Whether our Lord had in view individual cases of unbelief among
His hearers, or whether He looked forward to the national remorse
which many would feel too late in the final siege of Jerusalem, are
points which we cannot perhaps decide. But that many Jews did
remember Christ's saying long after He had ascended up into heaven,
and did in a way seek Him and wish Him when it was too late, we may
be very sure.

It is far too much forgotten that there is such a thing as finding out
truth too late. There may be convictions of sin, discoveries of our own
folly, desires after peace, anxieties about heaven, fears of hell – but all
too late. The teaching of Scripture on this point is clear and express. It
is written in Proverbs, 'Then shall they call upon me, but I will not
answer; they shall seek me early, but they shall not find me' (Prov. 1:28).
It is written of the foolish virgins in the parable, that when they found
the door shut, they knocked in vain, saying, 'Lord, Lord, open to us'
(Matt. 25:11). Awful as it may seem, it is possible, by continually resisting
light and warnings, to sin away our own souls. It sounds terrible, but it
is true.

Let us take heed to ourselves lest we sin after the example of the
unbelieving Jews, and never seek the Lord Jesus as a Saviour till it is too
late. The door of mercy is still open. The throne of grace is still waiting
for us. Let us give diligence to make sure of our interest in Christ,
which it is called today. Better never have been born than hear the Son
of God say at last, 'where I am, thither ye cannot come'.

October 30

I said therefore unto you, that ye shall die in your sins:
for if ye believe not that I am he, ye shall die in your sins.
John 8:24

How awful is the end to which unbelief can bring man. Our Lord says to His enemies 'if ye believe not that I am he, ye shall die in your sins'.

These solemn words are invested with peculiar solemnity when we consider from whose lips they came. Who is this that speaks of men dying in their sins, unpardoned, unforgiven, unfit to meet God – of men going into another world with all their sins upon them? He that says this is no other than the Saviour of mankind, who laid down His life for His sheep – the loving, gracious, merciful, compassionate Friend of sinners. It is Christ Himself! Let this simple fact not be overlooked.

They are greatly mistaken who suppose that it is harsh and unkind to speak of hell and future punishment. How can such persons get over such language as that which is before us? How can they account for many a like expression which our Lord used, and specially for such passages as those in which He speaks of the 'worm [that] dieth not, and the fire [that] is not quenched' (Mark 9:46)? They cannot answer these questions. Misled by a false charity and a morbid amiability, they are condemning the plain teaching of Scripture, and are wise above that which is written.

Let us settle it in our minds, as one of the great foundation truths of our faith, that there is a hell. Just as we believe firmly that there is an eternal heaven for the godly, so let us believe firmly that there is an eternal hell for the wicked. Let us never suppose that there is any want of charity in speaking of hell. Let us rather maintain that it is the highest love to warn men plainly of danger. And to beseech them to 'flee from the wrath to come'. It was Satan, the deceiver, murderer and liar, who said to Eve in the beginning, 'Ye shall not surely die' (Gen. 3:4). To shrink from telling men, that except they believe they will die in their sins, may please the devil, but surely it cannot please God. Let us never forget that unbelief is the special sin that ruins men's souls. Let us watch and pray hard against it.

October 31

Jesus said unto them, If ye were blind, ye should have no sin:
but now ye say, We see; therefore your sin remaineth.
John 9:41

How dangerous it is to possess knowledge, if we do not make a good use of it.

The rulers of the Jews were fully persuaded that they knew all religious truth. They were indignant at the very idea of being ignorant and devoid of spiritual eyesight. 'Are we blind also?' they cried. And then came the mighty sentence, 'If ye were blind, ye should have no sin: but now ye say, We see; therefore your sin remaineth'.

Knowledge undoubtedly is a very great blessing. The man who cannot read, and is utterly ignorant of Scripture, is in a pitiable condition. He is at the mercy of any false teacher who comes across him, and may be taught to take up any absurd creed, or to follow any vicious practice. Almost any education is better than no education at all.

But when knowledge only sticks in a man's head, and has no influence over his heart and life, it becomes a most perilous possession. And when, in addition to this, its possessor is self-conceited and self-satisfied, and fancies he knows everything, the result is one of the worst states of soul into which man can fall. There is far more hope about him who says, 'I am a poor blind sinner and want God to teach me', than about him who is ever saying, 'I know it, I know it, I am not ignorant', and yet cleaves to his sins. The sin of that man 'remaineth'.

Let us use diligently whatever religious knowledge we possess, and ask continually that God would give us more. Let us never forget that the devil himself is a creature of vast head-knowledge, and yet none the better for it, because it is not rightly used. Let our constant prayer be that which David so often sent up in the hundred and nineteenth Psalm, 'Lord ... teach me thy statutes ... give me understanding', unite my heart to fear Thy name.

NOVEMBER

November 1

But though he had done so many miracles before them,
yet they believed not on him ...
John 12:37

The desperate hardness of the human heart.
It is written of our Lord's hearers at Jerusalem, that 'though he
had done so many miracles before them, yet they believed not
on him'.

We err greatly if we suppose that seeing wonderful things will ever
convert souls. Thousands live and die in this delusion. They fancy if they
saw some miraculous sight, or witnessed some supernatural exercise
of divine grace, they would lay aside their doubts, and at once become
decided Christians. It is a total mistake. Nothing short of a new heart
and a new nature implanted in us by the Holy Ghost, will ever make us
real disciples of Christ. Without this, a miracle might raise within us a
little temporary excitement, but, the novelty once gone, we should
find ourselves just as cold and unbelieving as the Jews.

The prevalence of unbelief and indifference in the present day ought
not to surprise us. It is just one of the evidences of that mighty foundation
doctrine, the total corruption and fall of man. How feebly we grasp
and realize that doctrine is proved by our surprise at human incredulity.
We only half believe the heart's deceitfulness. Let us read our Bibles
more attentively, and search their contents more carefully. Even when
Christ wrought miracles and preached sermons, there were numbers
of his hearers who remained utterly unmoved. What right have we to
wonder if the hearers of modern sermons in countless instances remain
unbelieving? 'The disciple is not above his master.' If even the hearers of
Christ did not believe, how much more should we expect to find unbelief
among the hearers of His ministers. Let the truth be spoken and
confessed. Man's obstinate unbelief is one among many indirect proofs
that the Bible is true. The clearest prophecy in Isaiah begins with the
solemn question, 'Who hath believed'? (Isa. 53:1).

November 2

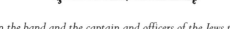

Then the band and the captain and officers of the Jews took Jesus,
and bound him ...
John 18:12

The amazing hardness of unconverted men.

We see this in the conduct of the men by whom our Lord was taken prisoner. Some of them most probably were Roman soldiers, and some of them were Jewish servants of the priests and Pharisees. But in one respect they were all alike. Both parties saw our Lord's divine power exhibited, when they 'went backward, and fell to the ground'. Both saw a miracle, according to St Luke's Gospel, when Jesus touched the ear of Malchus and healed him. Yet both remained unmoved, cold, indifferent and insensible, as if they had seen nothing out of the common way. They went on coolly with their odious business. They 'took Jesus, and bound him, And led him away ...'

The degree of hardness and insensibility of conscience to which men may attain, when they live twenty or thirty years without the slightest contact with religion, is something awful and appalling. God and the things of God seem to sink out of sight and disappear from their mind's eye. The world and the things of the world seem to absorb their whole attention. In such cases we may well believe miracles would produce little or no effect, as in the case before us. The eye would gaze on them, like the eye of a beast looking at a romantic landscape, without any impression being made on the heart. He who thinks that seeing a miracle would convert him into a thorough Christian, has got much to learn.

Let us not wonder if we see cases of hardness and unbelief in our own day and generation. Such cases will continually be found among those classes of mankind, who from their profession or position are completely cut off from means of grace. Twenty or thirty years of total irreligion, without the influence of Sunday, Bible or Christian teaching, will make a man's heart 'hard as the nether mill-stone'. Painful as these cases are, we must not think them peculiar to our own times. They existed under Christ's own eyes, and they will exist until Christ returns.

November 3

━━━━━◦◦◦◦━━━━━

Moreover if thy brother shall trespass against thee, go and tell him his
fault between thee and him alone: if he shall hear thee,
thou hast gained thy brother.
Matthew 18:15

How admirable are the rules laid down by our Lord for the healing of differences among brethren.
If we have unhappily received any injury from a fellow member of Christ's Church, the first step to be taken is to visit him 'alone', and tell him his fault. He may have injured us unintentionally, as Abimelech did Abraham (Gen. 21:26); his conduct may admit of explanation, like that of the tribes of Reuben, Gad and Manasseh, when they built an altar, as they returned to their own land (Josh. 22:24): at any rate, this friendly, faithful, straightforward way of dealing is the most likely course to win a brother, if he is to be won. '[A] soft tongue breaketh the bone' (Prov. 25:15). Who can tell but he may say at once, 'I was wrong', and make ample reparation?

If, however, this course of proceeding fails to produce any good effect, a second step is to be taken. We are to 'take with us one or two' companions, and tell our brother of his fault in their presence and hearing. Who can tell but his conscience may be stricken, when he finds his misconduct made known, and he may be ashamed and repent? If not, we shall at all events have the testimony of witnesses, that we did all we could to bring our brother to a right mind, and that he deliberately refused, when appealed to, to make amends.

Finally, if this second course of proceeding prove useless, we are to refer the whole matter to the Christian congregation of which we are members: we are to 'tell it unto the church'. Who can tell but the heart which has been unmoved by private remonstrances, may be moved by the fear of public exposure? If not, there remains but one view to take of our brother's case: we must sorrowfully regard him as one who has shaken off all Christian principles, and will be guided by no higher motives than 'an heathen man and a publican'. Differences and divisions there will be, so long as the world stands; but many of them would be extinguished at once, if the course recommended in these verses was tried.

November 4

And if a kingdom be divided against itself, that kingdom cannot stand.
Mark 3:24

Ｈow great is the evil of dissensions and divisions. This is a lesson which is strongly brought out in the beginning of our Lord's reply to the scribes. He shows the absurdity of supposing that Satan would 'cast out Satan', and so help to destroy his own power. He appeals to the notorious fact, which even His enemies must allow, that there can be no strength where there is division. 'And if a kingdom be divided against itself, that kingdom cannot stand.'

This truth is one which does not receive sufficient consideration. On no point has the abuse of the right of private judgment produced so much evil. The divisions of Christians are one great cause of the weakness of the visible Church. They often absorb energy, time and power, which might have been well bestowed on better things. They furnish the infidel with a prime argument against the truth of Christianity. They help the devil. Satan, indeed, is the chief promoter of religious divisions. If he cannot extinguish Christianity, he labours to make Christians quarrel with one another, and to set every man's hand against his neighbour. None knows better than the devil, that to divide is to conquer.

Let us resolve, so far as in us lies, to avoid all differences, dissensions and disputes in religion. Let us loathe and abhor them as the plague of the Churches. We cannot be too jealous about all saving truths. But it is easy to mistake morbid scrupulosity for conscientiousness, and zeal about mere trifles for zeal about the truth. Nothing justifies separation from a Church but the separation of that Church from the gospel. Let us be ready to concede much, and make many sacrifices for the sake of unity and peace.

November 5

And entered into the house of Zacharias, and saluted Elisabeth.
Luke 1:40

The benefit of fellowship and communion between believers.

We read of a visit paid by the Virgin Mary to her cousin Elisabeth. We are told in a striking manner how the hearts of both these holy women were cheered, and their minds lifted up by this interview. Without this visit, Elisabeth might never have been so filled with the Holy Ghost, as we are here told she was; and Mary might never have uttered that song of praise which is now known all over the Church of Christ. The words of an old divine are deep and true: 'Happiness communicated doubles itself. Grief grows greater by concealing: joy by expression.'

We should always regard communion with other believers as an eminent means of grace. It is a refreshing break in our journey along the narrow way, to exchange experience with our fellow travellers. It helps us insensibly and it helps them, and so is a mutual gain. It is the nearest approach that we can make on earth to the joy of heaven. As 'Iron sharpeneth iron; so a man sharpeneth the countenance of his friend.' We need reminding of this. The subject does not receive sufficient attention, and the souls of believers suffer in consequence. There are many who fear the Lord and think upon His name, and yet forget to speak often one to another (Mal. 3:16). First let us seek the face of God. Then let us seek the face of God's friends. If we did this more, and were more careful about the company we keep, we should oftener know what it is to feel 'filled with the Holy Ghost'.

November 6

And they said unto him, Why do the disciples of John fast often, and make
prayers, and likewise the disciples of the Pharisees; but thine eat and drink?
Luke 5:33

Men may disagree on the lesser points of religion,
while they agree on its weightier matters.
We have this brought out in the alleged difference between
the disciples of John the Baptist, and the disciples of Christ. The question
was put to our Lord, 'Why do the disciples of John fast often, and make
prayers, and likewise the disciples of the Pharisees; but thine eat and
drink?'

We cannot suppose that there was any essential difference between
the doctrines held by these two parties of disciples. The teaching of
John the Baptist was doubtless clear and explicit upon all the main points
necessary to salvation. The man who could say of Jesus, 'Behold the
Lamb of God, which taketh away the sin of the world', was not likely to
teach his followers anything contrary to the gospel. His teaching of
course lacked the fullness and perfection of his divine Master's teaching,
but it is absurd to suppose that it contradicted it. Nevertheless there
were points of practice on which his disciples differed from those of
Christ. Agreeing, as they doubtless did, about the necessity of
repentance, and faith, and holiness, they disagreed about such matters
as fasting, eating, drinking and manner of public devotion. One in heart,
and hope, and aim, as they were in matters of inner religion, they were
not entirely of one mind about outward matters.

We must make up our minds to see differences of this kind among
Christians so long as the world stands. We may regret them much,
because of the handle they give to an ignorant and prejudiced world.
But they will exist, and are one of the many evidences of our fallen
condition.

Let us, however, bless God that there are many points on which all
true servants of God are thoroughly agreed. About sin and salvation,
about repentance, and faith, and holiness, there is a mighty unity among
all believers, of every name, and nation, and people, and tongue. Let us
make much of these points in our own personal religion.

November 7

That they all may be one; as thou,
Father, art in me, and I in thee, that they also may be one in us:
that the world may believe that thou hast sent me.
John 17:21

How Jesus prays for the unity and oneness of His people.

'That they all may be one … that they also may be one in us … that they may be one, even as we are one', and that so the world may believe and 'know that thou hast sent me' – these are leading petitions in our Lord's prayer to His Father.

We can ask no stronger proof of the value of unity among Christians, and the sinfulness of divisions, than the great prominence which our Master assigns to the subject in this passage. How painfully true it is that in every age divisions have been the scandal of religion, and the weakness of the Church of Christ! How often Christians have wasted their strength in contending against their brethren, instead of contending against sin and the devil! How repeatedly they have given occasion to the world to say, 'When you have settled your own internal differences we will believe!' All this, we need not doubt, the Lord Jesus foresaw with prophetic eye. It was the foresight of it which made Him pray so earnestly that believers might be 'one'.

Let the recollection of this part of Christ's prayer abide in our minds, and exercise a constant influence on our behaviour as Christians. Let no man think lightly, as some men seem to do, of schism, or count it a small thing to multiply sects, parties and denominations. These very things, we may depend, only help the devil and damage the cause of Christ. 'If it be possible, as much as lieth in you, live peaceably with all men' (Rom. 12:18). Let us bear much, concede much, and put up with much, before we plunge into secessions and separations. So long as we have Christ and a good conscience, let us patiently hold on our way, follow the things that make for peace and strive to promote unity. It was not for nothing that our Lord prayed so fervently that His people might be 'one'.

November 8

And, behold, one came and said unto him,
Good Master, what good thing shall I do, that I may have eternal life?
Matthew 19:16

A person may have desires after salvation, and yet not be saved.

Here is one who in a day of abounding unbelief comes of his own accord to Christ. He comes not to have a sickness healed; he comes not to plead about a child: he comes about his own soul. He opens the conference with the frank question, 'Good Master, what good thing shall I do, that I may have eternal life?' Surely we might have thought, 'This is a promising case: this is no prejudiced ruler or Pharisee: this is a hopeful inquirer.' Yet by and by this very young man goes 'away sorrowful'; and we never read a word to show that he was converted! We must never forget that good feelings alone in religion are not the grace of God. We may know the truth intellectually; we may often feel pricked in conscience; we may have religious affections awakened within us, have many anxieties about our souls and shed many tears: but all this is not conversion. It is not the genuine saving work of the Holy Ghost.

Unhappily this is not all that must be said on this point. Not only are good feelings alone not grace, but they are even positively dangerous, if we content ourselves with them, and do not act as well as feel. It is a profound remark of that mighty master on moral questions, Bishop Butler, that passive impressions, often repeated, gradually lose all their power; actions, often repeated, produce a habit in man's mind; feelings often indulged in, without leading to corresponding actions, will finally exercise no influence at all.

Let us apply this lesson to our own state. Perhaps we know what it is to feel religious fears, wishes and desires. Let us beware that we do not rest in them. Let us never be satisfied till we have the witness of the Spirit in our hearts, that we are actually born again and new creatures; let us never rest till we know that we have really repented, and laid hold on the hope set before us in the gospel. It is good to feel; but it is far better to be converted.

November 9

But they made light of it, and went their ways, one to his farm,
another to his merchandise ...
Matthew 22:5

The salvation of the gospel is rejected by many to whom it is offered.

The Lord Jesus tells us that those whom the king's servants bade to the wedding 'made light of it, and went their way'.

There are thousands of hearers of the gospel who derive from it no benefit whatever. They listen to it Sunday after Sunday, and year after year, and do not believe to the saving of the soul. They feel no special need of the gospel; they see no special beauty in it; they do not perhaps hate it, or oppose it, or scoff at it, but they do not receive it into their hearts. They like other things far better. Their money, their land, their business or their pleasures, are all far more interesting subjects to them than their souls. It is an awful state of mind to be in, but awfully common. Let us search our own hearts, and take heed that it is not our own. Open sin may kill its thousands; but indifference and neglect of the gospel kill their tens of thousands. Multitudes will find themselves in hell, not so much because they openly broke the Ten Commandments, as because they made light of the truth. Christ died for them on the cross, but they neglected Him.

November 10

*O Jerusalem, Jerusalem, thou that killest the prophets, and stonest them which
are sent unto thee, how often would I have gathered thy children together, even
as a hen gathereth her chickens under her wings, and ye would not!*
Matthew 23:37

Those who are lost for ever, are lost through their own
fault.

The words of our Lord Jesus Christ are very remarkable. He
says, I would 'have gathered thy children together ... and ye would
not'.

There is something peculiarly deserving of notice in this expression:
it throws light on a mysterious subject, and one which is often darkened
by human explanations. It shows that Christ has feelings of pity and
mercy for many who are not saved, and that the grand secret of man's
ruin is his want of will. Impotent as man is by nature, unable to think a
good thought of himself, without power to turn himself to faith and
calling upon God – he still appears to have a mighty ability to ruin his
own soul. Powerless as he is to good, he is still powerful to evil. We say
rightly that a man can do nothing of himself, but we must always
remember that the seat of impotence is his will. A will to repent and
believe no man can give himself, but a will to reject Christ and have his
own way, every man possesses by nature, and if not saved at last, that
will shall prove to have been his destruction. 'And ye will not come to
me,' says Christ, 'that ye might have life' (John 5:40).

Let us leave the subject with the comfortable reflection that with
Christ nothing is impossible. The hardest heart can be made willing in
the day of His power. Grace beyond doubt is irresistible, but never let
us forget that the Bible speaks of man as a responsible being, and that it
says of some, 'ye do always resist the Holy Ghost' (Acts 7:51). Let us
understand that the ruin of those who are lost, is not because Christ
was not willing to save them, nor yet because they wanted to be saved,
but could not, but because they would not come to Christ.

November 11

But there were certain of the scribes sitting there,
and reasoning in their hearts ...
Mark 2:6

What great spiritual privileges some persons enjoy, and yet make no use of them.
This is a truth which is strikingly illustrated by the history of Capernaum. No city in Palestine appears to have enjoyed so much of our Lord's presence, during His earthly ministry, as did this city. It was the place where He dwelt, after He left Nazareth (Matt. 4:13). It was the place where many of his miracles were worked, and many of His sermons delivered. But nothing that Jesus said or did seems to have had any effect on the hearts of the inhabitants. They crowded to hear Him, as we read in this passage, till 'there was no room ... about the door'. They were amazed. They were astonished. They were filled with wonder at His mighty works. But they were not converted. They lived in the full noontide blaze of the Sun of Righteousness, and yet their hearts remained hard. And they drew from our Lord the heaviest condemnation that He ever pronounced against any place, except Jerusalem: 'thou, Capernaum, which art exalted unto heaven, shalt be brought down to hell: for if the mighty works, which have been done in thee, had been done in Sodom, it would have remained until this day. But I say unto you, That it shall be more tolerable for the land of Sodom, in the day of judgment, than for thee' (Matt. 11:23, 24).

It is good for us all to mark well this case of Capernaum. We are all too apt to suppose that it need nothing but the powerful preaching of the gospel to convert people's souls, and that if the gospel is only brought into a place everybody must believe. We forget the amazing power of unbelief, and the depth of man's enmity against God. We forget that the Capernaites heard the most faultless preaching, and saw it confirmed by the most surprising miracles, and yet remained dead in trespasses and sins. We need reminding that the same gospel which is the savor of life to some, is the savor of death to others, and that the same fire which softens the wax will also harden the clay.

November 12

If any man have ears to hear, let him hear.
Mark 4:23

The importance of hearing well what we hear.
This is a point to which our Lord evidently attaches great weight. We have seen it already brought out in the parable of the sower. We see it here enforced in two remarkable expressions. 'If any man have ears to hear, let him hear.' 'Take heed what ye hear …' Hearing the truth is one principal avenue through which grace is conveyed to the soul of man. '[F]aith cometh by hearing' (Rom. 10:17). One of the first steps towards conversion is to receive from the Spirit a hearing ear. Seldom are men brought to repentance and faith in Christ without 'hearing'. The general rule is that of which St Paul reminds the Ephesians, 'Ye also trusted, after that ye heard the word of truth' (Eph. 1:13).

Let us bear this in mind when we hear preaching decried as a means of grace. There are never wanting men who seek to cast it down from the high place which the Bible gives it. There are many who proclaim loudly that it is of far more importance to the soul to hear liturgical forms read, and to receive the Lord's Supper, than to hear God's Word expounded. Of all such notions let us beware. Let it be a settled principle with us that hearing the Word is one of the foremost means of grace that God has given man. Let us give to every other means and ordinance its proper value and proportion. But never let us forget the words of St Paul, 'Despise not prophesyings'; and his dying charge to Timothy, 'Preach the word' (1 Thess. 5:20; 2 Tim. 4:2).

November 13

For John had said unto Herod,
It is not lawful for thee to have thy brother's wife.
Mark 6:18

How boldly a faithful minister of God ought to rebuke sin.

John the Baptist spoke plainly to Herod about the wickedness of his life. He did not excuse himself under the plea that it was imprudent, or impolitic, or untimely, or useless to speak out. He did not say smooth things, and palliate the King's ungodliness by using soft words to describe his offence. He told his royal hearer the plain truth, regardless of all consequences: 'It is not lawful for thee to have thy brother's wife'.

Here is a pattern that all ministers ought to follow. Publicly and privately, from the pulpit and in private visits, they ought to rebuke all open sin, and deliver a faithful warning to all who are living in it. It may give offence. It may entail immense unpopularity. With all this they have nothing to do. Duties are theirs. Results are God's.

No doubt it requires great grace and courage to do this. No doubt a reprover, like John the Baptist, must go to work wisely and lovingly in carrying out his Master's commission and rebuking the wicked. But it is a matter in which his character for faithfulness and charity are manifestly at stake. If he believes a man is injuring his soul, he ought surely to tell him so. If he loves him truly and tenderly, he ought not to let him ruin himself unwarned. Great as the present offence may be, in the long run the faithful reprover will generally be respected. 'He that rebuketh a man afterwards shall find more favour than he that flattereth with the tongue' (Prov. 28:23).

November 14

And he charged them, saying, Take heed, beware of the leaven of the
Pharisees, and of the leaven of Herod.
Mark 8:15

Notice the solemn warning which our Lord gives to His disciples at the beginning of this passage.
He says, 'Take heed, beware of the leaven of the Pharisees, and of the leaven of Herod'.

We are not left to conjecture the meaning of this warning. This is made clear by the parallel passage in St Matthew's Gospel. We there read that Jesus did not mean the leaven of 'bread', but the leaven of 'doctrine'. The self-righteousness and formalism of the Pharisees, the worldliness and scepticism of the courtiers of Herod, were the objects of our Lord's caution. Against both He bids His disciples be on their guard.

Such warnings are of deep importance. It would be well for the Church of Christ if they had been more remembered. The assaults of persecution from without have never done half so much harm to the Church as the rise of false doctrines within. False prophets and false teachers within the camp have done far more mischief in Christendom than all the bloody persecutions of the emperors of Rome. The sword of the foe has never done such damage to the cause of truth as the tongue and the pen.

The doctrines which our Lord specifies, are precisely those which have always been found to inflict most injury on the cause of Christianity. Formalism, on the one hand, and scepticism, on the other, have been chronic diseases in the professing Church of Christ. In every age multitudes of Christians have been infected by them. In every age men need to watch against them, and be on their guard.

Let us often examine 'ourselves whether we be in the faith' and 'beware of the leaven'. Let us no more trifle with a little false doctrine than we would trifle with a little immorality, or a little lie. Once admit it into our hearts, and we never know how far it may lead us astray. The beginning of departure from the pure truth is like the letting out of waters – first a drop, and at last a torrent.

November 15

Whosoever therefore shall be ashamed of me and of my words in this adulterous and sinful generation; of him also shall the Son of man be ashamed, when he cometh in the glory of his Father with the holy angels.
Mark 8:38

The great danger of being ashamed of Christ. What saith our Lord? We are guilty of it when we are ashamed of letting people see that we believe and love the doctrines of Christ, that we desire to live according to the commandment of Christ, and that we wish to be reckoned among the people of Christ. Christ's doctrine, laws and people were never popular, and never will be. The man who boldly confesses that he loves them, is sure to bring on himself ridicule and persecution. Whosoever shrinks from this confession from fear of this ridicule and persecution, is ashamed of Christ, and comes under the sentence of the passage before us.

Perhaps there are few of our Lord's sayings which are more condemning than this. 'The fear of man' does indeed 'bringeth a snare' (Prov. 29:25). There are thousands of men who would face a lion, or storm a breach, if duty called them, and fear nothing – and yet would be ashamed of being thought 'religious', and would not dare to avow that they desired to please Christ rather than man. Wonderful indeed is the power of ridicule! Marvellous is the bondage in which men live to the opinion of the world!

Let us all pray daily for faith and courage to confess Christ before men. Of sin, or worldliness, or unbelief, we may well be ashamed. We ought never to be ashamed of Him who died for us on the cross. In spite of laughter, mockery and hard words, let us boldly avow that we serve Christ. Let us often look forward to the day of His second coming, and remember what He says in this place. Better a thousand times confess Christ now, and be despised by man, than be disowned by Christ before His Father in the day of judgment.

November 16

And when he was gone forth into the way, there came one running,
and kneeled to him, and asked him,
Good Master, what shall I do that I may inherit eternal life?
Mark 10:17

The self-ignorance of man.

We are told of one who 'came ... running' to our Lord, 'and kneeled to him, and asked' the solemn question, 'what shall I do that I may inherit eternal life?' At first sight there was much that was promising in this man's case. He showed anxiety about spiritual things, while most around him were careless and indifferent. He showed a disposition to reverence our Lord, by kneeling to Him, while scribes and Pharisees despised Him. Yet all this time this man was profoundly ignorant of his own heart. He hears our Lord recite those commandments which make up our duty to our neighbour, and at once declares, 'all these have I observed from my youth'. The searching nature of the moral law, its application to our thoughts, and words, as well as actions, are matters with which he is utterly unacquainted.

The spiritual blindness here exhibited is unhappily most common. Myriads of professing Christians at the present day have not an idea of their own sinfulness and guilt in the sight of God. They flatter themselves that they have never done anything very wicked: they have never murdered, or stolen, or committed adultery, or borne false witness; they cannot surely be in much danger of missing heaven. They forget the holy nature of that God with whom they have to do. They forget how often they break His law in temper, or imagination, even when their outward conduct is correct. They never study such portions of Scripture as the fifth chapter of St Matthew, or at any rate they study it with a thick veil over their hearts, and do not apply it to themselves. The result is, that they are wrapped up in self-righteousness. Like the church of Laodicea, they are 'rich, and increased with goods, and have need of nothing' (Rev. 3:17). Self-satisfied they live, and self-satisfied too often they die.

November 17

And they come to Jerusalem: and Jesus went into the temple, and began to cast out them that sold and bought in the temple, and overthrew the tables of the money changers, and the seats of them that sold doves …
Mark 11:15

The great danger of unfruitfulness and formality in religion.

This is a lesson which our Lord teaches in a remarkable typical action. We are told that coming to a fig tree in search of fruit, and finding on it 'nothing but leaves', He pronounced on it the solemn sentence, 'No man eat fruit of thee hereafter for ever'. And we are told that the next day the fig tree was found 'dried up from the roots'. We cannot doubt for a moment that this whole transaction was an emblem of spiritual things. It was a parable in deeds, as full of meaning as any of our Lord's parables in words.

But who were they to whom this withered fig tree was intended to speak? It was a sermon of threefold application, a sermon that ought to speak loudly to the consciences of all professing Christians. Though withered and dried up, that fig tree yet speaks. There was a voice in it for the Jewish Church. Rich in the leaves of a formal religion, but barren of all fruits of the spirit, that Church was in fearful danger at the very time when this withering took place. Well would it have been for the Jewish Church if it had had eyes to see its peril!

There was a voice in the fig tree for all the branches of Christ's visible Church, in every age and every part of the world. There was a warning against an empty profession of Christianity unaccompanied by sound doctrine and holy living, which some of those branches would have done well to lay to heart. But above all there was a voice in that withered fig tree for all carnal, hypocritical and false-hearted Christians. Well would it be for all who are content with a name to live while in reality they are dead, if they would only see their own faces in the glass of this passage.

November 18

And he spake a parable unto them, Can the blind lead the blind?
Shall they not both fall into the ditch?
Luke 6:39

The great danger of listening to false teachers in religion.

Our Lord compares such teachers and their hearers to the blind leading the blind, and asks the reasonable question, 'shall they not both fall into the ditch?' He goes on to confirm the importance of His warning, by declaring, that 'The disciple is not above his master', and the scholar cannot be expected to know more than his teacher. If a man will hear unsound instruction, we cannot expect him to become otherwise than unsound in the faith himself.

The subject which our Lord brings before us here deserves far more attention than it generally receives. The amount of evil which unsound religious teaching has brought on the Church in every age is incalculable. The loss of souls which it has occasioned is fearful to contemplate. A teacher who does not know the way to heaven himself is not likely to lead his hearers to heaven. The man who hears such a teacher runs a fearful risk himself of being lost eternally. 'If the blind lead the blind both must fall into the ditch.'

If we would escape the danger against which our Lord warns us, we must not neglect to prove the teaching that we hear by the holy Scriptures. We must not believe things merely because ministers say them. We must not suppose, as a matter of course, that ministers can make no mistakes. We must call to mind our Lord's words on another occasion: 'Beware of false prophets' (Matt. 7:15). We must remember the advice of St Paul and St John: 'Prove all things'. '[T]ry the spirits whether they are of God' (1 Thess. 5:21; 1 John 4:1). With the Bible in our hands, and the promise of guidance from the Holy Ghost to all who seek it, we shall be without excuse if our souls are led astray. The blindness of ministers is no excuse for the darkness of people. The man who from indolence, or superstition, or affected humility, refuses to distrust the teaching of the minister whom he finds set over him, however unsound it may be, will at length share his minister's portion.

November 19

And stood at his feet behind him weeping, and began to wash his feet
with tears, and did wipe them with the hairs of her head, and kissed
his feet, and anointed them with the ointment.

Luke 7:38

Men may show some outward respect to Christ, and yet remain unconverted.

The Pharisee before us is a case in point. He showed our Lord Jesus Christ more respect than many did. He even 'desired him that he would eat with him'. Yet all this time he was profoundly ignorant of the nature of Christ's gospel. His proud heart secretly revolted at the sight of a poor contrite sinner being allowed to wash our Lord's feet. And even the hospitality he showed appears to have been cold and niggardly. Our Lord Himself says, 'thou gavest me no water for my feet ... Thou gavest me no kiss ... My head with oil thou didst not anoint'. In short, in all that the Pharisees did there was one great defect. There was outward civility, but there was no heart-love.

We shall do well to remember the case of this Pharisee. It is quite possible to have a decent form of religion, and yet to know nothing of the gospel of Christ – to treat Christianity with respect, and yet to be utterly blind about its cardinal doctrines – to behave with great correctness and propriety at church, and yet to hate justification by faith, and salvation by grace, with a deadly hatred. Do we really feel affection toward the Lord Jesus? Can we say, 'Lord thou knowest all things, thou knowest that I love Thee'? Have we cordially embraced His whole gospel? Are we willing to enter heaven side by side with the chief of sinners, and to owe all our hopes to free grace? These are questions which we ought to consider. If we cannot answer them satisfactorily, we are in no respect better than Simon the Pharisee, and our Lord might say to us, 'I have somewhat to say unto thee'.

November 20

A sower went out to sow his seed: and as he sowed, some fell by the way side;
and it was trodden down, and the fowls of the air devoured it.
Luke 8:5

Beware of the devil when we hear the Word.
Our Lord tells us that the hearts of some hearers are like 'the way side'. The seed of the gospel is plucked away from them by the devil almost as soon as it is sown. It does not sink down into their consciences. It does not make the least impression on their minds.

The devil, no doubt, is everywhere. That malicious spirit is unwearied in his efforts to do us harm. He is ever watching for our halting, and seeking occasion to destroy our souls. But nowhere perhaps is the devil so active as in a congregation of gospel-hearers. Nowhere does he labour so hard to stop the progress of that which is good, and to prevent men and women being saved. From him come wandering thoughts and roving imaginations, listless minds and dull memories, sleepy eyes and fidgety nerves, weary ears and distracted attention. In all these things Satan has a great hand. People wonder where they come from, and marvel how it is that they find sermons so dull, and remember them so badly! They forget the parable of the sower. They forget the devil.

Let us take heed that we are not way side hearers. Let us beware of the devil. We shall always find him at church. He never stays away from public ordinances. Let us remember this, and be upon our guard. Heat, and cold, and draughts, and damp, and wet, and rain, and snow, are often dreaded by churchgoers, and alleged as reasons for not going to church. But there is one enemy whom they ought to fear more than all these things together. That enemy is Satan.

November 21

And some fell upon a rock; and as soon as it was sprung up, it
withered away, because it lacked moisture.
Luke 8:6

Beware of resting on mere temporary impressions when we have heard the Word.

Our Lord tells us that the hearts of some hearers are like rocky ground. The seed of the Word springs up immediately, as soon as they hear it, and bears a crop of joyful impressions, and pleasurable emotions. But these impressions, unhappily, are only on the surface. There is no deep and abiding work done in their souls. And hence, so soon as the scorching heart of temptation or persecution begins to be felt, the little bit of religion which they seemed to have attained, withers and vanishes away.

Feelings, no doubt, fill a most important office in our personal Christianity. Without them there can be no saving religion. Hope, and joy, and peace, and confidence, and resignation, and love, and fear, are things which must be felt, if they really exist. But it must never be forgotten that there are religious affections which are spurious and false, and spring from nothing better than animal excitement. It is quite possible to feel great pleasure, or deep alarm, under the preaching of the gospel, and yet to be utterly destitute of the grace of God. The tears of some hearers of sermons, and the extravagant delight of others, are no certain marks of conversion. We may be warm admirers of favourite preachers, and yet remain nothing better than stony-ground hearers. Nothing should content us but a deep, humbling, self-mortifying work of the Holy Ghost, and a heart-union with Christ.

November 22

And some fell among thorns; and the thorns sprang up with it, and choked it.
Luke 8:7

Beware of the cares of the world.

Our Lord tells us that the hearts of many hearers of the Word are like thorny ground. The seed of the Word, when sown upon them, is choked by the multitude of other things, by which their affections are occupied. They have no objection to the doctrines and requirements of the gospel. They even wish to believe and obey them. But they allow the things of earth to get such hold upon their minds, that they leave no room for the Word of God to do its work. And hence it follows that however many sermons they hear, they seem nothing bettered by them. A weekly process of truth-stifling goes on within. They bring no fruit to perfection.

The things of this life form one of the greatest dangers which beset a Christian's path. The money, the pleasures, the daily business of the world, are so many traps to catch souls. Thousands of things, which in themselves are innocent, become, when followed to excess, little better than soul-poisons, and helps to hell. Open sin is not the only thing that ruins souls. In the midst of our families, and in the pursuit of our lawful callings, we have need to be on our guard. Except we watch and pray, these temporal things may rob us of heaven, and smother every sermon we hear. We may live and die thorny-ground hearers.

November 23

And other fell on good ground, and sprang up, and bare fruit an
hundredfold. And when he had said these things, he cried,
He that hath ears to hear, let him hear.
Luke 8:8

Beware of being content with any religion which does not bear fruit in our lives.

Our Lord tells us that the hearts of those who hear the Word aright, are like good ground. The seed of the gospel sinks down deeply into their wills, and produces practical results in their faith and practice.

They not only hear with pleasure, but act with decision. They repent. They believe. They obey.

For ever let us bear in mind that this is the only religion that saves souls. Outward profession of Christianity, and the formal use of Church ordinances and sacraments, never yet gave man a good hope in life, or peace in death, or rest in the world beyond the grave. There must be fruits of the Spirit in our hearts and lives, or else the gospel is preached to us in vain. Those only who bear such fruits, shall be found at Christ's right hand in the day of His appearing.

Let us leave the parable with a deep sense of the danger and responsibility of all hearers of the gospel. There are four ways in which we may hear, and of these four only one is right, there are three kinds of hearers whose souls are in imminent peril. How many of these three kinds are to be found in every congregation! There is only one class of hearers which is right in the sight of God. And what are we? Do we belong to that one?

Finally let us leave the parable with a solemn recollection of the duty of every faithful preacher to divide his congregation, and give to each class his portion. The clergyman who ascends his pulpit every Sunday, and addresses his congregation as if he thought everyone was going to heaven, is surely not doing his duty to God or man. His preaching is flatly contradictory to the parable of the sower.

November 24

Then the whole multitude of the country of the Gadarenes round
about besought him to depart from them; for they were taken with
great fear: and he went up into the ship, and returned back again.
Luke 8:37

Then Gadarenes besought our Lord to depart from them,
and their request was granted.

We read these painfully solemn words, 'he went up into the
ship, and returned back again'.

Now why did these unhappy men desire the Son of God to leave
them? Why, after the amazing miracle of mercy which had just been
wrought among them, did they feel no wish to know more of Him who
wrought it? Why, in a word, did they become their own enemies, forsake
their own mercies and shut the door against the gospel? There is but
one answer to these questions. The Gadarenes loved the world, and the
things of the world, and were determined not to give them up. They
felt convinced, in their own consciences, that they could not receive
Christ among them and keep their sins, and their sins they were resolved
to keep. They saw, at a glance, that there was something about Jesus
with which their habits of life would never agree, and having to choose
between the new ways and their own old ones, they refused the new
and chose the old.

And why did our Lord Jesus Christ grant the request of the
Gadarenes, and leave them? He did it in judgment, to testify His sense
of the greatness of their sin. He did it in mercy to His Church in every
age, to show how great is the wickedness of those who wilfully reject
the truth. It seems an eternal law of His government, that those who
obstinately refuse to walk in the light shall have the light taken from
them. Great is Christ's patience and long-suffering! His mercy endureth
for ever. His offers and invitations are wide, and broad, and sweeping,
and universal. He gives every Church its day of grace and time of
visitation (Luke 19:44). But if men persist in refusing His counsel, He
has nowhere promised to persist in forcing it upon them. People who
have the gospel, and yet refuse to obey it, must not be surprised if the
gospel is removed from them.

November 25

For whosoever shall be ashamed of me and of my words, of him shall
the Son of man be ashamed, when he shall come in his own glory,
and in his Father's, and of the holy angels.
Luke 9:26

The guilt and danger of being ashamed of Christ and His words.

We read that He says, 'whosoever shall be ashamed of me and of my words, of him shall the Son of man be ashamed, when he shall come in his own glory, and in his Father's, and of the holy angels'.

There are many ways of being ashamed of Christ. We are guilty of it whenever we are afraid of letting men know that we love His doctrines, His precepts, His people and His ordinances. We are guilty of it whenever we allow the fear of man to prevail over us, and to keep us back from letting others see that we are decided Christians. Whenever we act in this way, we are denying our Master, and committing a great sin.

The wickedness of being ashamed of Christ is very great. It is a proof of unbelief. It shows that we care more for the praise of man whom we can see, than that God whom we cannot see. It is a proof of ingratitude. It shows that we fear confessing Him before man, who was not ashamed to die for us upon the cross. Wretched indeed are they who give way to this sin. Here, in this world, they are always miserable. A bad conscience robs them of peace. In the world to come they can look for no comfort. In the day of judgment they must expect to be disowned by Christ to all eternity, if they will not confess Christ for a few years upon earth.

November 26

*Then goeth he, and taketh to him seven other spirits more wicked than
himself; and they enter in, and dwell there:
and the last state of that man is worse than the first.*
Luke 11:26

How dangerous it is to be content with any change in religion short of through conversion to God. This is a truth which our Lord teaches by an awful picture of one from whom a devil has been cast forth, but into whose heart the Holy Spirit has not entered. He describes the evil spirit, after his expulsion, as seeking rest and finding none. He describes him planning a return to the heart which he once inhabited, and carrying his plan into execution. He describes him finding that heart empty of any good, and like a house 'swept and garnished' for his reception. He describes him as entering in once more, with seven spirits worse than himself, and once more making it his abode. And he winds up all by the solemn saying, 'the last state of that man is worse than the first'.

We must feel in reading these fearful words, that Jesus is speaking of things which we faintly comprehend. He is lifting a corner of the veil which hangs over the unseen world. His words, no doubt, illustrate the state of things which existed in the Jewish nation during the time of His own ministry. But the main lesson of His words, which concerns us, is the danger of our own individual souls. They are a solemn warning to us never to be satisfied with religious reformation without heart conversion.

There is no safety excepting in thorough Christianity. To lay aside open sin is nothing, unless grace reigns in our hearts. To cease to do evil is a small matter, if we do not also learn to do well. The house must not only be swept and whitewashed; a new tenant must be introduced, or else the leprosy may yet appear again in the walls. The outward life must not only be garnished with the formal trappings of religion; the power of vital religion must be experienced in the inward man. The devil must not only be cast out; the Holy Ghost must take his place. Christ must dwell in our hearts by faith. We must not only be moralized, but spiritualized. We must not only be reformed, but born again.

November 27

And he said unto them, Take heed, and beware of covetousness: for a man's life consisteth not in the abundance of the things which he possesseth.
Luke 12:15

What a solemn warning our Lord pronounces against covetousness.

'[H]e said unto them, Take heed, and beware of covetousness.'

It would be vain to decide positively which is the most common sin in the world. It would be safe to say that there is none, at any rate, to which the heart is more prone, than covetousness. It was this sin which helped to cast down the angels who fell. They were not content with their first estate: they coveted something better. It was this sin which helped to drive Adam and Eve out of paradise, and bring death into the world. Our first parents were not satisfied with the things which God gave them in Eden: they coveted, and so they fell. It is a sin which, ever since the fall, has been the fertile cause of misery and unhappiness upon earth. Wars, quarrels, strifes, divisions, envyings, disputes, jealousies, hatreds of all sorts, both public and private, may nearly all be traced up to this fountain head.

Let the warning which our Lord pronounces, sink down into our hearts, and bear fruit in our lives. Let us strive to learn the lesson which St Paul has mastered, when he says, 'I have learned, in whatsoever state I am, therewith to be content' (Phil. 4:11). Let us pray for a thorough confidence in God's superintending providence over all our worldly affairs, and God's perfect wisdom in all His arrangements concerning us. If we have little, let us be sure that it would not be good for us to have much. If the things that we have are taken away, let us be satisfied that there is a needs-be. Happy is he who is persuaded that whatever is, is best, and has ceased from vain wishing, and become 'content with such things as' he has (Heb. 13:5).

November 28

*But he that knew not, and did commit things worthy of stripes, shall
be beaten with few stripes. For unto whomsoever much is given,
of him shall be much required: and to whom men have committed
much, of him they will ask the more.*
Luke 12:48

The awful danger of those who neglect the duties of
their calling.

Of such our Lord declares, that they shall be 'cut in sunder, and
their portion appointed with the unbelievers.' These words no doubt
apply especially to the ministers and teachers of the gospel; yet we
must not flatter ourselves that they are confined to them: they are
probably meant to convey a lesson to all who fill offices of high
responsibility. It is a striking fact that when Peter says at the beginning
of the passage, 'speakest thou this parable unto us, or even to all?' our
Lord gives him no answer. Whosoever occupies a position of trust, and
neglects his duties, would do well to ponder this passage, and learn
wisdom.

The language which our Lord Jesus uses about slothful and unfaithful
servants is peculiarly severe. Few places in the Gospels contain such
strong expressions as this. It is a vain delusion to suppose that the gospel
speaks nothing but 'smooth things'. The same loving Saviour who holds
out mercy to the uttermost to the penitent and believing, never shrinks
from holding up the judgments of God against those who despise His
counsel. Let no man deceive us on this subject. There is a hell for such
an one as goeth on still in his wickedness, no less than a heaven for the
believer in Jesus. There is such a thing as 'the wrath of the Lamb' (Rev.
6:16).

Let us strive so to live that whenever the heavenly Master comes we
may be found ready to receive Him. Let us watch our hearts with a
godly jealousy, and beware of the least symptom of unreadiness for the
Lord's appearing. Specially let us beware of any rising disposition to
lower our standard of Christian holiness, to dislike persons who are
more spiritually minded than ourselves, and to conform to the world.
The moment we detect such a disposition in our hearts we may be sure
that our souls are in great peril.

November 29

Ye hypocrites, ye can discern the face of the sky and of the earth; but
how is it that ye do not discern this time?
Luke 12:56

The duty of noticing the signs of the times.
The Jews in our Lord's days neglected this duty. They shut their eyes against events occurring in their own day of the most significant character. They refused to see that prophecies were being fulfilled around them which were bound up with the coming of Messiah, and that Messiah Himself must be in the midst of them. The sceptre had departed from Judah, and the Lawgiver from between his feet. The seventy weeks of Daniel were fulfilled (Gen. 49:10; Dan. 9:24). The ministry of John the Baptist had excited attention from one end of the land to the other. The miracles of Christ were great, undeniable and notorious. But still the eyes of the Jews were blinded: they still obstinately refused to believe that Jesus was the Christ; and hence they drew from our Lord the question, 'how is it that ye do not discern this time?'

It becomes the servants of God, in every age, to observe the public events of their own day, and to compare them with the predictions of unfulfilled prophecy. There is nothing commendable in an ignorant indifference to contemporary history. The true Christian should rather watch the career of governments and nations with a jealous watchfulness, and hail with gladness the slightest indication of the day of the Lord being at hand. The Christian who cannot see the hand of God in history, and does not believe in the gradual movement of all kingdoms towards the final subjection of all things to Christ, is as blind as the Jew.

Let us remember the words of our Lord in the passage before us, and not err after the manner of the Jews. Let us not be blind, and deaf, and insensible to all that God is doing, both in the Church and in the world. The things of which we have just been reminded are surely not without meaning. They have not come on the earth by chance or accident, but by the appointment of God. We ought not to doubt that they are a call to watchfulness and to preparation for the day of God. May we all have an ear to hear, and a heart to understand!

November 30

And the lord commended the unjust steward, because he had done
wisely: for the children of this world are in their generation wiser than
the children of light.
Luke 16:8

D o not draw from these verses lessons which they were never meant to teach.

The steward, whom our Lord describes, is not set before us as a pattern of morality. He is distinctly called the 'unjust steward'. The Lord Jesus never meant to sanction dishonesty, and unfair dealing between man and man. This steward cheated his master, and broke the eighth commandment: his master was struck with his cunning and forethought, when he heard of it, and 'commended' him, as a shrewd and far-seeing man; but there is no proof that his master was pleased with his conduct. Above all, there is not a word to show that the man was praised by Christ. In short, in his treatment of his master the steward is a beacon to be avoided and not a pattern to be followed.

The caution now laid down is very necessary. Commercial dishonesty is unhappily very common in these latter days: fair dealing between man and man is increasingly rare: men do things in the way of business which will not stand the test of the Bible. In 'making haste to be rich,' thousands are continually committing actions which are not strictly innocent (Prov. 28:20).

Sharpness and smartness in bargaining, and buying and selling, and pushing trade, are often covering over things that ought not to be. The generation of 'the unjust steward' is still a very large one. Let us not forget this. Whenever we do to others what we would not like others to do to us, we may be sure, whatever the world may say, that we are wrong in the sight of Christ.

DECEMBER

WARNINGS

December 1

*And he spake this parable unto certain which trusted in themselves
that they were righteous, and despised others ...*
Luke 18:9

The sin against which our Lord Jesus Christ warns us in
these verses.

There is no difficulty in finding out this. St Luke tells us expressly,
that 'he spake this parable unto certain which trusted in themselves
that they were righteous, and despised others'. The sin which our Lord
denounces is self-righteousness.

We are all naturally self-righteous: it is the family-disease of all the
children of Adam; from the highest to the lowest we think more highly
of ourselves than we ought to do. We secretly flatter ourselves that we
are not so bad as some, and that we have something to recommend us
to the favour of God. 'Most men will proclaim every one his own
goodness' (Prov. 20:6).

We forget the plain testimony of Scripture: 'in many things we offend
all'. '[T]here is not a just man upon earth, that doeth good, and sinneth
not'. 'What is man, that he should be clean? and he which is born of a
woman, that he should be righteous?' (Jas. 3:2; Eccles. 7:20; Job 15:14).

The true cure for self-righteousness is self-knowledge. Once let
the eyes of our understanding be opened by the Spirit, and we shall talk
no more of our own goodness. Once let us see what there is in our own
hearts, and what the holy law of God requires, and self-conceit will die.
We shall lay our hand on our mouths, and cry with the leper, 'Unclean,
unclean' (Lev. 13:45).

December 2

And take heed to yourselves, lest at any time your hearts be
overcharged with surfeiting, and drunkenness, and cares of this life,
and so that day come upon you unawares.
Luke 21:34

The spiritual danger to which even the holiest believers are exposed in this world.

Our Lord says to His disciples, 'take heed to yourselves, lest at any time your hearts be overcharged with surfeiting, and drunkenness, and cares of this life, and so that day come upon you unawares'.

These words are exceedingly startling. They were not addressed to carnal-minded Pharisees, or sceptical Sadducees, or worldly Herodians: they were addressed to Peter, James, and John, and the whole company of the apostles. They were addressed to men who had given up everything for Christ's sake, and had proved the reality of their faith by loving obedience and steady adhesion to their Master; yet even to them our Lord holds out the peril of surfeiting, and drunkenness, and worldliness! Even to them He says, '[T]ake heed to yourselves'.

The exhortation before us should teach us the immense importance of humility. There is no sin so great but a great saint may fall into it: there is no saint so great but he may fall into a great sin. Noah escaped the pollutions of the world before the flood; and yet he was afterwards overtaken by drunkenness. Abraham was the father of the faithful, and yet through unbelief he said falsely that Sarah was his sister. Lot did not take part in the horrible wickedness of Sodom, and yet he afterwards fell into foul sin in the cave. Moses was the meekest man on earth, and yet he so lost self-command that he spoke angrily and unadvisedly. David was a man after God's own heart, and yet he plunged into most heinous adultery. These examples are all deeply instructive: they all show the wisdom of our Lord's warning in the passage before us. They teach us to be 'clothed with humility'. '[L]et him that thinketh he standeth take heed lest he fall' (1 Pet. 5:5; 1 Cor. 10:12).

December 3

Then entered Satan into Judas surnamed Iscariot,
being of the number of the twelve.
Luke 22:3

How far men may fall after making a high profession. We read that the second step towards our Lord's crucifixion was the treachery of one of the twelve apostles: 'Then entered Satan into Judas surnamed Iscariot, being of the number of the twelve.' These words are peculiarly awful. To be tempted by Satan is bad enough, to be sifted, buffeted, led captive by him is truly terrible: but when Satan enters into a man, and dwells in him, the man becomes indeed a child of hell.

Judas Iscariot ought to be a standing beacon to the Church of Christ. This man, be it remembered, was one of our Lord's chosen apostles. He followed our Lord during the whole course of His ministry; he forsook all for Christ's sake; he heard Christ preach, and saw Christ's miracles; he preached himself; he spoke like the other apostles; there was nothing about him to distinguish him from Peter, James and John; he was never suspected of being unsound at heart – and yet this man turns out at length a hypocrite, betrays his Master, helps his enemies to deliver Him up to death and dies himself a 'son of perdition' (John 17:12). These are fearful things. But they are true.

Let the recollection of Judas Iscariot constrain every professing Christian to pray much for humility. Let us often say, 'Search me, O God, and know my heart: try me, and know my thoughts' (Ps. 139:23). At best we have but a faint conception of the deceitfulness of our hearts. The length to which men may go in religion, and yet be without grace, is far greater than we suppose.

December 4

And when they had kindled a fire in the midst of the hall,
and were set down together, Peter sat down among them.
Luke 22:55

How small and gradual are the steps by which men may go down into great sins.

The various steps in Peter's fall are clearly marked out by the Gospel-writers. They ought always to be observed in reading this part of the apostle's history. The first step was proud self-confidence. Though all men denied Christ, yet he never would: he was ready to go with Him both to prison and to death! The second step was indolent neglect of prayer. When his Master told him to pray, lest he should enter into temptation, he gave way to drowsiness, and was found asleep. The third step was vacillating indecision. When the enemies of Christ came upon Him, Peter first fought, then ran away, then turned again and finally 'followed afar off'. The fourth step was mingling with bad company. He went into the high priest's house and sat among the servants by the fire, trying to conceal his religion, and hearing and seeing all manner of evil. The fifth and last step was the natural consequence of the preceding four. He was overwhelmed with fear when suddenly charged with being a disciple: the snare was round his neck: he could not escape. He plunged deeper into error than ever: he denied his blessed Master three times. The mischief, be it remembered, had been done before; the denial was only the disease coming to a head.

Let us beware of the beginnings of backsliding, however small. We never know what we may come to, if we once leave the King's highway. The professing Christian who begins to say of any sin or evil habit, 'It is but a little one', is in imminent danger. He is sowing seeds in his heart, which will one day spring up and bear bitter fruit. It is a homely saying, that 'if men take care of the pence the pounds will take care of themselves'; we may borrow a good spiritual lesson from the saying: the Christian who keeps his heart diligently in little things shall be kept from great falls.

December 5

Even as the Son of man came not to be ministered unto, but to
minister, and to give his life a ransom for many.
Matthew 20:28

The Lord Jesus Christ is intended to be the example of all true Christians.

What saith the Scripture? We ought to serve one another, 'even as the Son of man came not to be ministered unto, but to minister'.

The Lord God has mercifully provided His people with everything necessary to their sanctification. He has given those who follow after holiness the clearest of precepts, the best of motives and the most encouraging of promises: but this is not all. He has furthermore supplied them with the most perfect pattern and example, – even the life of His own Son. By that life He bids us frame our own; in the steps of that life He bids us walk (1 Pet. 2:21). It is the model after which we must strive to mould our tempers, our words and our works, in this evil world. 'Would my Master have spoken in this manner? Would my Master have behaved in this way?' These are the questions by which we ought daily to try ourselves.

How humbling this truth is! What searchings of heart it ought to raise within us! What a loud call it is to 'lay aside every weight, and the sin which doth so easily beset us' (Heb. 12:1). What manner of persons ought they to be who profess to copy Christ! What poor unprofitable religion is that which makes a man content with talk and empty profession, while his life is unholy and unclean! Alas, those who know nothing of Christ as an example, will find at last that He knows nothing of them as His saved people. 'He that saith he abideth in him ought himself also so to walk, even as he walked' (1 John 2:6).

December 6

Then said Jesus unto them, Be not afraid: go tell my brethren that they
go into Galilee, and there shall they see me.
Matthew 28:10

The gracious message which the Lord sent to the disciples after His resurrection.

He appeared in person to the women who had come to do honour to His body. Last at the cross and first at the tomb, they were the first privileged to see Him after He rose; and to them He gives commission to carry tidings to His disciples. His first thought is for His little scattered flock: 'go tell my brethren'.

There is something deeply touching in those simple words, 'my brethren': they deserve a thousand thoughts. Weak, frail, erring as the disciples were, Jesus still calls them His 'brethren'. He comforts them, as Joseph did his brethren who had sold him, saying, 'I am Joseph your brother'. Much as they had come short of their profession, sadly as they had yielded to the fear of man, they are still His 'brethren'. Glorious as He was in Himself – a conqueror over death and hell, and the grave, the Son of God is still 'meek and lowly of heart'. He calls His disciples 'brethren'.

Let us turn from the passage with comfortable thoughts, if we know anything of true religion. Let us see in these words of Christ an encouragement to trust and not be afraid. Our Saviour is One who never forgets His people; He pities their infirmities: He does not despise them. He knows their weakness, and yet does not cast them away. Our great High Priest is also our elder brother.

December 7

But the woman fearing and trembling, knowing what was done in her, came and fell down before him, and told him all the truth.
Mark 5:33

How much it becomes Christians to confess before men the benefits they receive from Christ.

We see that this woman was not allowed to go home, when cured, without her cure being noticed. Our Lord inquired who had touched Him, and 'looked round about to see her that had done this thing'. No doubt He knew perfectly the name and history of the woman. He needed not that any should tell Him. But He desired to teach her, and all around Him, that healed souls should make public acknowledgment of mercies received.

There is a lesson here which all true Christians would do well to remember. We are not to be ashamed to confess Christ before men, and to let others know what He has done for our souls. If we have found peace through His blood, and been renewed by His Spirit, we must not shrink from avowing it on every proper occasion. It is not necessary to blow a trumpet in the streets, and force our experience on everybody's notice. All that is required is a willingness to acknowledge Christ as our Master, without flinching from the ridicule or persecution, which by so doing we may bring on ourselves. More than this is not required; but less than this ought not to content us. If we are ashamed of Jesus before men, He will one day be ashamed of us before His Father and the angels.

December 8

Return to thine own house, and shew how great things God hath done
unto thee. And he went his way and published throughout the whole
city how great things Jesus had done unto him.
Luke 8:39

The man out of whom the devils were departed, besought our Lord that he might be with Him: but his request was not granted. We read that Jesus sent him away, saying 'Return to thine house, and shew how great things God hath done unto thee'.

We can easily understand the request that this man made. He felt deeply grateful for the amazing mercy which he had just received in being cured. He felt full of love and warm affection toward Him who had so wonderfully and graciously cured him. He felt that he could not see too much of Him, be too much in His company, cleave to Him too closely. He forgot everything else under the influence of these feelings. Family relations, friends, home, house, country, all seemed as nothing in his eyes. He felt that he cared for nothing but to be with Christ. And we cannot blame him for his feelings. They may have been tinged with something of enthusiasm and inconsideration. There may have been about them a zeal not according to knowledge. In the first excitement of a newly felt cure he may not have been fit to judge what his future line of life should be. But excited feelings in religion are far better than no feelings at all. In the petition he made there was far more to praise than to blame.

But why did our Lord Jesus Christ refuse to grant this man's request? Why, at a time when He had a few disciples, did He send this man away? Why, instead of allowing him to take place with Peter and James and John, did he bid him return to his own house? – Our Lord did what He did in infinite wisdom. He would have us know that there are various ways of glorifying Him, that He may be honoured in private life as well as in the apostolic office, and that the first place in which we should witness for Christ is our own house.

December 9

*And a woman having an issue of blood twelve years, which had spent
all her living upon physicians, neither could be healed of any ...*
Luke 8:43

How much our Lord desires that those who have received benefit from Him should confess Him before men.

We are told that He did not allow this woman, whose case we have been reading, to retire from the crowd unheeded. He inquired 'who had touched Him.' He inquired again, until the woman came forward and 'declared' her case before all the people. And then came the gracious words, 'Daughter, be of good comfort: thy faith hath made thee whole'. Confession of Christ is a matter of great importance. Let this never be forgotten by true Christians. The work that we can do for our blessed Master is little and poor. Our best endeavours to glorify Him are weak and full of imperfections. Our prayers and praises are sadly defective. Our knowledge and love are miserably small. But do we feel within that Christ has healed our souls? Then can we not confess Christ before men? Can we not plainly tell others that Christ has done everything for us – that we were dying of a deadly disease, and were cured – that we were lost, and now are found – that we were blind, and now see? Let us do this boldly, and not be afraid. Let us not be ashamed to let all men know what Jesus has done for our souls. Our Master loves to see us doing so. He likes His people not to be ashamed of His name. It is a solemn saying to St Paul, 'if thou shalt confess with thy mouth the Lord Jesus, and shalt believe in thy heart that God hath raised him from the dead, thou shalt be saved' (Rom. 10:9). It is a still more solemn saying of Christ Himself, 'whosoever shall be ashamed of me and of my words, of him shall the Son of man be ashamed' (Luke 9:26).

December 10

No man, when he hath lighted a candle, putteth it in a secret place,
neither under a bushel, but on a candlestick, that they which come in
may see the light.
Luke 11:33

The importance of making a good use of religious light and privileges.

We are reminded of what men do when they light a candle. They do not put 'it in a secret place', under a bushel measure. They place it on a candlestick, that it may be serviceable and useful by giving light.

When the gospel of Christ is placed before a man's soul, it is as if God offered to him a lighted candle. It is not sufficient to hear it, and assent to it, and admire it, and acknowledge its truth. It must be received into the heart, and obeyed in the life. Until this takes place the gospel does him no more good than if he were an African heathen, who has never heard the gospel at all. A lighted candle is before him, but he is not turning it to account. The guilt of such conduct is very great. God's light neglected will be a heavy charge against many at the last day.

But even when a man professes to value the light of the gospel he must take care that he is not selfish in the use of it. He must endeavour to reflect the light on all around him. He must strive to make others acquainted with the truths which he finds good for himself. He must let his light so shine before men, that they may see whose he is and whom he serves, and may be induced to follow his example, and join the Lord's side. He must regard the light which he enjoys as a loan, for the use of which he is accountable. He must strive to hold his candle in such a way that many may see it, and as they see it, admire and believe.

We should labour to make all men see that we have found 'the pearl of great price', and that we want them to find it as well as ourselves. A man's religion may well be suspected, when he is content to go to heaven alone. The true Christian will have a large heart. The Christian who is satisfied to burn his candle alone, is in a very weak and sickly state of soul.

December 11

Also I say unto you, Whosoever shall confess me before men, him shall the Son of man also confess before the angels of God ...
Luke 12:8

We must confess Christ upon earth, if we expect Him to own us as His saved people at the last day.

We must not be ashamed to let all men see that we believe in Christ, and serve Christ, and love Christ, and care more for the praise of Christ than for the praise of man.

The duty of confessing Christ is incumbent on all Christians in every age of the Church. Let us never forget that. It is not for martyrs only, but for all believers, in every rank of life. It is not for great occasions only, but for our daily walk through an evil world. The rich man among the rich, the labourer among labourers, the young among the young, the servant among servants – each and all must be prepared, if they are true Christians, to confess their Master. It needs no blowing a trumpet. It requires no noisy boasting. It needs nothing more than using the daily opportunity. But one thing is certain: if a man loves Jesus, he ought not to be ashamed to let people know it.

The difficulty of confessing Christ is undoubtedly very great. It never was easy at any period. It never will be easy as long as the world stands. It is sure to entail on us laughter, ridicule, contempt, mockery, enmity and persecution. The wicked dislike to see any one better than themselves. The world which hated Christ will always hate true Christians. But whether we like it or not, whether it be hard or easy, our course is perfectly clear. In one way or another Christ must be confessed.

The grand motive to stir us up to bold confession is forcibly brought before us in the words which we are now considering. Our Lord declares that if we do not confess Him before men He will not confess us 'before the angels of God' at the last day. He will leave us to reap the consequences of our cowardice, and to stand before the bar of God helpless, defenceless and unforgiven.

December 12

For the Holy Ghost shall teach you in the same hour what ye ought to say.
Luke 12:12

Christians need not be over-anxious as to what they shall say, when suddenly required to speak for Christ's cause.
The promise which our Lord gives on this subject has a primary reference no doubt to public trials, like those of Paul before Felix and Festus. It is a promise which hundreds in similar circumstances have found fulfilled to their singular comfort. The lives of many of the Reformers, and others of God's witnesses, are full of striking proofs that the Holy Ghost can teach Christians what to say in time of need.

But there is a secondary sense, in which the promise belongs to all believers, which ought not be overlooked. Occasions are constantly arising in the lives of Christians when they are suddenly and unexpectedly called upon to speak on behalf of their Master, and to render a reason for their hope. The home circle, the family fireside, the society of friends, the intercourse with relatives, the very business of the world, will often furnish such sudden occasions. On such occasions the believer should fall back on the promise now before us. It may be disagreeable, and especially to a young Christian, to be suddenly required to speak before others of religion, and above all if religion is attacked. But let us not be alarmed, and flurried, or cast down, or excited. If we remember the promise of Christ, we have no cause to be afraid.

Let us pray for a good memory about Bible promises. We shall find it an inestimable comfort. There are far more, and far wider promises laid down in Scripture for the comfort of Christ's people, than most of Christ's people are aware of. There are promises for almost every position in which we can be placed, and every event that can befall us. We are sometimes called upon to go into company which is not congenial to us, and we go with a troubled and anxious heart: we fear saying what we ought not to say, and not saying what we ought. At such seasons, let us remember this blessed promise, and put our Master in remembrance of it also.

December 13

Blessed is that servant, whom his lord when he cometh shall find so doing.
Luke 12:43

The importance of doing, in our Christianity.
Our Lord is speaking of His own second coming. He is comparing His disciples to servants waiting for their master's return, who have each their own work to do during His absence. 'Blessed', He says, 'is that servant, whom his lord when he cometh shall find so doing.'

The warning has doubtless a primary reference to ministers of the gospel. They are the stewards of God's mysteries, who are specially bound to be found 'doing', when Christ comes again. But the words contain a further lesson, which all Christians, would do well to consider. That lesson is, the immense importance of a working, practical, diligent, useful religion.

The lesson is one which is greatly needed in the Churches of Christ. We hear a great deal about people's intentions, and hopes, and wishes, and feelings, and professions: it would be well if we could hear more about people's practice. It is not the servant who is found wishing and professing, but the servant who is found 'doing', whom Jesus calls 'blessed'.

The lesson is one which many, unhappily, shrink from giving, and many more shrink from receiving. We are gravely told that to talk of 'working' and 'doing', is legal, and brings Christians into bondage! Remarks of this kind should never move us. They savour of ignorance or perverseness. The lesson before us is not about justification, but about sanctification – not about faith, but about holiness; the point is not what a man should do to be saved – but what ought a saved man to do. The teaching of Scripture is clear and express upon this subject. A saved man ought to be careful to maintain good works (Titus 3:8). The desire of a true Christian ought to be, to be found 'doing'.

If we love life, let us resolve by God's help, to be 'doing' Christians. This is to be like Christ: He 'went about doing good' (Acts 10:38). This is to be like the apostles: they were men of deeds even more than of words. This is to glorify God: 'Herein is my Father glorified, that ye bear much fruit' (John 15:8).

December 14

But when thou makest a feast, call the poor,
the maimed, the lame, the blind …
Luke 14:13

The duty of caring for the poor.

Our Lord teaches this lesson in a peculiar manner. He tells the Pharisee who invited Him to his feast, that when he made 'a dinner or a supper', he ought not to 'call his friends, or kinsmen, or rich neighbours'; on the contrary, He says, 'when thou makest a feast, call the poor, the maimed, the lame, the blind'.

The precept contained in these words must evidently be interpreted with considerable limitation. It is certain that our Lord did not intend to forbid men showing any hospitality to their relatives and friends. It is certain that He did not mean to encourage a useless and profuse expenditure of money in giving to the poor. To interpret the passage in this manner would make it contradict other plain Scriptures. Such interpretations cannot possibly be correct.

But when we have said this, we must not forget that the passage contains a deep and important lesson. We must be careful that we do not limit and qualify that lesson till we have pared it down and refined it into nothing at all. The lesson of the passage is plain and distinct. The Lord Jesus would have us care for our poorer brethren, and help them according to our power. He would have us know that it is a solemn duty never to neglect the poor, but to aid them and relieve them in their time of need.

Let the lesson of this passage sink down deeply into our hearts. '[T]he poor shall never cease out of the land' (Deut. 15:11). A little help conferred upon the poor judiciously and in season, will often add immensely to their happiness, and take away immensely from their cares, and promote good feeling between class and class in society. This help it is the will of Christ that all His people, who have the means, should be willing and ready to bestow. It is not for nothing that St Paul writes to the Galatians, 'they would that we should remember the poor; the same which I also was forward to do' (Matt. 25:42; Gal. 2:10).

December 15

*And Zacchaeus stood, and said unto the Lord; Behold, Lord, the half
of my goods I give to the poor; and if I have taken any thing from any
man by false accusation, I restore him fourfold.*
Luke 19:8

Converted sinners will always give evidence of their conversion.

We are told that Zacchaeus 'stood, and said unto the Lord ... the half of my goods I give to the poor; and if I have taken any thing from any man by false accusation, I restore him fourfold'. There was reality in that speech: there was unmistakable proof that Zacchaeus was a new creature. When a wealthy Christian begins to distribute his riches, and an extortioner begins to make restitution, all things become new (2 Cor. 5:17). There was decision in that speech. 'I give', says Zacchaeus: 'I restore'.

He does not speak of future intentions; he does not say, 'I will': but 'I do'. Freely pardoned, and raised from death to life, Zacchaeus felt that he could not begin too soon to show whose he was and whom he served.

He that desires to give proof that he is a believer should walk in the steps of Zacchaeus. Like him, let him thoroughly renounce the sins which have formerly most easily beset him; like him, let him follow the Christian graces which he has formerly most habitually neglected. In any case a believer should so live that all may know that he is a believer: faith that does not purify the heart and life, is not faith at all; grace that cannot be seen, like light, and tasted, like salt, is not grace, but hypocrisy.

The man who professes to know Christ and trust Him, while he cleaves to sin and the world, is going down to hell with a lie in his right hand. The heart that has really tasted the grace of Christ will instinctively hate sin.

Once saved and converted we shall say, 'What shall I render unto the Lord for all his benefits' (Ps. 116:12). Once saved, we shall not complain that self-denial, like that of Zacchaeus, is a grievous requirement.

December 16

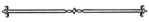

And he called his ten servants, and delivered them ten pounds,
and said unto them, Occupy till I come.
Luke 19:13

The present position of all professing Christians. Our Lord compares them to servants who have been left in charge of money by an absent master with strict directions to use that money well. They are to 'occupy till He comes'.

The countless privileges which Christians enjoy, compared to the heathen, are 'pounds' given to them by Christ, for which they must one day give account. We shall not stand side by side in the judgment day with the African and Chinese, who never heard of the Bible, the Trinity and the crucifixion. The most of us, it may be feared, have little idea of the extent of our responsibility. To whomsoever much is given, of them much will be required.

Are we 'occupying'? Are we living like men who know to whom they are indebted, and to whom they must one day give account? This is the only life which is worthy of a reasonable being. The best answer we can give to those who invite us to plunge into worldliness and frivolity, is the Master's commandment which is before us: let us tell them that we cannot consent, because we look for the coming of the Lord. We would fain be found 'occupying' when He comes.

We are told that when the master returned, he 'commanded these servants to be called that he might know how much every man had gained'. There is a day coming when the Lord Jesus Christ shall judge His people, and give to every one according to His works. High and low, rich and poor, gentle and simple, all shall at length give account to God, and all shall receive an eternal sentence.

Let the thought of this judgment exercise an influence on our hearts and lives.

December 17

*Then said he unto them, But now, he that hath a purse,
let him take it, and likewise his scrip: and he that hath no sword,
let him sell his garment, and buy one.*
Luke 22:36

The servant of Christ ought to use all reasonable means in doing his Master's work.

We read that our Lord said to His disciples, 'he that hath a purse, let him take it, and likewise his scrip: and he that hath no sword, let him sell his garment, and buy one'.

It is safest to take these remarkable words in a proverbial sense. They apply to the whole period of time between our Lord's first and second advents. Until our Lord comes again believers are to make a diligent use of all the faculties which God has implanted in them: they are not to expect miracles to be worked, in order to save them trouble; they are not to expect bread to fall into their mouths, if they will not work for it; they are not to expect difficulties to be surmounted, and enemies to be overcome, if they will not wrestle, and struggle, and take pains. They are to remember that it is 'the hand of the diligent [which] maketh rich' (Prov. 10:4).

We shall do well to lay to heart our Lord's words in this place, and to act habitually on the principle which they contain. Let us labour, and toil, and give, and speak, and act, and write for Christ, as if all depended on our exertions. And yet let us never forget that success depends entirely on God's blessing! To expect success by our own 'purse' and 'sword' is pride and self-righteousness; but to expect success without the 'purse' and 'sword' is presumption and fanaticism. Let us do as Jacob did when he met his brother Esau. He used all innocent means to conciliate and appease him; but when he had done all, he spent all night in prayer (Gen. 32:1-24).

December 18

And they talked together of all these things which had happened.
Luke 24:14

W hat encouragement there is to believers to speak to one another about Christ.

We are told of two disciples walking together to Emmaus, and talking of their Master's crucifixion; and then come the remarkable words, 'while they communed together and reasoned, Jesus himself drew near, and went with them'.

Conference on spiritual subjects is a most important means of grace. As iron sharpeneth iron, so does exchange of thoughts with brethren sharpen a believer's soul: it brings down a special blessing on all who make a practice of it. The striking words of Malachi were meant for the Church in every age: 'Then they that feared the LORD spake often one to another: and the LORD hearkened, and heard it, and a book of remembrance was written before him for them that feared the LORD, and that thought upon his name. And they shall be mine saith the LORD of hosts, in that day when I make up my jewels' (Mal. 3:16, 17).

What do we know ourselves of spiritual conversation with other Christians? Perhaps we read our Bibles, and pray in private, and use public means of grace. It is all well, very well; but if we stop short here we neglect a great privilege and have yet much to learn. We ought to 'consider one another to provoke unto love and to good works'; we ought to exhort and 'edify one another' (Heb. 10:24; 1 Thess. 5:11). Have we no time for spiritual conversation? Let us think again. The quantity of time wasted on frivolous, trifling and unprofitable talk, is fearfully great. Do we find nothing to say on spiritual subjects? Do we feel tongue-tied and dumb on the things of Christ? Surely if this is the case there must be something wrong within. A heart right in the sight of God will generally find words. '[O]ut of the abundance of the heart the mouth speaketh' (Matt. 12:34).

Let us learn a lesson from the two travellers to Emmaus. Let us speak of Jesus, when we are sitting in our houses and when we are walking by the way, whenever we can find a disciple to speak to (Deut. 6:7).

December 19

And that repentance and remission of sins should be preached in his
name among all nations, beginning at Jerusalem.
Luke 24:47

The peculiar position which believers, and especially ministers, are meant to occupy in this world.

Our Lord defines it in one expressive word: He says, 'ye are witnesses'.

If we are true disciples of Christ, we must bear a continual testimony in the midst of an evil world. We must testify to the truth of our Master's gospel, the graciousness of our Master's heart, the happiness of our Master's service, the excellence of our Master's rules of life, and the enormous danger and wickedness of the ways of the world. Such testimony will doubtless bring down upon us the displeasure of man: the world will hate us, as it did our Master, because we testify of it, that its works are evil (John 7:7). Such testimony will doubtless be believed by few comparatively, and will be thought by many offensive and extreme; but the duty of a witness is to bear his testimony, whether he is believed or not. If we bear a faithful testimony, we have done our duty, although, like Noah, and Elijah, and Jeremiah, we stand almost alone.

What do we know of this witnessing-character? What kind of testimony do we bear? What evidence do we give that we are disciples of a crucified Saviour, and, like Him, are 'not of the world' (John 17:14)? What marks do we show of belonging to Him who said: I came 'that I should bear witness unto the truth' (John 18:37)? Happy is he who can give a satisfactory answer to these questions, and whose life declares plainly that he seeks a country (Heb. 11:14).

December 20

And looking upon Jesus as he walked, he saith, Behold the Lamb of God!
John 1:36

W hat good is done by continually testifying of Christ. The first time that John the Baptist cried, 'Behold the Lamb of God', no result appears to have followed. We are not told of any who heard, inquired and believed. But when he repeated the same words the next day, we read that two of His disciples 'heard him speak, and they followed Jesus'. They were received most graciously by Him whom they followed. 'They came and saw where he dwelt, and abode with him that day'. Truly it was a day in their lives most eventful, and most blessed! From that day they became fast and firm disciples of the new-found Messiah. They took up the cross. They continued with Him in His temptations. They followed Him whithersoever He went. One of them at least, if not both, became a chosen apostle, and a master builder in the Christian temple. And all was owing to John the Baptist's testimony: 'Behold the Lamb of God'. That testimony was a little seed. But it bore mighty fruits.

This simple story is a pattern of the way in which good has been done to souls in every age of the Christian Church. By such testimony as that before us, and by none else, men and women are converted and saved. It is by exalting Christ, not the Church; Christ, not the sacraments; Christ, not the ministry; it is by this means that hearts are moved, and sinners are turned to God. To the world such testimony may seem weakness and foolishness. Yet, like the ram's horns before whose blast the walls of Jericho fell down, this testimony is mighty to the pulling down of strongholds. The story of the crucified Lamb of God has proved, in every age, the power of God unto salvation. Those who have done most for Christ's cause in every part of the world, have been men like John the Baptist. They have not cried, behold me, or, behold the Church, or behold the ordinances, but 'Behold the Lamb'. If souls are to be saved, men must be pointed directly to Christ.

December 21

He first findeth his own brother Simon, and saith unto him,
We have found the Messias, which is, being interpreted, the Christ.
John 1:41

What good a believer may do to others, by speaking to them about Christ.

No sooner does Andrew become a disciple, than he tells his brother Simon what a discovery he has made. Like one who has unexpectedly heard good tidings, he hastens to impart it to the one nearest and dearest to him. He says to his brother, 'We have found the Messias', and he brings him to Jesus. Who can tell what might have happened if Andrew had been of a silent, reserved and uncommunicative spirit, like many a Christian in the present day? Who can tell but his brother might have lived and died a fisherman on the Galilean lake? But happily for Simon, Andrew was not a man of this sort. He was one whose heart was so full that he must speak. And to Andrew's outspoken testimony, under God, the great Apostle Peter owed the first beginning of light in his soul.

The fact before us is most striking and instructive. Out of the three first members of the Christian Church, one at least was brought to Jesus, by the private, quiet word of a relative. He seems to have heard no public preaching. He saw no mighty miracle wrought. He was not convinced by any powerful reasoning. He only heard his brother telling him that he had found a Saviour himself, and at once the work began in his soul. The simple testimony of a warm-hearted brother was the first link in the chain by which Peter was drawn out of the world and jointed to Christ. The first blow in that mighty work by which Peter was made a pillar of the Church, was struck by Andrew's words: 'We have found the ... Christ'.

Well would it be for the Church of Christ, if all believers were more like Andrew! Well would it be for souls if men and women who have been converted themselves, would speak to their friends and relatives on spiritual subjects, and tell them what they have found! How much good might be done! How many might be led to Jesus, who now live and die in unbelief!

December 22

The day following Jesus would go forth into Galilee,
and findeth Philip, and saith unto him, Follow me.
John 1:43

How various are the paths by which souls are led into the narrow way of life.

We are told of a man, named Philip, being added to the little company of Christ's disciples. He does not appear to have been moved, like Andrew and his companions, by the testimony of John the Baptist. He was not drawn, like Simon Peter, by the outspoken declaration of a brother. He seems to have been called directly by Christ Himself, and the agency of man seems not to have been used in his calling. Yet in faith and life he became one with those who were disciples before him. Though led by different paths, they all entered the same road, embraced the same truths, and served the same Master, and at length reached the same home.

The fact before us is a deeply important one. It throws light on the history of all God's people in every age, and of every tongue. There are diversities of operations in the saving of souls. All true Christians are led by one Spirit, washed in one blood, serve one Lord, lean on one Saviour, believe one truth and walk by one general rule. But all are not converted in one and the same manner. All do not pass through the same experience. In conversion, the Holy Ghost acts as a sovereign. He calleth every one severally as He will.

A careful recollection of this point may save us much trouble. We must beware of making the experience of other believers the measure of our own. We must beware of denying another's grace, because he has not been led by the same way as ourselves. Has a man got the real grace of God? This is the only question that concerns us. Is he a penitent man? Is he a believer? Does he live a holy life? Provided these inquiries can be answered satisfactorily, we may well be content. It matters nothing by what path a man has been led, if he has only been led at last into the right way.

December 23

Come, see a man, which told me all things that ever I did:
is not this the Christ?
John 4:29

How zealous a truly converted person is to do good to others.

We are told that the Samaritan woman 'went her way into the city, and saith to the men, Come, see a man, which told me all things that ever I did: is not this the Christ?' In the day of her conversion she became a missionary. She felt so deeply the amazing benefit she had received from Christ, that she could not hold her peace about Him. Just as Andrew told his brother Peter about Jesus, and Philip told Nathanael that he had found Messiah, and Saul, when converted, straightway preached Christ; so, in the same way, the Samaritan woman said, come and see Christ. She used no abstruse arguments. She attempted no deep reasoning about our Lord's claim to be the Messiah. She only said, come and see. Out of the abundance of her heart her mouth spoke.

That which the Samaritan woman here did, all true Christians ought to do likewise. The Church needs it. The state of the world demands it. Common sense points out that it is right. Everyone who has received the grace of God, and tasted that Christ is gracious, ought to find words to testify of Christ to others. Where is our faith, if we believe that souls around us are perishing, and that Christ alone can save them, and yet hold our peace? Where is our charity if we can see others going down to hell, and yet say nothing to them about Christ and salvation? We may well doubt our own love to Christ, if our hearts are never moved to speak of Him. We may well doubt the safety of our own souls, if we feel no concern about the souls of others.

Do we ever talk to others about God, and Christ, and eternity, and the soul, and heaven, and hell? If not, what is the value of our faith? Where is the reality of our Christianity?

December 24

Jesus saith unto them, My meat is to do the will of him that sent me,
and to finish his work.
John 4:34

A n instructive pattern of zeal for the good of others. We read, that our Lord Jesus Christ declares, 'My meat is to do the will of him that sent me, and to finish his work'. To do good was not merely duty and pleasure to Him. He counted it as His food, meat and drink. Job, one of the holiest Old Testament saints, could say, that he esteemed God's word 'more than his necessary food' (Job. 23:12). The great Head of the New Testament Church went even further. He could say the same of God's work.

Do we do any work for God? Do we try, however feebly, to set forward His cause on earth, to check that which is evil, to promote that which is good? If we do, let us never be ashamed of doing it with all our heart, and soul, and mind, and strength. Whatsoever our hand finds to do for the souls of others, let us do it with our might (Eccles. 9:10). The world may mock and sneer, and call us enthusiasts. The world can admire zeal in any service but that of God, and can praise enthusiasm on any subject but that of religion. Let us work on unmoved. Whatever men may say and think, we are walking in the steps of our Lord Jesus Christ.

Let us, beside this, take comfort in the thought that Jesus Christ never changes. He that sat by the well of Samaria, and found it 'meat to drink' to do good to an ignorant soul, is always in one mind. High in heaven at God's right hand, He still delights to save sinners, and still approves zeal and labour in the cause of God. The work of the missionary and the evangelist may be despised and ridiculed in many quarters. But while man is mocking, Christ is well pleased. Thanks be to God, Jesus is the same yesterday, and today, and for ever.

December 25

And the angel said unto her, Fear not, Mary: for thou hast found favour with God. And, behold, thou shalt conceive in thy womb, and bring forth a son, and shalt call his name JESUS. He shall be great, and shall be called the Son of the Highest: and the Lord God shall give unto him the throne of his father David: And he shall reign over the house of Jacob for ever; and of his kingdom there shall be no end.

Luke 1:30-33

The lowly and unassuming manner in which the Saviour of mankind came amongst us.

The angel who announced His advent, was sent to an obscure town of Galilee, named Nazareth. The woman who was honoured to be our Lord's mother, was evidently in a humble position of life. Both in her station and her dwelling-place there was an utter absence of what the world calls 'greatness'.

We need not hesitate to conclude that there was a wise providence in all this arrangement. The almighty counsel, which orders all things in heaven and earth, could just as easily have appointed Jerusalem to be the place of Mary's residence as Nazareth, or could as easily have chosen the daughter of some rich scribe to be our Lord's mother, as a poor woman. But it seemed good that it should not be so. The first advent of Messiah was to be an advent of humiliation. That humiliation was to beg even from the time of his conception and birth.

Let us beware of despising poverty in others, and of being ashamed of it if God lays it upon ourselves. The condition of life which Jesus voluntarily chose, ought always to be regarded with holy reverence. The common tendency of the day to bow down before rich men, and make an idol of money, ought to be carefully resisted and discouraged. The example of our Lord is a sufficient answer to a thousand grovelling maxims about wealth, which pass current among men. '[T]hough he was rich, yet for your sakes he became poor' (2 Cor. 8:9).

Let His example daily bring home to our conscience the precept of Scripture: 'Mind not high things, but condescend to men of low estate' (Rom. 12:16).

December 26

Ye sent unto John, and he bare witness unto the truth.
John 5:33

The honour Christ puts on His faithful servants.
See how He speaks of John the Baptist. '[H]e bare witness unto the truth'; 'He was a burning and a shining light.' John had probably passed away from his earthly labours when these words were spoken. He had been persecuted, imprisoned, and put to death by Herod – none interfering, none trying to prevent his murder. But this murdered disciple was not forgotten by his divine Master. If no-one else remembered him, Jesus did. He had honoured Christ, and Christ honoured him.

These things ought not to be overlooked. They are written to teach us that Christ cares for all His believing people, and never forgets them. Forgotten and despised by the world, perhaps, they are never forgotten by their Saviour. He knows where they dwell, and what their trials are. A book of remembrance is written for them. Their tears are all in His bottle (Ps. 56:8). Their names are graven on the palms of His hands. He notices all they do for Him in this evil world, though they think it not worth notice, and He will confess it one day publicly, before His Father and the holy angels. He that bore witness to John the Baptist never changes. Let believers remember this. In their worst estate they may boldly say with David, 'I am poor and needy; yet the Lord thinketh upon me' (Ps. 40:17).

December 27

I must work the works of him that sent me, while it is day:
the night cometh, when no man can work.
John 9:4

What a solemn lesson Christ gives us about the use of opportunities.

He says to the disciples who asked Him about the blind man, 'I must work ... while it is called today: the night cometh, when no man can work.'

That saying was eminently true when applied to our Lord Himself. He knew well that his own earthly ministry would only last three years altogether, and knowing this He diligently redeemed the time. He let slip no opportunity of doing works of mercy, and attending to His Father's business. Morning, noon and night he was always carrying on the work which the Father gave him to do. It was his meat and drink to do His Father's will, and to finish His work. His whole life breathed one sentiment, 'I must work ... the night cometh, when no man can work.'

The saying is one which should be remembered by all professing Christians. The life that we now live in the flesh is our day. Let us take care that we use it well, for the glory of God and the good of our souls. Let us work out our salvation with fear and trembling, while it is called today. There is no work nor labour in the grave, toward which we are all fast hastening. Let us pray, and read, and keep our Sabbaths holy, and hear God's Word, and do good in our generation, like men who never forget that the night is at hand. Our time is very short. Our daylight will soon be gone. Opportunities once lost can never be retrieved. A second lease of life is granted to no man. Then let us resist procrastination as we would resist the devil. Whatever our hand findeth to do, let us do it with our might. '[T]he night cometh, when no man can work'.

December 28

Then Jesus said unto them, Yet a little while is the light with you. Walk
while ye have the light, lest darkness come upon you: for he that
walketh in darkness knoweth not whither he goeth.
John 12:35

The duty of using present opportunities.
The Lord Jesus says to us all, 'Yet a little while is the light with you. Walk while ye have the light ... believe in the light'. Let us not think that these things were only spoken for the sake of the Jews. They were written for us also, upon whom the ends of the world are come.

The lesson of the words is generally applicable to the whole professing Church of Christ. Its time for doing good in the world is short and limited. The throne of grace will not always be standing: it will be removed one day, and the throne of judgement will be set up in its place. The door of salvation by faith in Christ will not always be open: it will be shut one day for ever, and the number of God's elect will be completed. The fountain for all sin and uncleanness will not always be accessible. The way to it will one day be barred, and there will remain nothing but the lake that burns with fire and brimstone.

These are solemn thoughts: but they are true. They cry aloud to sleeping churchmen and drowsy congregations, and ought to arouse great searchings of heart. 'Can nothing more be done to spread the Gospel at home and abroad? Has every means been tried for extending the knowledge of Christ crucified? Can we lay our hands on our hearts, and say that the Churches have left nothing undone in the matter of missions? Can we look forward to the Second Advent with no feelings of humiliation, and say that the talents of wealth and influence and opportunities have not been buried in the ground?' Such questions may well humble us, when we look, on one side, at the state of professing Christendom, and, on the other, at the state of the heathen world. We must confess with shame that the Church is not walking worthy of its light.

December 29

I am the vine, ye are the branches: He that abideth in me, and I in him,
the same bringeth forth much fruit: for without me ye can do nothing.
John 15:5

The fruits of the Spirit are the only satisfactory evidence of a man being a true Christian.

The disciple that abides in Christ, like a branch abiding in the vine, will always bear fruit.

He that would know what the word 'fruit' means, need not wait long for an answer. Repentance toward God, faith toward our Lord Jesus Christ, holiness of life and conduct – these are what the New Testament calls 'fruit'. These are the distinguishing marks of the man who is a living branch of the true Vine. Where these things are wanting, it is vain to talk of possessing 'dormant' grace and spiritual life. Where there is no fruit there is no life. He that lacks these things is dead while he lives (1 Tim. 5:6).

True grace, we must not forget, is never idle. It never slumbers and never sleeps. It is a vain notion to suppose that we are living members of Christ, if the example of Christ is not to be seen on our characters and lives. 'Fruit' is the only satisfactory evidence of saving union between Christ and our souls. Where there is no fruit of the Spirit to be seen, there is no vital religion in the heart. The Spirit of Life in Christ Jesus will always make Himself known in the daily conduct of those in whom He dwells. The Master Himself declares, 'every tree is known by his own fruit' (Luke 6:44).

God will often increase the holiness of true Christians by His providential dealings with them. '[E]very branch', it is written, 'that beareth fruit, he purgeth it, that it may bring forth more fruit'.

The meaning of this language is clear and plain. Just as the vine-dresser prunes and cuts back the branches of a fruitful vine, in order to make them more fruitful, so does God purify and sanctify believers by the circumstances of life in which He places them.

This is the process by which He 'purges' them, and makes them more fruitful.

December 30

Herein is my Father glorified, that ye bear much fruit;
so shall ye be my disciples.
John 15:8

Fruitfulness in Christian practice will not only bring glory to God, but will supply the best evidence to our own hearts that we are real disciples of Christ. Assurance of our own interest in Christ, and of our consequent eternal safety, is one of the highest privileges in religion. To be always doubting and fearing is miserable work. Nothing is worse than suspense in any matter of importance, and above all in the matters of our souls. He that would know one of the best receipts for obtaining assurance, should diligently study Christ's works now before us. Let him strive to bear 'much fruit' in his life, his habits, his temper, his words and his works. So doing he shall feel the 'witness of the Spirit' in his heart, and give abundant proof that he is a living branch of the true Vine. He shall find inward evidence in his own soul that he is a child of God, and shall supply the world with outward evidence that cannot be disputed. He shall leave no room for doubt that he is a disciple.

Would we know why so many professing Christians have little comfort in their religion, and go fearing and doubting along the road to heaven? The question receives a solution in the saying of our Lord we are now considering. Men are content with a little Christianity, and a little fruit of the Spirit, and do no labour to be 'holy in all manner of conversation' (1 Pet. 1:15). They must not wonder if they enjoy little peace, feel little hope and leave behind them little evidence. The fault lies with themselves. God has linked together holiness and happiness; and what God has joined together we must not think to put asunder.

The Christian who is careful over his words and tempers and works, will generally be the most happy Christian. 'Joy and peace in believing', will never accompany an inconsistent life.

December 31

Then said Jesus to them again, Peace be unto you:
as my Father hath sent me, even so send I you.
John 20:21

The remarkable commission which our Lord conferred
upon His eleven apostles.

We are told that He said, 'as my Father hath sent me, even so
send I you. And when he had said this, he breathed on them, and saith
unto them, Receive ye the Holy Ghost: Whose soever sins ye remit,
they are remitted unto them; and whose soever sins ye retain, they are
retained.' It is vain to deny that the true sense of these solemn words
has been for centuries a subject of controversy and dispute. It is useless
perhaps to expect that the controversy will ever be closed. The utmost
that we can hope to do with the passage is to supply a probable
exposition.

It seems then highly probable that our Lord in this place solemnly
commissioned His apostles to go into all the world, and preach the
gospel as He had preached it. He also conferred on them the power of
declaring with peculiar authority whose sins were forgiven, and whose
sins were not forgiven. That this is precisely what the apostles did is a
simple matter of fact, which anyone may verify for himself by reading
the book of the Acts. When Peter proclaimed to the Jews, 'Repent ye
therefore, and be converted' – and when Paul declared at Antioch of
Iconium, 'to you is the word of this salvation sent', '[T]hrough this man
is preached ... the forgiveness of sins: And by him all that believe are
justified' – they were doing what this passage commissioned the apostles
to do. They were opening with authority the door of salvation, and
inviting with authority all sinners to enter in by it and be saved (Acts
3:19; 13:26-38).

No higher honour can be imagined than that of being Christ's
ambassadors, and proclaiming in Christ's name the forgiveness of sins
to a lost world.

LIST OF TOPICS

List of Texts

TEXTS

OTHER BOOKS
OF INTEREST

That Man of Granite with the Heart of a Child

A new biography of J.C. Ryle

Eric Russell

"*It is very good to have Ryle's story told afresh by someone who understands it so well...Ryle was an Anglican to remember.*"

J. I. Packer

John Charles Ryle was born into a comfortable English family background – his father was a politician and businessman. Ryle was intelligent, a great sportsman (captain of cricket at Eton and Oxford), and was set for a career in his father's business, and then politics – a typical, well-to-do, 19th century family.

Then – disaster. The family awoke to find that their father's bank had failed, taking all the other businesses with it. Ryle had lost his job and his place in society. He resigned his commission in the local yeomanry and went to comfort his parents, brother and sisters. One moment a popular man with good prospects, the next the son of a bankrupt with no trade or profession.

Almost as a last resort, he was ordained into the ministry of the church. Who could have thought that such an uninspiring entry into the ministry could have such an impact on the spiritual life of a nation.

Ryle's reputation as a pastor and leader grew until he was appointed the first Bishop of Liverpool, a post he held for twenty years. He was an author who is still in print today (he put aside royalties to pay his father's debts) and a man once described by his successor as 'that man of granite with the heart of a child'. He changed the face of the English church.

ISBN 1-85792-631-5

Regeneration

Being 'Born Again': What it means and why it's necessary

J.C. Ryle

REGENERATION
Being 'Born Again':
What it means and why it's necessary

J.C.RYLE

John Charles Ryle (1816 – 1900) was the first Bishop of Liverpool, England. Since then there have been countless other Bishops throughout the Anglican World. But none have had the impact on the wider evangelical world of J.C. Ryle. His extensive writings have remained continuously in print for over one hundred years, being treasured by hundreds of thousands both within and without the Anglican Church.

Ryle found himself faced with the difficult task of being an evangelical leader of a mixed diocese in the most sectarian of English cities. It was a recipe for strife, division and resentment, but throughout his period in office Ryle was respected by his colleagues to the extent that even one of his most strident opponents broke down and wept at the news of his death. He was able to master the difficult task of being firm in his beliefs and loving in his application of them. His gracious spirit is an example to us today.

In this powerful work, Ryle explains that divisive, often derided (so often misapplied by advertising) term 'born again'. He explains what being 'born again' means, why it is necessary and how you can tell whether you are.

Much of the value of this publication, though, lies in what Ryle writes next. In his gracious yet firm way Ryle devotes the majority of the book to explaining how the objections people have had to the doctrine should be handled and overcome with gentle persuasion.

It is a supreme example of the art of persuasion, one that we all need to consider.

ISBN 1-85792-741-9

Our Daily Walk
Daily Readings
F. B. Meyer

What better way than to start each day with the words of God in our minds. F.B. Meyer brings us short readings on a variety of themes to encourage, challenge and remind us of our obligations. Our Daily Walk is a treasury of wisdom distilled into brief and memorable readings which can be enjoyed by anyone – whether they have an hour to meditate or five minutes of peace in a hectic schedule.

F. B. Meyer(1847-1929) was Prolific author, convention speaker and pastor of a late 1800s 'megachurch' - Meyer had an influential effect on the Christian landscape of his time. With their easy readibility and evident relevance, his books and devotionals are still widely read and treasured.

ISBN 1-85792-048-1

Morning and Evening
C. H. Spurgeon

A Luxury Gift edition of Spurgeon's classic devotional that is full of challenge, encouragement and arresting comments. This is the original text that has been a comfort and inspiration to millions. One full year of starting and finishing each day with CH Spurgeon as he directs you to Christ will provide spiritual nourishment that will not be forgotten.

White ISBN 1-85792-300-6
Black ISBN 1-85792-125-9
Blue ISBN 1-85792-104-6
Burgundy ISBN 1-85792-126-7
Green ISBN 1-85792-127-5

Cheque Book of the Bank of Faith
C. H. Spurgeon

A short reading for everyday. Spurgeon wrote this selection of readings to encourage believers to enter into the full provision, that their relationship to Jesus entitled them to realise, on a daily basis. He explains we have to present the promises of Scripture to God in prayer and faith, anticipating that he will honour what he has said.

Red 1-85792-221-2
Blue 1-85792-495-9
Burgundy 1-85792-494-0

Known as the 'Prince of Preachers' C. H. Spurgeon(1834-1892) was perhaps one of the most famous preachers of the 19th Century. For 38 years he pastored the same congregation, which, to handle the crowds coming to hear him, built Metropolitan Tabernacle. To this day his writings continue to be read worldwide.

Christian Focus Publications

publishes books for all ages

Our mission statement —

STAYING FAITHFUL

In dependence upon God we seek to help make His infallible Word, the Bible, relevant. Our aim is to ensure that the Lord Jesus Christ is presented as the only hope to obtain forgiveness of sin, live a useful life and look forward to heaven with Him.

REACHING OUT

Christ's last command requires us to reach out to our world with His gospel. We seek to help fulfil that by publishing books that point people towards Jesus and help them to develop a Christ-like maturity. We aim to equip all levels of readers for life, work, ministry and mission.

Books in our adult range are published in three imprints.

Christian Focus contains popular works including biographies, commentaries, basic doctrine and Christian living. Our children's books are also published in this imprint.

Mentor focuses on books written at a level suitable for Bible College and seminary students, pastors, and other serious readers. The imprint includes commentaries, doctrinal studies, examination of current issues and church history.

Christian Heritage contains classic writings from the past.

For a free catalogue of all our titles, please write to
Christian Focus Publications, Ltd
Geanies House, Fearn,
Ross-shire, IV20 1TW, Scotland, United Kingdom
info@christianfocus.com

For details of our titles visit us on our website
www.christianfocus.com